Business Intelligence and Big Data

Business Intelligence and Big Data: Drivers of Organizational Success

By Celina M. Olszak

CRC Press
Taylor & Francis Group
Boca Raton London New York

CRC Press is an imprint of the
Taylor & Francis Group, an **informa** business

AN AUERBACH BOOK

To my husband for his unconditional love and support

Contents

About the Author

 **Celina M. Olszak** is a professor of Computer Science and Management Information Systems. She received MSc in Computer Science from Wroclaw University of Science (Poland) and Technology and was awarded PhD and a title of professor in Management Information Systems from the University of Economics in Katowice (Poland). Celina is also a scholarship holder at the Swiss Federal Institute of Technology in Zurich (Switzerland), German Academic Exchange Service at Trier University in Germany, and was elected to a fellowship at University of Technology, Sydney in Australia. She has visited and delivered different courses at universities in Europe (London University, Vienna University, ESC of Toulouse, and ESC of Clermont Ferrand).

Celina has performed various functions during her academic career. She was a deputy director of the Silesian International School of Economics in Katowice, a dean of the Faculty of Computer Science of the Silesian University of Management, a vice dean of Science at the Faculty of Economics, and a dean of Faculty of Economics at the University of Economics in Katowice. Currently, she is the chair of the Department of Business Informatics and a rector of the University of Economics in Katowice.

Celina is the author of 15 books and over 300 research papers. Her research focuses on decision support systems, knowledge management, management information systems, design of management information systems, business intelligence systems, big data, artificial intelligence as well as organizational creativity, innovation, and digital economy. She is currently teaching: Business Information Systems, Business Intelligence, E-business, and Information Systems Design.

She is a member of the Informing Science Institute in the United States, PGV New York (Pays du Groupe De Vysegrad), Canadian Centre of Science and Education, the American Research Foundation's Centre for European and Middle Eastern Studies, the Polish Academy of Sciences, as well as a member of many committees of international scientific conferences and journals. For several years, she has been the chair of Minitrack *Business Intelligence & Big Data for Innovative and Sustainable Development of Organizations* at Hawaii International Conference on System Sciences.

Preface

The 21st century is a time of intensified rivalry, competition, and progressing digitization. Individual employees, managers, and entire organizations are under increasing pressure to succeed. The question then arises what success actually means, is success a matter of chance and luck, or maybe success is a category that can be planned and properly supported.

In this book, I try to show that the success of an organization largely depends on the ability to anticipate and quickly respond to challenges from the market, customers, and other stakeholders. What is more, success is associated with the potential to process and analyze a variety of information and the means to use modern information and communication technologies (ICTs). Success also requires creative behaviors and organizational cleverness from an organization.

There is a lot of evidence in the research literature that ICTs can play a crucial role in achieving competitive advantage, improving decision-making, and achieving organizational efficiency. Unfortunately, there is still too little research focused on exploring the issues of using Business Intelligence and Big Data (BI&BD) systems in organizations and the economy.

Analysis of the research literature clearly confirms that organizations insufficiently utilize at all times the potential of the opportunities offered by BI&BD systems. The reasons for this are extremely complex and not sufficiently researched and analyzed. That is why there is an absolute need to intensify research on the effective use of BI&BD, answering, among others, the question of what determines the success of their use and how to design and implement BI&BD systems in organizations.

The discussion on the BI&BD issues in this monograph is presented in light of modern management paradigms, stating that: (1) intangible resources such as information and knowledge are strategic resources of each organization and the ability to intelligently process and analyze them is becoming a key competence; (2) thanks to modern ICTs, such as BI&BD, new business models are created that enable organizations to gain a competitive advantage and stand out in the market; (3) BI&BD are tools that can be used, not only for operational activities but also for strategic decisions to deal with upcoming economic setbacks; (4) modern technologies, such as BI&BD, are necessary for new knowledge discovery and in-depth data mining, which are the basis for predicting market trends, customer behaviors, economic, demographic, epidemic, fraud threads, and socioeconomic sentiment; and (5) BI&BDs are a means by which organizations and their participants can create significant, permanent value for various stakeholders.

The principal objective of this monograph is to conduct theoretically and empirically grounded discussion on the chances and the possibilities of BI&BD application in organizations. The main goal of the monograph is connected with the implementation of many specific objectives, including: (1) analysis and interpretation of the essence of BI&BD; (2) examination of the BI&BD decision support issue; (3) identification and characterization of potential areas of BI&BD utilization in organizations; (4) description of various approaches, methods, and tools for developing BI&BD in organizations; (5) recognition of BI&BD maturity measurement methods in organizations; (6) examination of factors determining the success of using BI&BD in organizations; (7) examination of the BI&BD role in value creation for organizations; and (8) identification of barriers and constrains related to the BI&BD design and implementation in organizations.

The book cites a lot of arguments and evidence confirming that BI&BD may be a trigger for making more effective decisions, improving business processes and business performance, as well as doing new business. The book proposes a comprehensive framework on how to design and use BI&BD to provide organizational success.

The structure of work, which consists of five chapters, is subordinated to the implementation of research objectives formulated. The first chapter of the book covers the characteristic of the complex environment and the impact of emerging technologies and information systems in driving continual change. The continual change poses challenges to design business models that address continual change. BI&BD plays a significant role in such design.

The second chapter is devoted to the theoretical foundations of using BI in organization management. It presents various interpretations of the term *Business Intelligence*, the most important generations of BI systems, as well as many BI models that can be used in organizations. The final part of the chapter presents a holistic approach to building BI systems in organizations.

The third chapter deals with the issue of analyzing large data sets. It was emphasized that data coming mainly from the Internet, social media, various government portals, distributed databases, as well as from mobile devices should be treated as a new form of capital and high business value. BD resources can provide valuable knowledge about customer behaviors and opinions, competition activities, the labor market, emerging ecological and environmental threats, trends in the economy, the popularity of various products and services, as well as social and political moods. In order to extract valuable knowledge from BD resources, it becomes necessary to use various methods and techniques for their exploration and analysis. To meet these requirements, a lot of attention in this chapter has been devoted to various technologies and techniques for BD processing.

The fourth chapter is a comprehensive compendium of knowledge about potential areas of BI&BD applications in organizations. Much space is devoted to the use of BI&BD in relational marketing, customer relationship management, and in planning and budgeting, sales and distribution, insurance, credit risk assessment, engineering and manufacturing, energy sector, financial and banking sector, logistics industry, as well as in health care and human resources management.

The last chapter deals with the measurement and assessment of BI&BD utilization in organizations. Various models for assessing BI&B maturity in organizations were presented. Using CSF theories, various factors determining the success of BI&BD in organizations were analyzed. The chapter builds on various research projects dealing with this issue as well as author's own research and recommendations that result from her many years of experience and interest in BI&BD issues. It ends with the problem of Big Data-based business value creation.

This book has been written for scientists who are conducting or intend to start researching the issues related to BI&BD use in organizations. The monograph may also be an interesting teaching material for students and postgraduate students. Furthermore, representatives of business practice and specialists from the ICT industry will find in it many tips on how to design and implement BI&BD systems in organizations, and above all, what benefits their application brings.

The multilayered research related to the use of BI&BD in organizations means that it has certainly not been possible in this book to discuss all issues in a comprehensive manner. I hope that the subsequent years will provide an opportunity to expand interest in BI&BD issues and bring new experience in this field.

Celina M. Olszak

Chapter 1

Changing Business Environments and Decision Support Systems

Changing Business Environments

The beginning of the 21st century brought huge changes in the management domain, people's way of thinking, perception of organizational success and information technologies. Modern organizations are expected to be able to anticipate the future, quickly establish cause-and-effect relationships, and propose new ways of doing things. Allocating intangible resources (information and knowledge in particular) at the center of wealth production and skillfully utilizing information technologies have become a crucial task of the organization. Intelligent technologies and IT systems that are able to match the requirements of modern management have gained importance (Bui, 2000; Kersten, 2000; Laudon & Laudon, 2018; Olszak, 2016; Power, 2001; Turban et al., 2014).

It is claimed that change is an inherent element in which contemporary organizations have to operate. Growing information flows, new business practices, customers, competition, employees, and dramatically changing technology are the primary driving force of the ongoing changes. Technology plays an important role in both inducing and carrying out changes (McNurlin, Sprague, & Bui, 2014; Sauter, 2010).

Many authors are of the opinion (Rivard et al., 2004) that understanding the essence of changes that take place, both within and in the environment of modern organizations, and responding quickly to these changes, is the basis for achieving competitive advantage, improving customer relationships and enhancing organizational efficiency(Figure 1.1).

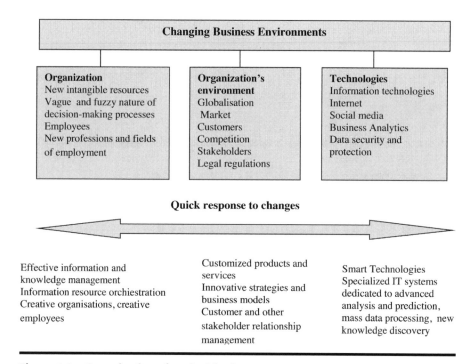

Figure 1.1 Organizations faced with changes.

Growing Information Flows

The modern world has been dominated by information and information flows are becoming increasingly complex. The problem for many organizations is not the lack of information but its excess, which causes informational noise and even informational chaos. Information on the basis of which organizations make decisions comes from various scattered resources. Information is often incomplete, inconsistent, and volatile (Laudon & Laudon, 2018).

The nature of many decision-making problems has become extremely vague and fuzzy. Many events cannot be predicted or should be treated as hypotheses based on highly speculative premises. This applies in particular to dependencies that characterize the external environment of the organization, e.g., sales markets and long-term capital cost. Managers are faced with the need to solve problems with varying degrees of structuralization – from well-structured to partially structured up to unstructured decisions. Solving many economic issues requires the use of an interdisciplinary approach, i.e., the ability to combine knowledge from various disciplines, especially management, economics, sociology, statistics, computer science, and even physics.

New Organizational Structures and a New Distribution of Decision-Making Powers

Today, flat, process, network, and contract structures are gaining in importance in modern organizations where team coordination, self-discipline, trust in employees, business partners, as well as individual responsibility for created relationships and communication play a crucial role. Projects where employees are focused on tasks aimed at achieving specific goals are a vehicle for many types of work in organizations. The criteria for selecting members for such project teams are knowledge, competence, and experience. Organizations are becoming a complex chain of networks and decision-making teams that go beyond their traditional boundaries (Kelly, 2001).

It is hard not to notice that in traditional organizations, built in accordance with the linear hierarchical model, decision-making powers were clearly defined, well demarcated, and precisely distributed in a horizontal and vertical system (Jamali, 2005). The distribution of decision-making powers and associated responsibilities is usually less defined, less rigid, and more blurred in organizations with flatter structures. In such organizations, there are no clear and permanent divisions of work, and the exchange of information takes place in a highly individualized manner. Information centers, and consequently power centers, are dispersed, and in many cases hidden. They change their boundaries and internal structure. Most decisions are made in the process of consultations, negotiations, and tenders. Power is usually obtained for a short time, without any institutional and social guarantees, since it is situational, i.e., connected with the system of variable forces, and it must be constantly sought.

New Professions and Fields of Employment

The need to make increasingly complex decisions, based on highly aggregated and processed data, creates demand for new professions and fields of employment. These include, in particular, analysts, statisticians, and specialists in the field of data science, as well as creators of electronic markets, webmasters, Internet service providers, information and knowledge brokers, application testers, and security specialists. Work can increasingly be done remotely, and employees face retraining, frequent job changes, and even profession changes. Notably, already in 2020, approximately 85% of all professions in North America and 80% in Europe required the use of knowledge resources, and specialized software and hardware. At the same time, there is a dramatic reduction in employment in the area of material production, both industrial and agricultural. Research shows that, in a 2030 perspective, there will be a global growing demand for competences related to the ability to solve complex problems, critical and creative thinking, having interdisciplinary knowledge and the ability to negotiate, communicate, and cooperate. The progressive development of information technologies, contrary to what may seem, requires from employees not only skills related to the operation of equipment, mobile devices, and Internet but also the soft skills mentioned above. In addition, progressing globalization means that employees and managers use different languages and often have different cultural roots. It can be assumed that just as the process of receiving and evaluating information itself may significantly differ in such multicultural teams, the premises that guide them in making decisions may also be different (Viehland, 2005). This means that organizations should clearly provide their employees with information about the organization's goals and how to achieve them, as well as care for developing common ethical behavior and understanding of values. Furthermore, in fact, employees also place more and more demands on their employers. They expect support from them in the area of professional development and promotion as well as creating conditions for safe and decent work.

Customers

Customers are believed to have become the driving force behind many changes that are taking place inside the organization and in its business environment. A modern customer is often a very inquisitive, well-educated person interested in highly personalized services and products; together with producers shaping the organization's value system (Brilman, 2002; Chapman, 2001). The customer's interest in a specific offer and maintenance of their long-term loyalty to the company has become extremely difficult, and also a priority task for many organizations. It is regarded that organizations can deal with these issues by developing the ability to quickly discover and satisfy customer needs by providing highly personalized products and services. However, it should be noted that personalization requires changes in virtually everything that the organization has done so far (from needs analysis, through product design, advertising, to distribution). The correct implementation of the individualization assumptions is associated with the development of various relationships with customers and suppliers, which should be based on trust and close integration. It must be admitted that we still know too little about how to anticipate those needs. Skills in customer segmentation and profiling, reaching the target group as soon as possible, developing individual customer relationships, and engaging them in the process of developing new products and services are extremely valuable (Tiwana, 2000).

Competition

More and more often one can come across the statement that for a contemporary organization what is happening in its environment has become more important than what is happening within it. This is due to the fact that in the past, organizations functioned in a predictable and even friendly environment. Contemporary business environment is turbulent and often hostile. It requires constant monitoring, anticipation, and quick response to any signals coming from the market. Systematic and professional analysis of competitors and markets, defined as benchmarking, has become an effective way of learning and gaining experience for many organizations. It casts competition in a completely different light than previously. Competition is treated as a valuable source of information and a partner for exchanging views. Today, we are witnessing the formation of joint interest groups and mergers of companies that have recently competed with each other. Strategic alliances, outsourcing, and joint ventures have already become a certain norm. They are concluded as the need for using the same raw materials, creating strong organization–supplier relationships, as well as joint research groups arises. As a consequence, this leads to the development of broad cooperation and collaboration.

Stakeholders

In modern management, which often takes on the characteristics of network management, an organization is a system of many groups of shareholders connected with each other. Organizations must cooperate with stakeholders who belong to different institutional spheres and thus support different views, interests, and values. The basic groups of stakeholders of an organization include owners (primarily interested in return on equity and share prices), employees (primarily interested in earnings, job satisfaction, and working conditions), customers (interested in the quality of products and services, price, and service), suppliers (interested in contract terms and liability regulations), lenders (interested in timely repayments and organization's development perspectives), local communities (interested in job creation and environmental protection) and state authorities (primarily interested in an efficient tax system and compliance with the law). This situation of increased pluralism is a new challenge for organizations. Not only do they have to deal with the dispersion of power, but also face the need to create strategies in the context of complex and often contradictory goals. The efficiency and effectiveness of modern business requires meeting the expectations of stakeholders in the economic area as well as in social and image-related areas.

New Conflicts and Threats

The development of modern organizations brings various fears and new threats (Rivard et al., 2004). Conflicts and anxieties are of a different nature than they used to be. Their source is, among others, lack of accessibility and ability to use information technologies which may consequently lead to digital division of the world. It is believed that organizations which will not keep up with technological development are at risk of isolation and exclusion from economic and social activity. Another escalating problem is terrorism and electronic attacks. It is mainly about hacker attacks on stock exchanges, banks, energy networks, water supply systems, military systems, air navigation, as well as electronic surveillance and invasion of privacy. In those circumstances, solutions (technological, legal, business and transnational) are needed to protect organizations against these types of threats and crimes.

At this point of considerations, we pose the fundamental question of how organizations can deal with such a diverse range of changes taking place within them and in their business environment, and, above all, how to use these changes to achieve competitive advantage and create new values.

We believe that the following are important to deal with changes: (1) the organization's ability to manage intangible assets, such as information and knowledge; (2) creative people and creative organizations; and (3) information technologies.

Resource-based View

Many authors are of the opinion that in the era of heavy computerization and digitization of information resources, the organization's success can be explained through the lens of Resource-based View (RBV). RBV asserts that the success of an organization's strategy depends on alignment of its resources and capabilities providing the basis to build key competences. Acquisition, configuration, reconfiguration, and development of available information resources are critical factors in gaining a competitive advantage and creating value (Cosic, Shanks, & Maynard, 2012; Olszak, Bartuś, & Lorek, 2018; Wade & Hulland, 2004). An extended approach to RBV resources entails intangible categories including organizational, human, and networks (Ahn & York, 2011). According to RBV, to lead to a competitive advantage, resources should be VRIN: Valuable (enable an organization to carry out a value-creating strategy), Rare (are in short supply), Inimitable (cannot be perfectly replicated by competitors) and Non-substitutable (cannot be countered by a rival with a substitute). This knowledge-based resource approach of RBV stimulates organizations to attain, access, and maintain intangible endowments since these resources are the ways in which firms combine and transform tangible input resources and assets.

The traditional RBV concept infers that the information resources are static and do not account for changes in the unstable environment of the organization. These challenges of the environment can be met with dynamic capabilities (DC). The resource adoption method is at least as consequential as the value of these resources (Hsu & Ziedonis, 2013). The benefits realized from the resource pool are transient; therefore, organizations need to concentrate on continuous acquisition of new resources (information and knowledge) and the creation of their new configurations (Sirmon et al., 2011). It may be useful to consider DC in the context of three clusters of activities and adjustments (Teece, Pisano, & Shuen, 1997): (1) identification and assessment of an opportunity (*sensing*), (2) mobilization of resources to address an opportunity and to capture value from doing so (*seizing*), and (3) continued renewal (*transforming*). These activities are essential if the organization wants to sustain itself as markets and technologies change, although some firms will be more efficient than others in performing some or all of these tasks. In the context of organizational support, sensing entails exploring technological opportunities, probing markets, and listening to customers. Seizing pertains to (Ortbach et al., 2012): (1) solution development (a firm's capability to generate different potential solutions, e.g., process design, concept development, idea refinement); (2) solution evaluation and selection (established procedures to allow informed decision-making, and thus selection of the most suitable solution for a specific problem); and (3) solution detailing (forward thinking and control mechanisms should constitute an action plan). The last activity –transforming consists of unfreezing, changing, and re-freezing sub-capabilities. When searching for new suggestions concerning new products and services, it is important to break up the existing work structures and procedures. The acceptance has to be promoted by active communication about the changes and benefits that result from them. Changing sub-capability refers to the actual implementation of the idea of change. The last sub-capability relates to all tasks necessary to promote internalization of the newly deployed ideas.

Information and Knowledge – Organization's Strategic Resources

The source of organization's power has shifted from land, finance, and material capital to intangible resources (Herschel & Jones, 2005; McGonagle & Vella, 2002; Negash & Gray, 2008; Wickramasinghe & von Lubitz, 2007). Organizations are more often governed by information, knowledge, intelligence, intellectual capital, and wisdom (Davenport & Harris, 2007; Liautaud & Hammond, 2001; Wixom & Watson, 2010). It is stated that the ability of an organization to take advantage of all available information and knowledge is its critical success factor. However, this challenge becomes more daunting with a constantly increasing volume of information and dynamic change in the environment (Schick, Frolick, & Ariyachandra, 2011). The ability to manage information, especially knowledge, is recognized as the main factor of organizational success (Davenport, Harris, & Morison, 2010; Drucker, 2002; Howson, 2008; Knox, 2014; Manyika et al., 2011).

Understanding the essence of knowledge requires clarifying the basic differences and relationships between such terms as data, information, and knowledge. This issue has been discussed in the literature a number of times (Laudon & Laudon, 2018; Tiwana, 2000; Wu, 2000). Data means a set of numbers, facts, transactions, and events that have been recorded, e.g., on some medium (in the computer's memory). They constitute the raw starting material on the basis of which information is created. Organizations collect data about their employees, customers, and suppliers. However, they must be processed and presented in the right context to become fully valuable to the organization and be considered information.

The complex socioeconomic reality means that information alone is not enough in decision-making processes. One should reach for knowledge which reveals various causal relationships, discovers new ways of acting, and serves to anticipate future. Knowledge is inseparable from learning, logical thinking, and discovering new facts and rules. Nowadays, this knowledge is recognized as the basis for effective decision-making.

At this point, it is worth mentioning that the term "knowledge" dates back to the time of Plato and Aristotle. Modern understanding of knowledge is manifested in the works of D. Bella, M. Polanyi, A. Toffler, and I. Nonaka. It is identified with organizational assets, organizational memory, and key competences (Davydow, 2000; Nonaka & Takeuchi, 2000). In 1960, P. Drucker, when discussing the role of knowledge in the organization, used terms such as "knowledge workers" and "knowledge-based work." He was also one of the first to state that the US economy shifted toward a knowledge-based economy and that its main resource is not material capital but knowledge.

Of the many opinions about the role of knowledge in decision-making, one is particularly interesting and important. It is claimed that today it is necessary to use first of all deep knowledge, which does not result directly from simple data analysis. Such knowledge is shaped in a long-term process of learning, gaining experience, accumulating information, organizing it into logical cognitive structures, bonding with emotions, and using it within various value systems. However, this requires creativity, innovation, experimentation, and organizational learning. Particular attention is paid to higher-level learning, the so-called generational learning, which, unlike adaptive learning, requires new ways of looking at the world, understanding customers, and understanding the need for better business management. This type of learning, referred to as a double learning loop, requires the organization to constantly experiment and test its results, while causing changes in the organizational knowledge base. Its effect is the embedding of knowledge in processes, products, services, in the structure and culture of the organization, and in relationships it creates with its close and distant environment (Figure 1.2).

The importance of knowledge for an organization results from the very characteristics of this resource. The following attributes are usually mentioned: (Nonaka & Takeuchi, 2000):

- Domination: it is stated that the competitive position of enterprises depends mostly on an effective use of knowledge. Other resources are in fact sidestepped to secondary manufacturing factors.
- Inexhaustibility: knowledge, unlike other resources, is not consumed, on the contrary, the more and more often it is used, the more its value increases.
- Simultaneity and mobility: it is noticed that the same knowledge can be used by many organizations and people, and in many places at the same time. Knowledge is mobile as opposed to traditional resources such as premises, machinery, etc.

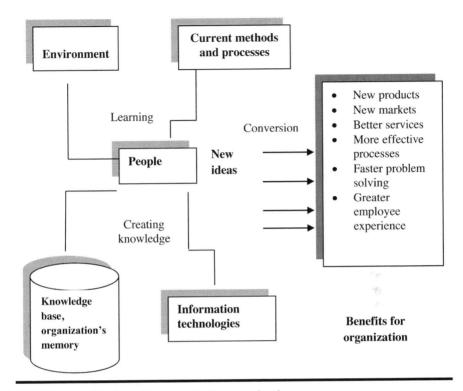

Figure 1.2 Adoption of knowledge in organization.

Source: Elaborated on (Awad & Ghaziri, 2004).

■ Non-linearity: it is pointed out that even a small amount of knowledge can have unimaginable consequences, and vice versa; a huge amount of knowledge may prove to be useless. The lack of linearity also means that the same body of knowledge can bring dramatically different effects in different enterprises.

■ Complexity: knowledge is a complex resource, comprising practical knowledge (know-how), theoretical knowledge (know-why), strategic knowledge (know-what) as well as informal relationships in the enterprise. Knowledge is an attribute of both individual members and the entire organization.

■ Learning: knowledge of individual employees and the entire organization is inseparably connected with the learning process, which means acquisition and implementation of knowledge in processes, products, services, and solutions in the field of organizational structures. Particular attention, as it has been emphasized earlier, is paid to higher-level learning, the so-called generational learning.

■ Applicability: knowledge has no value until it is applied. In addition, to be effective, it must be developed and managed in conjunction with human resources.

It is people and information technologies that create intellectual capital. While information technologies are responsible for collecting, processing, and sending information, people are important when converting data into information, especially their deep vertical knowledge and ability to reason.

■ Costliness: it should also be noted that knowledge is an extremely costly resource in production, but usually cheap (and sometimes free) in reproduction.

Naturally, knowledge is not a resource which can be taken for granted. Its value changes over time. In this situation, organizations must continually acquire new knowledge resources and create new configurations from them. In other words, knowledge, like any other resource, requires adequate power, revitalization, configuration, and reconfiguration. The ability of an organization to dynamically acquire, modify, configure information resources, and create unique configurations from them becomes a key competence of a modern organization (Sirmon et al., 2011; Wade & Hulland, 2004).

Recognition of knowledge as the main resource of an organization, determining its success, justifies the need for effective management of this resource. The experience of many firms in knowledge management illustrates that this process is associated with many problems. They may result from various reasons:

■ Knowledge is located in many places.
■ Knowledge is often of an informal nature.
■ There is a blurred division of knowledge into public and private.
■ Much of the knowledge is obtained interactively and used jointly in subgroups or networks.
■ Knowledge consists of many types and carriers.

Some difficulties in using knowledge to make decisions stem from the fact that it is usually located in different places, both inside and outside the organization. Most often these are internal documents and files, correspondence, information systems, databases, e-mail, Internet sources, social media, newsletters, etc. In many cases, access to these resources is difficult due to not only their dispersion, but difficulties in identifying them and their informal character.

A large body of knowledge, extremely valuable for the decision-making process, is knowledge which includes cognitive and social skills that result from the experience and relationships that organization's employees, customers, and stakeholders create. Such knowledge, to a large extent, is informal and extremely difficult to codify (formalize), but it is visible in action. This category primarily includes experience, intuition, premonition, and organizational culture. The use of such knowledge requires the skill of locating experts, creating knowledge maps, coding and integrating knowledge, and the development of various techniques enabling access to such knowledge (Sanchez & Heene, 1997).

Today, a large body of knowledge arises as a result of the development of various networks of relationships (Jashapara, 2006) which can be created at many levels, especially at the level of a single unit, organizational groups, and relationships of the organization with its environment. A single individual and their cognitive capabilities have always played an unquestionable role in creating knowledge. However, such an individual model of creating knowledge in contemporary management has somewhat lost its importance. The focus has shifted to collective work, which means team learning and pursuit of group consensus. This way of creating knowledge depends to a great extent on the quality of communication of individual people. However, it should be noted that this approach has become somewhat outdated. It is now claimed that the success of an organization can be explained by analyzing the network of relationships it has entered into. What happens outside is more important for the organization's success than what happens within it. Relationship networks provide strategic weight to creation of knowledge resources. The network, together with the resources obtained through it, can become a source of relatively lasting competitive advantage and a source difficult to imitate. Therefore, competences in creating such connections, using appropriate supervision mechanisms, building ways of knowledge sharing, improving partner systems, and maintaining a central position in the network are important.

As it has already been stressed, using knowledge in decision making is not a simple task, *inter alia*, due to the fact that knowledge consists of many carriers and types. For example, an organization's knowledge can be classified into one of four categories (Knowledge Management, KPMG Consulting, Research Report, 2000):

■ Know-what – refers to knowledge of facts. In this case, knowledge is synonymous with information.
■ Know-why – concerns knowledge of principles and laws of nature. Access to this type of knowledge accelerates technical progress and reduces the frequency of error in testing procedures.
■ Know-how – refers to skills, i.e., the ability to do something. It applies to both employee skills and new product development.
■ Know-who – identifies knowledge holders and describes the knowledge they possess.

An interesting division of knowledge was introduced by Japanese scientists Nonaka and Takeuchi (2000) who distinguished formal (explicit) and informal (implicit) knowledge. Formal knowledge is the part of knowledge that has been presented through procedures, words, signs, or symbols. It is therefore systematized and relatively easy to transfer. In turn, the essence of informal knowledge is sometimes difficult to explain. It is created on the basis of experience and intuition, and it is a kind of know-how of an employee, project team, or the entire organization. It is difficult to copy and imitate.

Within formal as well as informal knowledge, procedural, declarative, semantic, and episodic knowledge can be distinguished. Procedural knowledge tells us how to perform specific tasks and procedures. Standard programming languages are usually used to encode it. Declarative knowledge, on the other hand, serves to describe certain situations, objects, and relationships between them. It indicates what the problem is and what the goal of the solution might be, not what steps should be taken to reach it. One could say that it refers to knowing if something is true or false. In coding such knowledge, the principles of formal and informal logic, known, e.g., from expert systems and neural networks, are helpful.

Semantic knowledge becomes useful in making decisions. It reflects the deeply hidden relationships between various events. Semantic networks, neural networks, knowledge maps, and data mining techniques are used to represent these types of relationships.

It has been shown many times that decision-makers learn by studying the past, and especially learn from their own experience as well as from customers and competitors. Information about past decisions and their consequences turns out to be valuable in identifying and forecasting organization's future successes and failures. Therefore, it is worth collecting episodic knowledge that refers to various facts, processes, and experiences which have taken place in the past. Case Base Reasoning (CBR) techniques, knowledge repositories, knowledge maps and data warehouses are particularly helpful in coding this type of knowledge.

Knowledge Management

Considering the essence of the term knowledge, it is difficult not to refer to knowledge management. It can be guessed that since information is different from knowledge, then information management should be different from knowledge management. In the first case, the focus is primarily on searching and finding objects (facts, events, etc.). On the other hand, knowledge management encompasses a broader spectrum of issues mainly related to the creation and use of knowledge, communication, and knowledge sharing (Nonaka & Takeuchi, 1995; Sirmon et al., 2011). It is assumed that knowledge management is a discipline which addresses various means used by people to create and share knowledge and to provide it a social context to implement various organizational and business activities properly. Due to the globalization and development of various information technologies, knowledge management is an important alternative for firms in creating and maintaining a competitive advantage.

At present, three main trends in the development of the concept of knowledge management can be distinguished. These are (a) the Japanese approach, (b) the resource approach, and (c) the process approach.

The Japanese approach, which is the result of the work of Nonaka and Takeuchi (2000), focuses on the issue of knowledge conversion, the so-called "spiral of knowledge" model that reflects four knowledge conversion processes. They include

- adaptation, involving the conversion of implicit knowledge into implicit knowledge;
- externalization, involving the conversion of implicit knowledge into explicit knowledge;
- combination, consisting in the conversion of explicit knowledge into explicit knowledge; and
- internalization, involving the conversion of explicit knowledge into implicit knowledge.

According to the Japanese concept, knowledge management is a repetitive cycle involving the four processes mentioned.

In the resource approach, special importance is attached to the "sources of knowledge" model (Leonard-Barton, 1995). In this model, created as a result of research into the innovativeness of industrial enterprises, it is assumed that for effective knowledge management, the following five elements are necessary: (1) key skills, (2) joint problem solving, (3) implementation and integration of new tools and technologies, (4) experimenting, and (5) importing knowledge. It is not difficult to notice that the individual elements of the above model refer both to the inside of the organization (implementation and integration of new tools and technologies) and its environment (knowledge import), include the present (joint problem solving), and also look into the future (experimenting). Key competences and skills perform the function of an integrating factor into one coherent and efficient system.

The process approach is a trend based on the experience and solutions developed in large consulting companies. Knowledge management is assumed to be all processes that enable the creation, dissemination, and use of knowledge to achieve the organization's goals (Drucker, 2002; Evenport & Prusak, 1998; Sanchez & Heene, 1997). The knowledge creation process includes a set of specific actions and initiatives that enterprises take to increase the amount and quality of organizational knowledge. The process of knowledge transfer concerns its transfer and sharing with others. The use of knowledge means the use of this resource to create new products, services, and business practices, and to develop original relationships with customers and suppliers.

To explain the mechanism of effective knowledge management in organizations, it is impossible not to refer to the theory of Critical Success Factors (CSFs), described in the literature by many authors (Daniel, 1961; Rockart, 1979; Wong, 2005).

D. Skyrme and D. Amidon (1997), researching knowledge management systems, identified seven key factors that determine their success, such as (1) a strong connection between the concept of knowledge management and the business imperative, (2) a convincing vision of knowledge management, (3) management support, (4) culture of knowledge creation and sharing, (5) continuous learning, (6) properly developed technological infrastructure, and (7) systematic process of knowledge organization. In turn, C. W. Holsapple and K. D. Joshi (2000), after analyzing various case studies and conducting research using the Delhi method, indicated three types of impacts on knowledge management: managerial, resource, and environment. Managerial impact consists of factors such as coordination, control, measurement of knowledge, and management support. Resource impact refers in particular to knowledge, human, and financial resources. On the other hand, factors related to the environment are primarily competition, markets, time, and economic factors.

T. H. Davenport (1998) and colleagues conducted knowledge management research that covered 31 projects in 24 firms. The purpose of this research was to identify the factors affecting the success of knowledge management. Eighteen projects have been recognized as successful projects. Eight common success factors were identified in these projects. They referred to the economic efficiency or value of the industry, clear business goals, standard and flexible knowledge structure, multi-channel knowledge transfer, knowledge-oriented culture, technical and organizational infrastructure, changes in motivational practices, and support of top management. In turn, the work of P. Chourides, D. Longbottom, and W. Murphy (2003) on the issue of knowledge management contributed to the identification of five areas important from the point of organizational success. These include strategy, human resources management, information technology, quality, and marketing. Whereas J. Liebowitz and Suen (2000), after conducting research into CSFs, proposed six key components that determine the success of knowledge management in organizations. They distinguished (1) knowledge management strategy and support from top management, (2) knowledge management infrastructure, (3) knowledge ontologies and knowledge repositories, (4) knowledge management systems and tools, (5) incentives (stimuli) to share knowledge, and (6) organizational culture. According to the research carried out by F. Hasanali (2003), success in knowledge management depends on factors such as management support, organizational culture, its structure, employee roles and responsibilities, technological infrastructure, and the ability to measure knowledge.

In addition, research in Polish small and medium-size organizations (Olszak, 2012) allowed to state that the management plays a key role in knowledge management. The management is responsible for the dissemination of knowledge sharing, learning, and search for new ideas. It significantly affects the behavior of other employees. Other competencies of the management, important from the point of knowledge management and organizational success are the ability to manage change in the firm and trust as well as creating a climate for the development of creative and innovative work. Research findings have highlighted the important role of work culture in SMEs and its direct impact on knowledge management. Culture should be understood as key beliefs, values, norms, and social behaviors that imply the way employees work in the organization. Knowledge-oriented culture encourages the creation of knowledge, development of various forms of cooperation, and knowledge sharing and its use. In the light of the conducted research, the importance of Information Communication Technology (ICT) in knowledge management also proved to be indisputable. ICTs allow firms to quickly identify and search for a variety of information, discover previously unknown relationships between data, as well as support cooperation and communication between individual employees, customers, and suppliers. It was recognized that the most important technologies supporting knowledge management in the organization include business intelligence, knowledge bases, management of cooperation, content and documentation, group work systems, knowledge portals, customer relationship management, and e-learning. The research also showed that one of the measures that guarantee success in knowledge management is a clear and well-developed strategy. It is the basis for enabling SMEs to develop their capabilities and resources in line with their objectives. It was emphasized that this strategy should correspond strictly with the business strategy and be understood by all employees.

To sum up the issue of the role of intangible resources (especially information and knowledge) for organizations, it should be recognized that the coordination of three important elements facilitates their efficient use:

- People – who create individual and collective knowledge through learning, sharing knowledge, solving problems, integrating it with the culture of the organization with the ultimate aim to market, e.g., better products and services.
- Processes – which should be regularly updated with current information, knowledge and improved respectively.
- Technology, especially information technology – the use of which should be correlated with the needs of the market, competitors' activities, and firm's resources.

Creative Employees and Creative Organizations

One can cite many examples confirming that organization's success is largely influenced by its employees, their competences and their ability to think and act creatively. Transforming information into knowledge, and especially into deep knowledge, requires not only individual employees, but also the entire organization, to think and act creatively (Amabile, 1988; Proctor, 2010). Creativity entails generating something new from existing information and knowledge (Baron, 2012). That is why it is often compared to the knowledge system (Basadur, Basadur, & Licina, 2012) which assists firms in solving various problems and increasing the level of effectiveness (Houghton & DiLiello, 2010). Creativity is particularly important in solving weak or generally unstructured problems (Mumford, Robledo, & Hester, 2011). Thanks to creativity, organizations generate new situations, added value and contribute, e.g., to the improvement in customer satisfaction. Organizational creativity is necessary to trigger new behaviors and interpretations in unexpected situations (Bechky & Okhuysen, 2011). Creativity is believed to be a means by which organizations and their participants can create significant lasting value for their diverse stakeholders (George, 2007). It is a kind of organizational ability, meaning adaptation to changing environmental conditions, by constantly acquiring new resources and creating new configurations from them (Arora & Nandkumar, 2012; Olszak & Kisielnicki, 2018; Sirmon et al., 2011; Zahra, Sapienza, & Davidsson, 2006).

Today, it is deemed that creativity in new technology sectors, as well as in traditional, mature organizations, seems to play a greater role in success than production systems (Styhre & Sundgren, 2005). Therefore, it is not surprising that many organizations and managers are looking for ways, tools, and infrastructure to improve organizational creativity and its computer support (Heweet et al., 2005; Shneiderman, 2007). Nakakoji (2006) assumes that ICTs can be used to (1) improve employees' ability to perform creative tasks, (2) support users in acquiring knowledge in a given problem area to unleash their creativity, and (3) provide users with new skills in problem solving. In contrast, Indurkhya (2013) claims that ICTs stimulate users' imagination, facilitate the creation of new ideas, and modeling of creative processes.

Information Communication Technology (ICT) as a Driver of Change and Innovation

Interest in ICT as a factor in socioeconomic development is not a new phenomenon and has long been the subject of numerous studies. Many authors agree (Rivard et al., 2004; Roztocki & Weistroffer, 2008; Tapscott & Williams, 2006) that the development of organizations and entire economies depends on the level of investment in science and technology. It is believed that ICTs, especially today, have become a strategic tool for economic growth, determining the competitiveness of many organizations and their innovative development (Drucker, 2014; Nonaka & Takeuchi, 1995; Tan, Steinbach, & Kumar, 2005; Steiger, 2010).

The development of the Internet and the spectacular successes of firms which quickly became market leaders and were valued by investors many times higher than traditional organizations, caused an increase in the interest in the strategic importance of information technologies. It was reflected, *inter alia*, in appointing IT managers to management boards and decision-making bodies. Rapid careers, but often also the failures of many Internet companies at the end of the 20th century, have shown that even the best ideas and technologies improperly implemented can plunge organizations financially. In fact, firms differ in their ability to extract business benefits from investments in information technologies.

The era of ICT development, which began in the 1960s, was mainly based on the principles of ordinary automation and support of simple, operational activities of the organization. Nowadays, the role of ICT has changed dramatically. ICTs are used to (1) develop modern strategies and business models, (2) create sources of competitive advantage, (3) make fundamental transformations in organizations, and (4) integrate and develop the entire ecosystem (Figure 1.3).

Not only do IT technologies support the basic tasks and functions of today's organization, but they have become a critical element in the development of business strategy. An example is Cisco which treats computer networks as an integral part of firm's strategy and uses these networks to interact with customers and suppliers. There are many examples of firms that, with the participation of ICT, are integrated with a modular, distributed, and global infrastructure that allows them

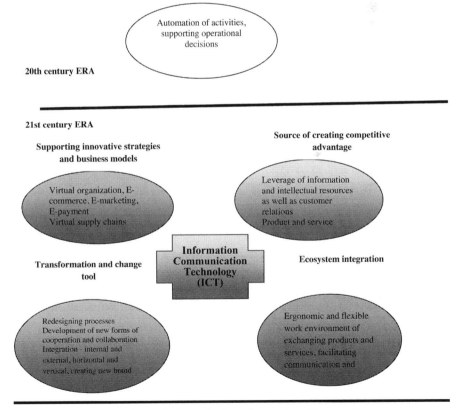

Figure 1.3   ICT as a factor in introducing changes and innovations.

Source: Own elaboration based on (Rivard et al., 2004).

to do work, regardless of time and distance. Technologies merge into social relations and include them in the consumer and corporate space. Many of the products and services produced are implemented in the cloud (cloud computing) and it is increasingly difficult to separate them from the ICT infrastructure and find out who is the producer and who is the customer.

Technologies enable crucial transformations as well as creation of new values for an organization and the whole society. They facilitate the organization of new markets, introduction of innovative products and services, and emergence of creative sectors (e.g., art, computer games, music, publishing). Information systems such as: MRP II (Manufacturing Resource Planning), ERP (Enterprise Resource Planning), CMS (Content Management Systems), and EDI (Electronic Data Interchange) have led to significant reengineering in workflow, organizational structures, ways of contacting customers, integrating, monitoring business processes, as well as intellectual and social capital management (Banker et al., 2006; Bharadwaj et al. 2013; Ettlie & Pavlou, 2006; Kohli & Grover, 2008; Straub & Watson, 2001; Subramaniam & Venkatraman, 2001; Rai et al., 2012).

ICTs are increasingly seen as a tool for gaining competitive advantage. CRM (Customer Relation Management), SCM (Supply Chain Management), and e-commerce systems enable the creation of unique virtual values, development of more effective and long-term relationships with customers, customization of products and creation of new organizational roles, and market structures. It should be highlighted that ICTs also have a huge impact on other sectors and industries, thus contributing to the creation of new jobs, professions, and specializations. In both large and small firms, ICTs are used to reduce labor costs, improve quality, provide a better level of service, design and production control, etc.

ICTs are extremely important in designing and integrating various information systems for firms and in developing flexible, multi-module, secure applications that meet the requirements of customers, employees, and suppliers and helps in creating an ergonomic, friendly and intuitive work environment. Therefore, one can share the opinions of many authors (Mitchell, Inouye & Blumenthal, 2003) that ICTs have become the cement binding various areas, especially science, business and culture, in which new, creative activities can be developed. For example, scientists can use computers to analyze huge amounts of data from the Internet and based on them discover new knowledge that could not be extracted using traditional means. The Internet of Things (IoT) technology has become a source of inspiration for many architects and designers. Advanced sensor and signal processing technologies open up unprecedented possibilities in composing and developing computer games, and e-book technology has introduced revolutionary changes in the publishing industry.

The impact of information technology on the economy and society at large is undeniable. It seems that this was largely determined by its characteristics: connectivity, convergence, ubiquity, and development of miscellaneous software (Rivard et al., 2004). Computers and telecommunications today create a global digital infrastructure that is the basis for economic transformation. This infrastructure is characterized by, *inter alia*, providing the opportunity to communicate to a growing group of people who send text, video, and voice data. It gives unlimited access to various information resources, the Internet and network services. Increasingly, connectivity is becoming wireless, which makes communication even simpler and unlimited. It is also worth noting that modern computers, laptops, television sets, radios, and projectors bear the hallmarks of convergence. In biology, the term means that unrelated organisms tend to become similar when they adapt to the same environment. Currently, the boundaries between many devices are somewhat blurred. There is also a trend to create multifunctional solutions with the features of computers, mailbox, fax, notebook, TV, radio, and open systems, providing the possibility of easy connection of new systems from various suppliers and the construction of modular and flexible architectures.

The advancing miniaturization of equipment together with its increasing power and decreasing manufacturing costs means that computers are ubiquitous in human life. By placing microprocessors, sensors in materials and various devices, firms are able to create objects that allow them to be closer to customers, suppliers, etc. An example is automatic control, monitoring of work processes, self-monitoring structures, automated factories and robots.

In recent years, the functioning of the organization has particularly been influenced by integrated MRP II, ERP class IT solutions, as well as CRM, BI, and group work systems, computer networks, artificial intelligence, and the Internet of Things. Another type of software that has undoubtedly changed the face of organization management is computer simulations and virtual reality. Computer simulations with elements of artificial intelligence allow users to create virtual scenarios without bearing real risk. Virtual reality allows organizations to go one step further, namely to create an environment visually similar to the real one on the computer.

Modern studies indicate that the greatest impact on the development of the organization will belong to technologies such as (UNCTAD, 2018):

- Big Data analysis (BD) – it can assist organizations in managing or resolving critical global issues, producing new scientific breakthroughs, advancing human health and improve decision-making, by providing real-time streams of information.
- The Internet of Things (IoT) – it enables the condition and actions of connected objects and machines to be monitored and managed, and provides more effective monitoring of the natural world, animals and people.
- Artificial intelligence (AI) – it can be employed in image recognition, problem solving, and logical reasoning that sometimes surpasses those of humans. Artificial intelligence, notably combined with robotics, also has the capacity to remodel production processes and business, in particular manufacturing.
- Biotechnology – it enables very specific gene editing for human medicine, making personalized treatments possible for certain conditions combined with AI and BD as well as for genetic modification of plants and animals.

Notably, these technologies offer the solutions and opportunities that are (UNCTAD, 2018):

- better – they offer more effective solutions to problems, provide new capabilities and opportunities, and enable much more efficient use of natural and human resources;
- cheaper – the cost of technologies such as microchips and renewable energy has decreased significantly as they have become more powerful and/or efficient;
- faster – the new technologies are disseminating ever more rapidly around the world, driven by Internet connectivity and sharply falling prices;
- scalable –they often provide small-scale solutions that can be quickly scaled up to satisfy human needs for energy, food, clean water, health care and education; and
- easy to use – they have altered previously complex, labor- and/or time-intensive tasks, such as searching for patterns in huge data sets, to become almost effortless, while growing increasingly transparent to users.

These technologies have beneficial applications in health care, agriculture, energy, water management and quality, construction, and education.

At the conclusion of these considerations, it should be mentioned that the ICT mission has changed significantly. ICTs cease to perform a subordinate function, focused on supporting business and catering to its needs (Bharadwaj et al., 2013; Kahre, Hoffmann, & Ahlemann, 2017). The Strategic Alignment Model (SAM), which has been in force for decades, developed by Henderson and Venkatraman (1993) and used to measure the adoption of ICT to business needs, and organizational efficiency mainly, has lost some importance. The roles have reversed – ICTs have become the moderator of change and the provider of new business opportunities. Until now, it was business that determined the scope and area of ICT use. Similarly to the leverage effect, we can talk today about the leverage effect of digital resources and new and distinctive values for the entire business and ecosystem powered by them. This means that, based on digital resources, firms compete in markets, develop original business models, and create value.

Information Communication Technology (ICT) in Business Value Creation

For a long time, many researchers have been asking themselves what exactly ICTs are and how much they can actually contribute to the improvement of organizational efficiency or innovative development and business success. In response to these questions, the indicated resource approach is partially helpful (Barney, 1991;Grant 1991). It says that only valuable and scarce resources can lead to competitive advantage. This advantage can be maintained in the long run if firms are able to protect their resources against imitation, transfer, and substitutability. Therefore, it is hard not to notice that not all ICT solutions can be a source of innovative success. Furthermore, business success cannot be automatically guaranteed by clean technological innovations. This issue has been extensively described in various papers (Teece, 2010) which pointed out that technological innovations without a proper commercialization strategy will not be successful; on the contrary, they can quickly lead to self-destruction of a creative organization. Numerous examples can be quoted of firms which have achieved success in the field of technological innovation, but have not been able to link it with the right business model. The experience of many organizations confirms that in designing ICT-based business models, the answer to the question of how to deliver new value to the customer and how to transform it into benefits for the firm becomes crucial. A model based on the contract theory can be the answer to this problem. According to this model, innovators can derive value from ICTs in two ways. The first is that the creator of ICT innovation takes responsibility for the introduction of an end-to-end value chain, including the design, manufacturing, and distribution of a new product. The second way, in turn, means that other firms are involved in creating the value chain, offering the production of specific products or sales support.

Creating ICT-based value has been described in an interesting way, *inter alia*, by J. Ross, C.M. Beath, & D.L. Goodhue(1996). The authors analyzed ICTs from the perspective of various assets. These include human assets (technical skills, business understanding, problem-solving orientation), technological (physical ICT infrastructure, databases, IS architecture, standards), and relationships between these assets (customer relationships, management support, and risk and responsibility management). In turn, Feeny and Willcocks (1998) identified nine key capabilities that are relevant to the development of ICT business value, which can be divided into four overlapping areas. These are ICT business and vision, ICT architecture design, ICT service delivery and network capability, related to ICT leadership and acquisition (purchase) of information. In contrast, Bharadwaj (2000) proposed six dimensions of ICTs, relevant from the point of creating value. These are ICT/business partnership, ICT external networks, strategic thinking in the ICT area, integration of ICT business processes, ICT management, and ICT infrastructure.

Research carried out by the authors mentioned earlier shows that the ICT infrastructure is the easiest asset to be captured and copied by competitors and, therefore, represents the most "sensitive" resource in creating business value. ICT-based value is derived by organizations mainly from intangible values, such as new skills, new business models, and new products (Wade & Hulland, 2004). They are much harder to copy and follow by competitors. For example, Amazon Web Server has expanded online models for suppliers by providing services in the "cloud." Google, Netflix, Microsoft, Facebook and Twitter also operate in a similar way that builds their competitive advantage not only on advanced equipment, specialized software and applications, but also original Internet communication and multilateral business models. This means that the delivery of specific products and services is increasingly more closely associated with other firms, e.g., telecommunications operators, publishing houses, and film producers.

To sum up this thread of considerations, it should be stressed that more and more firms, including start-ups, imitate leaders such as Google and Amazon, who base their services and offers on information digitization, analytics, original resource orchestration and supply chain integration. Unfortunately, the topic of value creation and achieving ICT-based success is still a poorly understood issue.

Computer Decision Support Systems

The beginnings of research on decision support systems can be found in works initiated in the 1960s. They were mainly related to the achievements of (a) H. Simon (1996), on solving psychological decision making problems;(b) Massachusetts researchers in the field of interactive human-computer computer systems;(3) R. Anthony (1965); and (4) MS Scott Morton and JD Little, regarding managerial activities (Little, 1970; Scott Morton, 1971). Early decision support systems, known as Transaction Systems (TS), supported organizations in implementing simple and routine operations. They were focused on supporting fragmentary, simple operational decisions related to production planning and scheduling, inventory and raw materials management, as well as sales and payroll, and human resources. The architecture of the first decision support systems was relatively simple and adapted to the batch mode of data processing. Over time, it has been enriched with components (modules) responsible for database management.

The development of computer technology, especially third-generation computers (in the 1970s), disk storage, data transmission, relational databases, multifunctional operating systems as well as reduction of hardware and software manufacturing costs have contributed to the development of Management Information Systems (MIS). In its assumptions, MIS was to support mid-level management (Bonczek, Holsapple, & Whinston, 1980). These systems have proved effective in supporting well-structured decisions. Above all, they enabled the analysis of the budget, financial expenses, making short-term predictions as well as simple purchase and sale analyses. The architecture of these systems was mainly based on relational databases, and relatively advanced algorithms were used for data processing.

Following MIS, in the 1980s, Decision Support Systems (DSS) appeared whose goal was to support the management in tactical and strategic planning (Alter, 1980). A novelty in the architecture of these systems, compared to MIS, was the model base and the model base management system. These components allowed users to model different events, e.g., portfolio, distribution systems, and product allocation on the markets. The development of DSS was fostered by interdisciplinary research in the field of organization and management, psychology, operational research, and the theory of computer science. The first DSS were dedicated to individual decision makers. However, practice quickly showed that effective decision-making is achieved through exchanges of views, negotiations, and brainstorming. In connection with the above, Group Decision Support Systems (GDSS) quickly developed, which supported parallel information processing, idea generation, and conflict resolution (DeSanctis & Brent, 1987). GDSS enabled a larger group of decision-makers to participate in the exchange of views, knowledge, and skills. Many empirical studies have confirmed that they contribute to increasing the efficiency of decision-making processes.

In the late 1980s and early 1990s, Executive Information Systems (EIS) were created. The EIS model was developed for managers for whom effective reporting, data visualization, and providing quick and reliable information about current values (indicators) and the expected directions of changes in these parameters were priority issues (McNurlin & Sprague, 1993). It was stressed at the time that the EIS architecture should be different from the current solutions because senior managers have their own distinctive style of decision-making. They need information in a synthetic form and have different preparation for work with computer equipment than middle managers. EIS were to prove themselves as tools that quickly generate general and cross-sectional analyses. The results presented in a graphical form allowed decision-makers to supplement knowledge in a rapidly changing environment (DeSanctis & Brent, 1987).

Fundamental progress in software development and intensive research into artificial intelligence have contributed to the development of Expert Systems (ES). In its assumption, ES was to provide suggestions or solve specific decision problems to a degree similar to that of an expert human being in a selected field. The basic distinguishing features of ES compared to previous systems were new ways of knowledge representation, use of different methods of problem-solving, and separation of the knowledge system from inference and control. ES enabled intelligent decision support, expert advice, explaining expert conclusions, and assistance in formulating questions. The first attempts of ES implementation mainly concerned medicine. However, over time, they have become interesting technologies for banks, insurance companies, and various consulting institutions. At this point, it is worth noting that although ES overcame many imperfections in the field of existing decision support, they did not support a decision-maker in a wider problem area well. Acquiring knowledge from field experts turned out to be an extremely difficult issue. Today, these problems (at least partially) are solved with the aid of intelligent agents. They enable better communication and cooperation of many expert systems from various fields of knowledge. The term "agent" means a special computer program that has the ability to communicate with other programs (agents), monitor the environment, and make or prepare decisions that will allow it to achieve the goal or objectives for which it was programmed (Poole & Mackworth, 2010; Wang & Wang, 2005). In other words, an agent is a system that has the ability to solve problems and operate efficiently in environments characterized by high dynamics and complexity (Wooldridge, 2009). It is regarded that an intelligent agent should have the following features (Rudowsky, 2004; Rykowski, 2006; Paprzycki, 2014): (a) learning, i.e., carrying out such processing that allows continuous access to the changing needs of the environment and use of acquired knowledge; (b) autonomy, i.e., the ability to make independent decisions or recommendations of proposed solutions; (c) communicativeness, understood as the ability to interact with other agents; and (d) flexibility, understood as the perception of and responding to any slight changes in the environment.

Depending on the purpose for which the agent was built, a number of features may change. The agent is often required to be friendly or to allow the use of natural language because of the users' skills, e.g., they are not always able to take a full advantage of ICT tools. Sometimes anthropomorphic features are attributed to agents, including responsibility, emotions, faith, and rationality, and the ability to predict (Russell & Norvig, 2003). Equipping the agent with such features as communicativeness and flexibility allows the creation of a multi-agent system (Weyns, 2010). Such a system is built of communicating and cooperating agents. Such agents, in addition to achieving their own specific goals, can also pursue common goals. Moreover, they can absorb information and knowledge from the environment, as well as use their own knowledge and optimize their operation.

At the end of the 1990s, we witnessed the increasingly effective integration of information technologies with various management concepts, such as balanced scorecard, SWOT analysis, and critical factor analysis (Bocij et al., 2003). It resulted in the development of such computer systems as MRP II (Manufacturing Resource Planning), ERP (Enterprise Resource Planning), CRM (Customer Relationship Management), SCM (Supply Chain Management), and e-business that have essentially changed the way in which a firm is managed, they altered customer and supplier relationship management. In addition, there have been bold attempts to implement information systems in new areas such as business planning, water and land management, food production and distribution, reduction of poverty and destitution, health services, administrative services, education, pollution control, environmental management, management and urban planning, and assistance in natural disasters (Beynon-Davies, 2009).

The beginning of the 21st century is a period of dynamic development of systems focused on advanced business analytics and decision support at all levels of management. Business Intelligence (BI), Competitive Intelligence (CI), and Big Data (BD) systems are developing. These systems are mainly focused on collecting, analyzing various data from many distributed, heterogeneous information resources (including the Internet), discovering new knowledge and its visualization to improve decision-making efficiency. The existing decision support systems with varying results, often not very satisfactory, allowed the use of external and internal information resources. Much valuable information was lost due to the lack of ability to store historical data, unify, aggregate, and discover relationships between them. These systems began to provide organizations with these capabilities. In addition, there have been opportunities to process large data sets, mainly from the Internet, referred to as Big Data (BD) (Laudon & Laudon, 2018; Turban, McLean, & Wetherebe, 2002). A synthetic summary of the most important decision support systems is presented in Table 1.1.

Table 1.1 Comparison of Selected Decision Support Systems

Characteristics	TS	SJK	SWD	SE	EIS	BI	BI&BD
Types of problems	Selected, well structured	Structured	Partly structured	Non-structured	Partly structured	Structured, partly structured and non-structured	Structured, partly structured and non-structured
Tasks	Providing simple reporting	Providing algorithms for problem-solving and simulations	Providing models to describe reality	Inference, explanation	Information visualization	Exploration and acquisition of knowledge	Analysis of data mainly from distributed internet resources, mobile devices
Time horizon	Past	Past and present	Present and future	Present	Present and future	Present, Future	Past, present, future
Decision area	Operational	Operational, tactical	Tactical, strategic	Operational, tactical	Strategic	Operational, tactical, strategic	Operational, tactical, strategic
Technology	Batch processing, files	Database	Model database, interface	Knowledge base, inference module	Interface	Data warehouse, OLAP, data mining	Web mining, sentimental analysis, real time analysis, analysis on demand
Typical applications	Payroll, HR	Accounting	Finance, production	Diagnostics, training	Analysis and visualization of trends	Market and financial analysis, anomaly detection	Analysis of customer behavior, and individuals and organizations in social media
Users	ICT specialists, selected management personnel	Analysts, middle management	Analysts, middle and senior management	Field experts, knowledge engineers	Top management decision makers	Management decision makers of all level, analysts, customers	Management decision makers of all levels, analysts, customers, individuals

Designing Decision Support Systems

The effective creation and use of any information system in an organization requires reliance on proven research methodologies and practices. They guarantee that the developed system will meet the users' expectations and support the implementation of the organization's various goals. Hevner et al. (2004) in their paper *Design Science in Information System Research* argue that the overarching goal of any information system in the organization should primarily improve organizational efficiency and effectiveness. Said efficiency and effectiveness are determined by various factors, in particular the specific nature of the organization, work system in the organization, skills of employees, capacities (capabilities) of the IT system, as well as methods used to design and implement IT systems. Exploration and understanding of these factors require to reach into different layers of knowledge, especially two paradigms that are related to behavioral and design sciences (March & Smith, 1995). The paradigm of behavioral sciences is derived from research conducted as part of life science research which mainly amounts to creating theories (principles, laws) that explain phenomena related to human and organizational behaviors as well as design, implementation, management, and use of information systems. These theories describe all interactions between people, technologies, and organizations that should be reflected in the information system.

The paradigm of design sciences is derived from engineering (Simon, 1996). This is a fundamental canon of knowledge that is used to solve and support all decision-making problems. The focus of this paradigm is primarily innovation, which means all ideas, practices, technological capabilities, and products, thanks to which analysis, design, implementation, management, and utilization of information systems can be implemented more effectively and efficiently. Terms such as analysis, design, and implementation are referred to as artifacts. They do not come from the laws of nature or theory of behavior. Their creation is based on kernel theories, which are applied, tested, modified, and extended with the participation of various experiments, creative practices, intuition, and the ability to solve research problems (Markus, Majchrzak, & Gasser, 2002; Walls, Widmeyer, & El Sawy, 1992). These theories focus on creating new approaches and techniques for effective design and construction of information systems for organizations.

The gist of research on information systems for organizations is the issue of integration of people, organizations, and technologies (March & Smith, 1995; Nunamaker, Chen, & Purdin, 1991; Ostrowski, Helfer, & Xie, 2012). This integration means the need to align business with information technology strategies, organizational infrastructure, and information systems infrastructure. Researchers denote that effective transition from strategy to infrastructure requires project activity, both on the organizational design side (to create an effective organizational infrastructure) and information system design (to create an effective information system infrastructure). These project activities should be closely related. In other words, authors involved in the design of decision support systems must take into account in their work the relationships between business strategy, ICT strategy, organizational infrastructure, and information system infrastructure.

Hevner et al. (2004) claim that information systems design is dichotomous. Design can mean both a process (sequence of activities) and a product (artifact). In the first case, the point is that economic reality can be described in terms of processes, while in the second, that the description of this reality is done in terms of various entities (artifacts).

Research in the design of decision support systems should take into account that the design process is a sequence of various expert activities which are to lead to the development of the system. The assessment of such a system is very important. It provides information on the need to modify/improve the product itself or to improve the entire (or part of) design process. In turn, the artifacts can be constructs, models, methods, or instantiations that describe the ontology of the studied reality in an abstract way, i.e., business processes, data flows, and data structures. Figure 1.4 reflects the heart of the research conducted by Hevner et al. (2004).

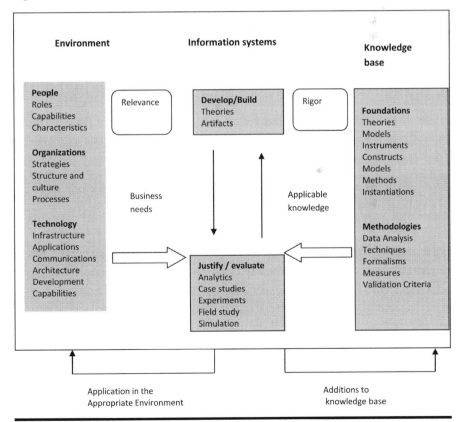

Figure 1.4 Designing information systems for organizations.

Source: Own elaboration based on (Hevner et al., 2004).

It shows that in order to understand, create, and evaluate computer systems, it is necessary to skillfully combine knowledge of behavioral sciences with the body of achievements in the field of design sciences.

Hevner et al. (2004) devoted a lot of attention to the issue of organization environment which consists of people, organizations, and technologies. These elements set goals, tasks, problems, as well as business opportunities and needs that are assessed and evaluated in terms of organizational strategies, structure, organizational culture, and existing business processes. In turn, Takeda et al. (1990) draw attention to the need to enumerate a business problem, while Rossi and Sein (2003) prove the importance of identifying information needs. Many authors agree that the process of designing an information system for an organization can be described in terms of six activities, which include (Hevner et al., 2004; Markus, Majchrzak, & Gasser, 2002; Peffers et al., 2007): (1) identifying the problem and motivating its solution; (2) defining system goals in the context of business needs; (3) system design and development – creation of artifacts; (4) description and use of artifacts to solve a specific problem; (5) assessment – observation of artifacts, leading to determination of how artifacts support the solution of a given problem; and (6) communication – meaning dissemination of the test results obtained.

To sum up, these considerations show that a decision support system is a complex concept (Seidel, Muller-Wienbergen, & Becker, 2010), covering issues related to hardware, software, information resources, people, functioning of the organization and its environment, as well as relations that take place between these elements. The purpose of such a system is to support organizations in making decisions related to all levels of management. A decision support system should be treated as a collection of many artifacts, i.e., unique mechanisms for acquiring and discovering knowledge, databases, knowledge bases, human communication interfaces, components for carrying out various event scenarios, suggesting ideas, reasoning mechanisms, and space for carrying out dialogue and sharing ideas. Such a system should have the ability to dynamically integrate, explore, and reconfigure organization's information resources (Teece, Pisano, & Shuen, 1997; Wade & Hulland, 2004). In other words, it should focus on generating original information resources and discovering new knowledge necessary for effective decision making.

References

Ahn, M.J., & York, A.S. (2011). Resource-based and institution-based approaches to biotechnology industry development in Malaysia. *Asia Pacific Journal of Management, 28*(2), 257–275.

Alter, S. L. (1980). *Decision support systems. Current practices and challenges.* New York: Addison-Wesley.

Amabile, T.M. (1988). A model of creativity and innovation in organizations. *"Research in Organizational Behavior", 10,* 123–167.

Anthony, R. (1965). Planning and control system. A framework for analysis. Boston: Harvard University.

Arora, A., & Nandkumar, A. (2012). Insecure advantage? Markets for technology and the value of resources for entrepreneurial ventures. *"Strategic Management Journal"*, *33*, 231–251.

Awad, E. M., & Ghaziri, H. M. (2004). *Knowledge management*. New Jersey: Prentice Hall.

Banker, R. D., Bardhan, I. R., Chang, H., & Lin, S. (2006). Plant information systems. manufacturing capabilities, and plant performance. *"MIS Quarterly"*, *30*(2), 315–337.

Barney, J. (1991). Firm resources and sustained competitive advantage. *Journal of Management*, *17*(1), 99–120.

Baron, R.A. (2012). *Entrepreneurship: An evidence-based guide*. Cheltenham, UK and Northampton: Edward Elgar Publishing.

Basadur, M., Basadur, T., & Licina, G. (2012). *Organizational development*. In: M.D. Mumford (Eds.), *Handbook of organizational creativity*, pp. 667–703. London: Academic Press/Elsevier.

Bechky, B.A., & Okhuysen, G.A. (2011). Expecting the unexpected? How SWAT officers and film crews handle surprises, *"Academy of Management Journal"*, *54*(2), pp. 239–261.

Beynon-Davies, P. (2009). *Business information systems*. Basingstoke: Palgrave MacMillan.

Bharadwaj, A.S. (2000). A resource-based perspective on information technology capability and firm performance: An empirical investigation. *"MIS Quarterly"*, *24*(1), 169–196.

Bharadwaj, A.S., El Sawy, O.A., Pavlou, P. A., & Venkatraman, N. (2013). Digital business strategy: Toward a next generation of insights. *"MIS Quarterly"*, *37*(2), Special Issue: Digital Business Strategy, 471–482.

Bocij, P., Chaffey, D., Greasley, A., & Hickie, S. (2003). *Business information systems: Technology, development and management for the e-business*. New York: Prentice Hall.

Bonczek, H. C., Holsapple, W., & Whinston, A. (1980). Evolving roles of models in decision support systems. *"Decision Science"*, *11*(2), pp. 337–356.

Brilman, J.(2002). *Nowoczesne koncepcje i metody zarządzania*. Warszawa: PWE.

Bui, T. (2000). Decision support systems for sustainable development. In: G. E. Kersten, Z. Mikolajuk, & A. Gar-on Yeh (Eds.), *Decision Support Systems for Sustainable Development. A resource book of methods and applications*. Kluwer Academic Publishers.

Chapman, J. A. (2001). The Work of managers in new organizational contexts. *"Journal of Management Development"*, *20*(1), 55–68.

Chourides, P., Longbottom, D., & Murphy, W. (2003). Excellence in knowledge management: An empirical study to identify critical factors and performance measures. *"Measuring Business Excellence"*, *7*(2), 29–45.

Cosic, R. Shanks, G., & Maynard, S. (2012). Towards a business analytics capability maturity model. In: Proceedings of the 23 Australasian Conference on Information Systems, Geelong.

Daniel, D.R. (1961). Management information crises. *Harvard Business Review*, *39*(5), 111–116.

Davenport, T.H. & Harris, J.G. (2007). *Competing on analytics: The new science on winning*. Boston Massachusetts: Harvard Business School Press.

Davenport, T. H., Harris, J. G., & Morison, R. (2010). *Analytics at work: smarter decisions, better results*. Cambridge: Harvard Business Press.

Davenport, T. H., de Long, D. W., & Beers, M. C. (1998). Successful knowledge management projects. *"Sloan Management Review"*, *39*(2), 43–57.

Davydow, M. M. (2000). The second wave of EIP. Intelligent Enterprise, *3*(4).

DeSanctis, G. & Brent, G. (1987). A foundation for the study of group decision support systems. *"Management Science"*, *33*(5), 589–609.

Drucker, P.F. (2002). *Managing in the next society*. Oxford: Butterworth-Heinemann.

Drucker, P. F. (2014). *Innovation and entrepreneurship*. New York; Routledge.

Ettlie, J., & Pavlou, P. (2006). Technology-based ew product development partnerships. *"Decision Science"*, *37*(2), 117–148.

Evenport, T. H., & Prusak, I. (1998). *Working knowledge: How organizations manage what they know*. Boston: Harvard Business School Press.

Feeny, D.F., & Willcocks, L.P. (1998). Core IS capabilities for exploiting information technology. *"Sloan Management Review"*, *39*(3), 9–21.

George, J.M. (2007). Creativity in organizations. *"The Academy of Management Annals"*, 3. London: Routledge, 439–477.

Grant, R.M. (1991). The resource-based theory of competitive advantage: implications for strategy formulation. *"California Management Review"*, *33*(1), 114–135.

Henderson, J., & Venkatraman, H. (1993). Srategicaligment: leveranging information technology for transforming organizations. *"IBM Systems Journal"*, *32*(1), 472–484.

Herschel, R. T., & Jones, N.E. (2005). Knowledge management and business intelligence: the importance of integration. *Journal of Knowledge Management*, *9*(4), 45–54.

Hevner, A.R., March, S. T., Park, J., & Ram S. (2004). Design science in information systems research. *"MIS Quarterly"*, *28*(1), 75–105.

Heweet, T., Czerwinski, M., Terry, M., Nunamaker, J.F., Candy, L., Kules, B., & Sylvan, E. (2005). Creativity support tools evaluation methods and metrics. In: *Creativity Support Tools*. A workshop sponsored by the National Science Foundation, Washington, retrieved from http://www.cs.umd.edu.hcil/CST.

Houghton, J.D., & DiLiello, T.C. (2010). Leadership development: The key to unlocking individual creativity in organizations. *"Leadership & Organization Development Journal"*, *11*, 230–245.

Howson, C. (2008). *Successful business intelligence: Secrets to making BI a killer application*. New York: McGraw-Hill.

Hasanali, F. (2003). Critical success factors of knowledge management. In: M. Koenig and K. Srikantaiahby(Eds.), Knowledge Management Lessons Learned, Information Today.

Holsapple, C. W., & Joshi, K. D. (2000). An investigation of factors that influence the management of knowledge in organizations. *"Journal of Strategic Information Systems"*, *9*(2), 235–261.

Hsu, D.H., & Ziedonis, R.H. (2013). Resource as dual sources of advantage: implications for valuing entrepreneurial – firm patents. *"Strategic Management Journal"*, *34*, 761–781.

Indurkhya, B. (2013). On the role of computers in creativity-support systems. *In:* A. Skulimowski (Eds.), *Looking into the future of creativity and decision support systems*, 233–244. Kraków: Progress & Business Publishers.

Jamali, D. (2005). Changing management paradigms: Implication for educational institutions. *"Journal of Management Development"*, Vol. 24, 104–115.

Jashapara, A.(2006). *Zarządzanie wiedzą*. Warszawa: PWN.

Kahre, C., Hoffmann, D., & Ahlemann, F. (2017). *Beyond Business-It Alignment – digital Business strategies as a Paradigmatic Shift: a review and research agenda*. Proceedings of the 50th Hawaii international Conference on Systems Sciences, Hawaii.

Kelly, K. (2001). *Nowe reguły nowej gospodarki. Dzisięć przełomowych strategii świata połączonych siecią*. Warszawa: Wig Press.

Kersten, G. E. (2000). Decision making and decision support. In: Kersten, G. E., Mikolajuk, Z., Gar-On Yeh, A. (Eds.), *Decision Support Systems for Sustainable Development. A Resource book of methods and applications*. Kluwer Academic Publishers.

Knox, K.T. (2014). The ambiguity that surrounds information strategy. *"International Journal of an Emerging Transdiscipline"*, *17*, 149–173.

Kohli R., & Grover, V. (2008). Business value of IT: An essay on expanding research directions to keep up with the times. *"Journal of Association for Information Systems"*, *9*(1), 23–39.

KPMG Consulting, Knowledge Management (2000). Research Report.

Laudon, K.C., & Laudon, J.P. (2018). *Management information systems. Managing the digital firm*[15 edn.]. Harlow, England: Pearson.

Leonard-Barton, D. (1995). *Wellsprings of knowledge: Building and sustaining the source of innovation*. Boston: Harvard Business.

Liautaud, B., & Hammond, M. (2001). *E-business intelligence, turning information into knowledge into profit*. New York: McGraw-Hill.

Liebowitz, J., & Suen, C. Y. (2000). Developing knowledge management metrics for measuring intellectual capital. *"Journal of Intellectual Capital"*, *1*(1), 54–67.

Little, J. D. (1970). Models and managers: The concept of a decision calculus. *"Management Science"*, *16*(8).

Manyika, J., Chui, M., Brown, B., Bughin, J., Dobbs, R., Roxburgh, C., & Byers, A. H. (2011). *Big data: The next frontier for innovation, competition, and productivity*. McKinsey Global Institute.

March, S. T., & Smith, G. (1995). Design and natural science research on information technology. *"Decision Support Systems"*, *15*(4), 251–266.

Markus, M.L., Majchrzak, A., & Gasser, L. (2002). A design theory for systems that support Emergent Knowledge Processes. *"MIS Quarterly"*, *26*(3), 179–212.

McGonagle, J.J., & Vella, C.M. (2002). *Bottom line competitive intelligence*. Westport, CT: Quorum Books.

McNurlin, B. C., Sprague, R.H., & Bui, T. (2014). *Information systems management*. Harlow, England: Pearson.

McNurlin, B. C., & Sprague, R. H. (1993). *Information systems management in practice*. Engelwood Cliffs: Prentice Hall.

Mitchell, W.J., Inouye, A.S., & Blumenthal, M.S. (2003). *Beyond productivity: information technology, innovation and creativity. technology and creativity*. Washington: National Research Council, National Academy of Science.

Mumford, M.D., Robledo, I.C., & Hester, K.S. (2011). *Creativity, innovation, and leadership: Models and findings*. In: A. Bryman, D. Collinson, K. Grint, B. Jackson & M. Uhl-Bien (Eds.), *The Sage handbook of leadership*, 405–421. Washington: Sage.

Nakakoji, K. (2006). *Meanings of tools, support, and uses for creative design process*. CREDITS Research Center: International Design Research Symposium'06, Seoul, 156–165.

Negash, S., & Gray, P. (2008). Business intelligence. In: F. Burstein and C.W. Holsapple (Eds.), *Decision Support Systems* (pp. 175–193). Berlin: Springer.

Nonaka, I., & Takeuchi, H. (1995). Knowledge creating organizations. New York: Oxford University Press.

Nonaka, I., & Takeuchi, H. (2000). Kreowanie wiedzy w organizacji. Warszawa: Poltex.

Nunamaker, J.F., Chen, M., & Purdin, T.D.M. (1991). Systems development in Information Systems Research. *"Journal of Management IS, 7*(3), 89–106.

Olszak, C. M. (2012). Krytyczne czynniki sukcesu wdrażania zarządzania wiedzą w małych i średnich przedsiębiorstwach. In: Gospodarka Elektroniczna. Wyzwania rozwojowe. Zeszyty Naukowe 702. Ekonomiczne Problemy Usług 87. Szczecin: Uniwersytet Szczeciński, 110–119.

Olszak, C. M. (2016). Toward better understanding and use of Business Intelligence in organizations. *Information Systems Management*, *33* (2), 105–123.

Olszak, C.M., & Kisielicki, J. (2018). A conceptual framework of information systems for organizational creativity support. Lessons from empirical investigations. *"Information Systems Management"*, *35* (1), 29–48.

Olszak, C.M., Bartuś, T., & Lorek, P. (2018). A comprehensive framework of information system design to provide organizational creativity support (2018). *Information & Management*, *55*, 94–108.

Ortbach, K., Plattfaut, R., Popelbuss, J., & Niehaves, B. (2012). A dynamic capability-based framework for business process management: Theorizing and empirical application. Proceedings of 45th Hawaii International Conference on System Sciences, IEEE Computer.

Ostrowski, Ł., Helfert, M., & Xie, S. (2012). A conceptual framework to construct an artefact for meta-abstract design knowledge in design science research. Proceedings of 45th International Conference on System Sciences, IEEE, computer society, Hawaii, 4074–4081.

Paprzycki, M. (2014). *Agenci programowi jako metodologia tworzenia oprogramowania*, *E-informatyka.pl*, retrieved from: http://www.e-informatyka.pl/attach/Agenci_programowi_jako_metodologia_tworzenia_oprogramowania/422.pdf.

Peffers, K., Tuunanen, T., Rothenberger, M. A., & Chatterjee, S. (2007). A design science research methodology for information systems research. *"Journal of Management Information Systems"*, *1*(3), 45–77.

Poole, D., & Mackworth, A. (2010). *Artificial intelligence: Foundations of computational agent.* Cambridge: University Press.

Power, D. J. (2001). Supporting decision-makers: An expanded framework. In:E. Cohen, & E. Boyd (Eds.), Informing Science and IT Education. Santa Rosa, California: The Informing Science Institute.

Proctor, T. (2010). *Creative problem solving for managers. Developing skills for decision making and innovation*, 3th edition. New York: Taylor & Francis e-Library.

Rai, A., Pavlou, P. A., Im, G., & Du, S. (2012). Interfirm IT capability profiles and communications for cocreating relational value: Evidence from the logistics industry. *"MIS Quarterly"*, *36*(1), 233–262.

Rivard, S. B., Aubert, B. A., Patry, M., Pare, G., & Smith, H. A. (2004). *Information technology and organizational transformation*, London: Elsevier.

Rockart, J. (1979). Chief executives define their own information needs. *Harvard Business Review*, March/April, 81–92.

Ross, J., Beath, C.M., & Goodhue, D.L. (1996). Develop long-term competitiveness trough IT assets. *"Sloan Management Review"*, *39*(1), 31–42.

Rossi, M. & Sein, M.K. (2003). Design research workshop: A proactive research approach. In: Proceedings of 26th Information Systems Research Seminar. Scanynavia, Haikko.

Roztocki, N., & Weistroffer, H.R. (2008). Information technology in transition economy. *"Journal of Global Information Technology Management"*, *11*(4), 2–9.

Rudowsky, I. (2004). Intelligent agents. *Proceedings of the Americas Conference on Information Systems*, New York.

Russell, S., & Norvig, P. (2003). *Artificial intelligence: A modern approach*. New Jersey: Prentice Hall.

Rykowski, J. (2006). *Personalized access to heterogeneous distributed information sources by means of software agents*. Poznań: Publishing House of University of Economics.

Sanchez, R., & Heene, A. (1997). A competence perspective on strategic learning and knowledge management. In: R. Sanchez & A. Heene (Eds.), *Strategic Learning and Knowledge Management*. New York: John Wiley & Sons.

Sauter, V.L. (2010). *Decision support systems for business intelligence*. Second edition, New Jersey, Wiley.

Schick, A., Frolick, M., & Ariyachandra, T. (2011). Competing with BI and analytics at Monster Worldwide. In: *Proceedings of the 44 Hawaii International Conference on System Sciences*, Hawaii.

Scott Morton, M. S. (1971). Management decision systems: Computer based support for decision making. Cambridge: Mass Division of Research, Harvard University.

Seidel, S., Muller-Wienbergen, F., & Becker, J. (2010). The concept of creativity in the information systems discipline, *"CAIS"*, *27*(1), 218–242.

Shneiderman, B. (2007). Creativity support tools: Accelerating discovery and innovation. *"Communications of the ACM"*, *50*(12), 20–32.

Simon, H.A. (1996). The sciences of the artificial (3 rded.). Cambridge, MA: MIT Press.

Sirmon, D.G., Hitt, M.A., Ireland, R.D., & Gilbert, B.A. (2011). Resource orchestration to create competitive advantage: Breadth, depth, and life cycle effects. *"Journal of Management"*, *37*, 1390–1412.

Skyrme, D., & Amidon, D. (1997). The *knowledge agenda*. *"Journal of Knowledge Management"*, *1*, 27–37.

Steiger, D.M. (2010). Decision support as knowledge creation: A business intelligence design theory. *"International Journal of Business Intelligence Research"*, *1*(1), 29–47.

Straub, D., & Watson, R. (2001). Transformational issues in researching IS and net-enabled organizations. *"Information Systems Research"*, *12*(4), 337–345.

Styhre, A., & Sundgren, M. (2005). *Managing creativity in organizations*. New York: Palgrave.

Subramaniam, M., & Venkatraman, N. (2001). Determinants of transnational new products development capability: Testing the influence of transferring and deploying tacit overseas knowledge. *"Strategic Management Journal"*, *22*(4), 359–378.

Tan, P.N., Steinbach, M., & Kumar V. (2005). *Introduction do data mining*. New York: Addison-Wesley.

Tapscott, D., & Williams, A.D. (2006). *Wikinomics: How mass collaboration changes everything*. New York: Penguin Group.

Teece, D.J., Pisano, G., & Shuen, A. (1997). Dynamic capabilities and strategic management, *"Strategic Management Journal"*, *18*, 509–533.

Teece, D.J. (2010). Business models, business strategy and innovation. *"Long Range Planning"*, *43*, 172–194.

Takeda, H., Veerkamp, P., Tomiyama, T., & Yoshikawam, H. (1990). Modelling Design Process. *"AI Magazine"*, *11*(4), 37–48.

Tiwana, A. (2000). *The knowledge management toolkit: Practical techniques for building a knowledge management systems*. New York: Prentice Hall.

Turban, R., Sharada, R., Delen, D., & King, D. (2014). *Business intelligence: A managerial approach*. London, England: Pearson.

Turban, E., McLean, E., & Wetherbe, J.C. (2002). *Information technology for management transforming business in the digital economy*. New York: John Wiley & Sons, Inc.

UNCTAD (2018). TECHNOLOGY AND INNOVATION REPORT 2018. Harnessing Frontier Technologies for Sustainable Development, United Nations Conference on Trade and Development. UNCTAD, United Nations.

Viehland, D. (2005). ISExpertNet: Facilitating knowledge sharing in the information systems academic community. In: E. Cohen, & E. Boyd (Eds.), *Informing Science and IT Education*. Santa Rosa, Calofornia: The Informing Science Institute.

Wade, M., & Hulland, J. (2004). The resource-based view and information systems research: Review, extension, and suggestions for future research. *"MIS Quarterly"*, *28*(1), 107–142.

Walls, J., Widmeyer, G., & El Sawy, O. (1992). Building an information system design theory for vigilant EIS. *"Information Systems Research"*, *3*(1), 36–59.

Wang, M., & Wang, H. (2005). Intelligent agent supported business process management. *Proceedings of the 38th Hawaii International Conference on System Sciences*.

Weyns, D. (2010). *Architecture-based design of multi-agent systems*. Berlin Heidelberg: Springer-Verlag.

Wickramasinghe, N., & von Lubitz, D. (2007). *Knowledge-based enterprise: Theories and fundamentals*. Hershey: IDEA Group Publishing.

Wixom, B.H., & Watson, H.J. (2010). The BI-based organization. *International Journal of Business Intelligence Research*, *1*(1), 13–28.

Wong, K. W. (2005). Critical success factors for implementing knowledge management in small and medium enterprises. *"Industrial Management & Data Systems"*, *105*(2), 261–279.

Wooldridge, M. (2009). *An introduction to multi agent systems*. New York: John Wiley & Sons Ltd.

Wu, J. (2000). *Business intelligence: The transition of data into wisdom*. DM Direct.

Zahra, S.A., Sapienza, H.J., & Davidsson, P. (2006). Entrepreneurship and dynamic capabilities: A review, model, and research agenda. *"Journal of Management Studies"*, *43*, 917–955.

Chapter 2

Business Intelligence in Management of Organizations

The Essence of Business Intelligence

The first chapter of the book stresses that the environment in which modern organizations operate is extremely complex and unstable. To respond quickly to market needs, organizations face the imperative to utilize various technologies and decision support systems. Organizations need intelligent solutions that would be able to analyze a variety of data from different, distributed sources and discover new knowledge for the decision-making process (Bui, 2000; Carlsson & Turban, 2002; Gray, 2003; Gray & Watson, 1998; Laudon & Laudon, 2004).

In the opinion of many authors, the solution that responds to the needs of modern organizations is Business Intelligence (BI) systems. Global reports from firms such as the Gartner Group, the Australian Computer Society, and Oracle and Teradata indicate that BI and advanced analytics have become an important area of research that reflects the importance of information in solving the problems of a modern organization. Research results reveal that BI systems can contribute to streamlining the decision-making process, improving customer relationship management, monitoring the environment, as well as detecting anomalies and business fraud (Kalakota & Robinson, 1999; Liautaud & Hammond, 2001; Moss & Alert, 2003; Olszak, 2016).

It is argued that a special role of BI was marked when managers faced the necessity of (a) taking into account many data in the decision-making process, often from different sources; (b) handling historical data; (c) manipulating synthetic data; (d) predicting the future and creating long-term plans; (e) conducting continuous control over the implementation of actions taken, both operational and strategic in nature; and (f) responding quickly to market changes and taking into account competition activities.

Although the BI issue has been developing for many years, there is still no consistency with the interpretation of this term. There are many reasons for this. The very term *intelligence* can be understood differently. *Intelligence* is sometimes associated with the intellectual abilities of a human being, skills in abstract thinking and learning, as well as perceiving the relationships between different facts and drawing various conclusions on this basis. The term "intelligence" can also mean the ability to adapt to new conditions and perform new tasks using the means of thinking. It is worth stressing that intelligent behavior and action have been attributed only to human beings for many years. Nowadays, this characteristic is also attributed to computers, software, various objects, products, as well as entire industries (sectors) and organizations. As a consequence, the term *Business Intelligence* (BI) appeared.

It is believed that the term *Business Intelligence* was first used in the 1980s by H. Dresner of the Gartner Group. However, some say that as early as 1958, H. P. Luhn used this term to describe data analysis tools (Anandarajan & Srinivasan, 2004). Today, it is often identified with: (a) data analysis tools and technologies, data warehouse (Inmon, Strauss, & Neushloss, 2008); (b) a decision support system (Alter, 2004; Baaras & Kemper, 2008; Negash, 2004); (c) Competitive Intelligence (Albescu, Pugna, & Paraschiv, 2008; Sauter, 2010; Styl, 2012); (d) knowledge management (Negash & Gray, 2008; Wells, 2008); (e) information- and knowledge-based organizational culture (Liautaud & Hammond, 2001); (f) process focused on collecting, analyzing and sharing information (Jourdan, Rainer, & Marschall, 2008); (g) analytics (Davenport & Harris, 2007); (h) Big Data (Schmarzo, 2013); and (i) a research field, denoting a holistic view of decision support (Gray, 2003; Liautaud & Hammond, 2001; Moss & Alert, 2003; Simmers, 2004). Selected interpretations of the term BI are presented in Table 2.1.

While interpreting the BI term, it is important to consider its two main approaches (Isik, Jones, & Sidorova, 2011; Moss & Atre, 2003): technical and managerial. In technical terms (and this first appeared in describing the essence of BI), BI means an integrated set of tools, technologies, and software products for collecting heterogeneous data from various distributed sources, integrating, analyzing, and sharing them (Reinschmidt & Francoise, 2000). These primarily include a data warehouse, Online Analytical Processing (OLAP) tools, and data mining techniques. The data warehouse is responsible for integrating various data from distributed sources. In turn, OLAP tools enable their multidimensional analysis, and data mining techniques are used to detect previously unknown correlations and relationships between data.

In a managerial approach, it is emphasized that information and knowledge are strategic resources of an organization, andhadvanced data analysis allows not only

Table 2.1 Selected Definitions of Business Intelligence

Author	Description
Adelman and Moss (2000)	A term comprising a wide range of software for collecting, consolidating, analyzing and sharing information that enables better decision-making for organizations
Alter (2004)	A term referring to decision support
Business Objects (2007)	Providing various data, information, and analyses to employees, customers, and suppliers to improve decision-making
Cognos (2007)	BI connects people and data, offering various ways of looking at information that support decision-making
Chang (2005)	Accurate, timely, and relevant data, information, and knowledge that support strategic and operational decisions, risk assessment in an uncertain and dynamic environment of the organization
Chung, Chen, and Nunamaker (2005)	Results obtained by collecting, analyzing, assessing, and using information in business
Davenport, Harris, and Morison (2010); Watson, (2010)	*An umbrella* that is commonly used to describe the technologies, applications, and processes for gathering, storing, accessing, and analyzing data to help users make better decisions
Dresner et al. (2002)	A term comprising a set of concepts and methods used to improve decision-making using decision support systems
Eckerson (2005)	A system that transforms data into various information products
Gangadharan and Swami (2004)	The result of using deep analyses on business data in databases
Gartner Research (Hostmann, 2007)	A term comprising analytical applications, infrastructure, platforms, and best practices
Hannula and Pirttimaki (2003)	An organized and systemic process that is used to collect, analyze, and share information to support operational and strategic decisions
IBM (Whitehorn & Whitehorn, 1999)	A term comprising a broadly understood process aimed at extracting valuable information from various organization's data resources

(Continued)

Table 2.1 Continued

Author	Description
Informatica, Teradata, MicroStrategy, Markarian, Brobst, and Bedell (2007)	Interactive process of exploration and analysis of structured, domain-specific information (stored in data warehouses) aimed at discovering trends and patterns
Isik, Jones, and Sidorova (2011)	BI means a holistic and sophisticated approach to cross-organizational decision support
Jourdan et al. (2008)	Processes and products that are used to create relevant information necessary for functioning in a global economy and predicting the behavior of the business environment
Kulkarni and King (1997)	A product of business data analysis using intelligent tools
Lonnqvist and Pirttimaki (2006)	Management philosophy and a tool that helps manage and make more effective decisions
Moss and Atre (2003)	Architecture and a collection of integrated operations as well as decision support applications and data warehouses that provide organizations with easy access to business data
Moss and Hoberman (2004)	Processes, technologies and tools that are necessary to transform data into information, information into knowledge, and knowledge into activities that benefit an organization. BI comprises data warehouses, analytical tools, and knowledge and content management
Negash (2004)	A system that integrates and stores data, manages knowledge using analytical tools so that decision-makers can convert information into a competitive advantage
Olszak and Ziemba (2006)	A set of concepts, methods, and processes whose goal is not only to improve business decisions but also to support an organization's strategy
Oracle (2007)	A portfolio of technologies and applications that provide an integrated organization management system, including finance, management, BI applications, and data warehouses

Table 2.1   Continued

Author	Description
SAS Institute (Ing, 2011)	Providing the right information to the right people, at the right time, to support better decision-making and competitive advantage
Turban et al. (2014)	A term that comprises tools, architectures, databases, data warehouses, performance management and methodologies which are integrated within unified software
Watson, Fuller, and Ariyachandra (2004)	A system that assists users in managing large quantities of data and in making decisions
White (2004)	A term comprising data warehouses, reporting, analytical processes, performance management, and predictive analyses
Williams and Williams (2007)	A combination of products, technologies, and methods for discovering key information to improve profits and productivity within the organization

faster decision-making but also enables the discovery of new business opportunities and the identification of factors on which this development depends (Laudon & Laudon, 2018). In other words, BI stands for the synergy of data, information, processes, tools, and technologies for data mining and multidimensional analysis (Wells & Hess, 2004; Liautaud & Hammond, 2001). Such synergy, according to many researchers (Kalakota & Robinson, 1999; Turban et al., 2014), serves to improve the decision-making process, in particular to improve the quality of expertise, forecasting event scenarios, developing good business practices, as well as building a network of experts and competence centers. It is also claimed that BI enables discovering new knowledge that is important from the point of organization's competitiveness, entering new markets, acquiring new customers, and introducing new sales channels. In the opinion of some authors, BI means a new work culture based on information sharing (Gray, 2003). It is also highlighted that BI facilitates the development of various strategic initiatives aimed at (Figure 2.1): (a) carrying out fundamental changes in an organization, establishing new relationships and introducing innovative products; (b) optimizing relationships with customers, suppliers, and other stakeholders; (c) modifying and improving business strategies in order to obtain a competitive advantage, improving business processes, increasing profitability and achieving set management goals; and (d) a better understanding of the functioning of organization, minimizing the risk of business operations, and improving organization's performance.

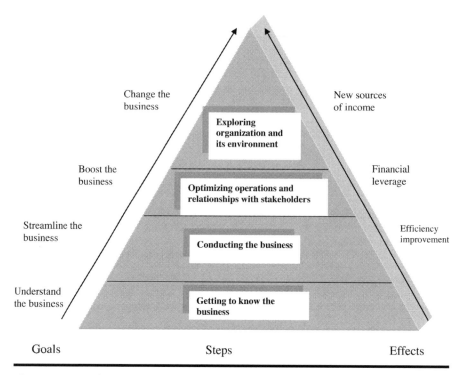

Figure 2.1   Business Intelligence in reinforcing organization's management.

Source: Own elaboration based on (Dresner et al., 2002).

The difficulty in interpreting the term *Business Intelligence* stems from the fact that BI can relate to various fields. Terms such as *Marketing Intelligence, Finance Intelligence,* and *Competitive Intelligence* are used more often. *Marketing Intelligence* primarily focuses on comprehensive customer analysis, market segmentation, direct marketing, as well as modeling and predicting market events. In turn, *Financial Intelligence* means integrating financial information from many sources, which is particularly important for capital groups and international corporations. It serves, *inter alia*, multidimensional financial reporting, and processing what-if scenarios using real-time data such as cash flow, financial performance, and measuring effectiveness of an organization using a scorecard. *Competitive Intelligence*, on the other hand, involves systematic identification and analysis all competitors' activities. This term is sometimes identified with BI, including all activities involving the search, processing, and dissemination of information useful to various economic entities (Kalakota & Robinson, 1999).

Analyzing the essence of BI, it is hard not to refer to the relationship of BI with decision support systems. Many authors are of the opinion that BI represents

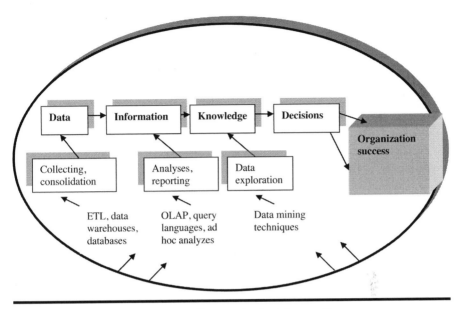

Figure 2.2   Place of Business Intelligence in decision-making.

a new generation of decision support systems aimed at transforming specific data into information and knowledge. Their goal is to increase the efficiency of decision-making at all levels of management, improve business processes and relations with stakeholders, and ultimately achieve organizational success (Figure 2.2).

It is stressed that BI systems differ from previous decision support systems (DSS, EIS, ES) not only in architecture, construction techniques but, above all, in much wider functionality (O'Brien & Marakas, 2007). BI systems integrate the possibilities of the mentioned solutions, which previously operated independently. They focus on supporting various business functions and supporting decisions at all levels of management, using advanced analytical techniques (Glancy & Yadav, 2011). In strategic planning, BI allows firms to precisely set goals and track their implementation. They allow for making various comparisons, e.g., historical results, profitability of individual offers, effectiveness of distribution channels, as well as conducting simulations and forecasting future results. By contrast, at the tactical level, BI systems provide the basis for making decisions in the areas of marketing, sales, finance, and capital management. They allow users to optimize future activities and properly modify the organizational, financial, and technological aspects of the enterprise's operation so that it can more effectively achieve its strategic goals. In turn, at the operational level, BI systems are used to perform *ad hoc* analyses, answer questions related to the current state of finances, sales, and the state of cooperation with suppliers, recipients, and customers.

BI systems, unlike earlier decision support systems, enable work with multidimensional, personalized information and knowledge (Reinschmidt & Francoise, 2000). Multidimensional analyses provide a holistic view of business processes, decision making, anticipation of the future, projection of various business event scenarios, as well as in-depth analysis and monitoring of organization's current situation.

It is emphasized that BI systems offer access to static and dynamic knowledge (created on the basis of *ad hoc* queries and information obtained from databases and data warehouses). Thus, they encourage decision-makers to seek new knowledge and show them the information in a new light. This can become an inspiration for the development of new forms of cooperation, new ways of acquiring customers, as well as creating new markets and original offers for customers. It is believed that by sharing various techniques in the field of analysis, data mining, and visualization, the openness, activeness, commitment, and creativity of users of such systems increase.

Business Intelligence Generations

In order to gain a deeper understanding of the BI subject, it is worth analyzing different generations in BI development. There are distinguished three generations: BI 1.0, BI 2.0, and BI 3.0.

The first generation of BI, called BI 1.0., falls in the time period between 1970s and 1980s. It is closely connected to MIS (Management Information Systems), EIS (Executive Information Systems), and DSS (Decision Support Systems) (Turban et al., 2014; Watson & Wixom, 2007). The technologies and applications commonly utilized in these information systems were underpinned by basic statistical methods and simple data mining techniques. Analyzed data were mostly structured, collected by firms through various legacy systems, and often stored in commercial relational database management systems. Data management and regional warehousing are considered to be the cornerstone of BI 1.0. Data marts and ETL (Extract-Transformation-Load) tools are fundamental for converting and integrating enterprise-specific data. Database query, OLAP, and reporting tools were used to explore important data features. Business performance management using scorecards and dashboards aids organizations in analyzing and visualizing a variety of performance metrics (Chen, Chiang, & Storey, 2012). BI 1.0 was able to process simple tasks for operational and tactical management. It was focused on *delivery to the consumer* and the market leaders include SAS and IBM (Gratton, 2012).

The second generation of BI (1990–2005) is associated with further development of advanced data warehouses, OLAP techniques, data mining, and most of all with the Internet and web technology (web search engines such as Google, Yahoo, etc.). These technologies enable organizations to demonstrate their business online and interact with their customers directly. Text and web analytics are widely used to process and analyze unstructured web content. The many Web 2.0 applications have also created ample user-generated content from various online social media, such as forums, online groups, web blogs, social networking sites, social media sites, and even virtual worlds and social games (Gratton, 2012). It is pointed out that BI 2.0 is dedicated to *creation and delivery for consumers* and market leaders include Business Objects, Cognos, Hyperion, Microsoft, Teradata, and Oracle.

BI 3.0 embodies a new generation in the BI evolution. Thanks to networking and mobile devices (iPad, iPhone, and other sensor-based Internet-enabled devices equipped with RFID, barcodes, radio tags) it seems possible to create innovative applications and intelligent business network for everyone (Chen, Chiang, & Storey, 2012). There is a growing acceptance of the idea that analysis is a collaborative (not only individual) and social effort. It addresses collaborative workgroups (which are self-regulated) and information outcomes within the limits of core business interaction with customers, employees, and regulators. It is widely viewed that BI 3.0 should not only go beyond reliance on structured data available in internal sources but should also utilize external, mostly unstructured, data in various formats (social media posts, common web content, images, and video files) (Nemec, 2012). BI 3.0 focuses on *creation, delivery, and management for consumers* (Gratton, 2012). According to Scott (2013), there are five core attributes that support BI 3.0 philosophy: proactive, real-time, integrated with business processes, operational (available to line workers) and extended to reach beyond the boundaries of organizations to improve information delivery, and decision support functionality for all. It is also indicated that there is no reason to underestimate BI 3.0 functions (known from BI 2.0), such as reporting, OLAP, and data mining. Their position is still strong. BI 3.0 philosophy is to increase the added value of BI tools' architecture by anchoring collaborative style of information search and analysis in intuitive and self-service user interface that delivers timely and highly relevant insights to anyone who is properly authorized and needs them (Nemec, 2012).

Finally, a new trend in BI, called *cloud BI* or *BI services on demand* has emerged. Cloud BI presents a model that provides on-demand access to software and hardware resources with minimal management efforts (Tamer et al., 2013). It is reported that cloud BI is a revolutionary concept of delivering BI capabilities "as service" using cloud-based architecture that comes at a lower cost yet faster deployment and flexibility (Gurjar & Rathore, 2013). Cloud BI solution is of special interest to organizations that desire to improve agility, while reducing IT costs and exploiting the benefits of cloud computing at the same time. According to Ouf and Nasr (2011), a cloud BI platform is typically used to satisfy one of the three primary customer needs:

■ As a horizontal BI tool to deliver standalone, internally facing reporting and analysis applications – probably using a traditional relational database (or data mart) as the primary source data system.

- As an application framework or pre-built reporting and analysis template for systems integrators to use for assembling customer-specific solutions more quickly. These solutions are probably function or domain specific and contain reusable components and application logic (but are assembled uniquely for each customer).
- As a development platform that enables embeddable, externally facing applications that solve a function-specific data analysis problem (e.g., CRM analytics, financial analytics, or supply chain analytics).

There are many options, both from traditional BI vendors and from newcomers, providing different BI functionalities based on different architectures and platforms (Table 2.2).

Despite the numerous benefits of adopting cloud BI, there are many risks and vulnerabilities. Cloud also raises significant challenges such as lack of cloud trust and security, insufficient availability, legal issues or the fear of vendor lock-in. Furthermore, in many cases, the integration of cloud solution may not make sense for economic reasons or simply can't be realized due to technological limits.

Table 2.2   Architectures and Platforms for Cloud Business Intelligence

Architecture and Platform	Representative Vendors
SaaS BI Solutions	Adaptive Planning, Analytix On Demand, Birst, BlinkLogic, GoodData, HostAnalytics, Indicee, LiteBI, Oco, PivotLink BI, SAP Business Objects on Demand
BI/DW Platform as a Service (PaaS)	AsterData MPP on Amazon EC2, IBM Cognos Express on Amazon EC2, Teradata Express on Amazon EC2, RightScale/ Talend/Vertica/Jaspersoft on Amazon EC2
Traditional BI hosted	Actuate, IBM Cognos, Information Builders, Jaspersoft, Kognitio, MicroStrategy, Oracle, Panorama Software, Pentaho, QlikView, SAS Institute, TIBCO Spotfire
SaaS BI Packaged Analytic Application Solutions	Cloud9 Analytics, IBM Cognos Analytic Applications, PivotLink, Rosslyn Analytics, SAS, SAP Business Objects BI On-demand for Salesforce
Cloud Based Data Integration Tools	IBM InfosphereDataStage, IBM CastIron, InformaticaPowercenter Cloud Edition, Snaplogic Dataflow, Talend Integration Suite on RightScale Managed Platform

Source: Elaborated on (Menon & Rehani, 2014).

According to Tamer et al. (2013) and Menon and Rehani (2014), there are also many inhibitors that have resulted in a very slow adoption rate to cloud BI so far. They concern mainly:

- Data security: Security concerns including confidentiality, integrity, and availability of the data to the cloud. For some organizations, the concerns over security may be a barrier that is impossible to overcome today. With cloud computing, data is stored and delivered across the Internet. As a result, there are many risks surrounding the loss or compromise of data. Data hosting may be untrusted or unsecure, with the potential for data leakage. However, in many cases, the cloud vendors provide a more secure environment than what exists at customer sites.
- On-premise integration: Data integration capability, one of the core BI capabilities, is crucial to defining a successful and robust BI solution. The cloud presents the potential for compromised data, metadata, and application integration. However, instant change into the cloud is not feasible and a phased approach is usually recommended. There will be a coexistence model until the cloud BI market is more mature.
- Lack of control: Tough to get Service Level Agreements (SLAs) from cloud providers. Data control and data ownership, reliability of service challenges are some of the main reasons for client concern. To mitigate this, organizations should already have in place thorough IT governance and service delivery standards and models.
- Vendor maturity: Too many cloud BI vendors, hosting providers with varying offerings, make it confusing to choose the right vendor based on required needs and vendor capabilities.
- Performance: Limits to the size and performance of data warehouses in the cloud, significant latency if BI applications exist in the cloud, but the data exists at a client site, especially when processing and returning large amounts of data.
- Pricing models: Lack of standardized pricing models makes it difficult for customers to select the right one.
- Some analytics consider that returns on investment in cloud-based BI solutions have not been fully proven nor yet measured.

Architecture of Business Intelligence Systems

The functionality of BI systems is greatly influenced by their architecture. It usually consists of four main elements (Figure 2.3):

- Data warehouse – a place of storing thematically aggregated and analyzed data.
- Data extraction and transmission tools – mainly responsible for the transfer of data from various sources, from transactional systems and the Internet to the data warehouse in particular.

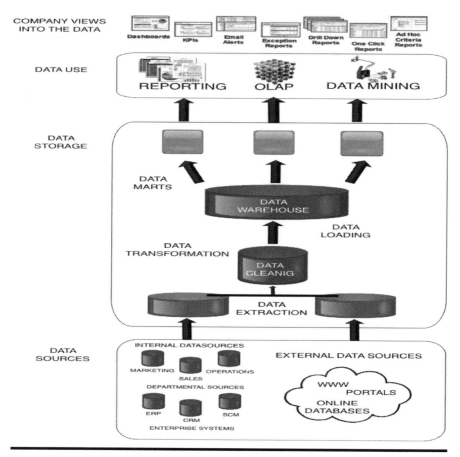

Figure 2.3 Architecture of Business Intelligence system.

- Data analysis and exploration tools – enabling users to access data as well as their comprehensive analysis and mining.
- Data visualization – tools and applications designed to provide information in a transparent and accessible form.

Data Warehouse

The problem of modern organizations is not lack of information but its excess and dispersion. To make effective decisions, various sources of information need to be reached and then integrated and comprehensively analyzed. Different data formats, lack of consistency and integration between data mean that a lot of information is lost or unused. A data warehouse is considered a technology that integrates data from various dispersed sources.

A data warehouse is a collection of thematically integrated, non-volatile and historical data to support organizational decisions (Inmon, 1996). It aids an enterprise in gaining a coherent, multidimensional view of the business (impossible to obtain by using transactional systems), which can be analyzed in various cross sections and perspectives, also in a historical context. In contrast to the classic database, a data warehouse provides the opportunity to track the most important indicators from the perspective of an organization, such as product profitability, credit risk, customer satisfaction level, customer turnover, and quality of the production process that affect strategic decision-making and ongoing tasks.

There are usually two approaches that dominate building a data warehouse, namely top-down and bottom-up. In the top-down approach, the construction of a central data warehouse system is assumed, on which thematic data warehouses are created. The bottom-up approach begins with the creation of thematic data warehouses, which only later are attempted to be integrated.

The data warehouse project should be created in such a way as to allow later creation of reporting mechanisms, queries, multidimensional analyses, and data mining in the easiest way. Experience shows that "star," "snowflake," or constellation models are usually aimed at. In the first case, the factual data are stored in a central table surrounded by reference tables, which contain data on individual dimensions needed to make decisions. In the snowflake pattern, each dimension can have several dimensions of its own. This means that reference tables are not denormalized. A constellation-type scheme is an intermediate solution. Some tables are denormalized and others are normalized.

Today, there are many different methodologies for building a data warehouse. These include, but are not limited to, the methodology of Oracle; Warehousing Institute; Rapid Warehouse Methodology, proposed by SAS Institute; and the methodology for implementing the SAFE/DW data warehouse by Sybase and its partners.

Extraction-Transformation-Load

The usefulness of a data warehouse, to a large extent, depends on the quality of data collected. Data must be obtained and integrated in advance before being entered into a repository which is a data warehouse. This involves implementing efficient data extraction mechanisms, standardization of data (coding and naming), cleaning, aggregating, and transforming data into a consistent form. The Extraction-Transformation-Load (ETL) tools are responsible for the implementation of these activities. ETL operation usually amounts to three stages: extraction, transformation, and data loading (Meyer, 2001).

Data extraction involves accessing data from various sources (databases, text files, HTML documents, XML, e-mail). This usually leads to data being saved in a relational database, which significantly facilitates their further processing at the transformation stage. The most important problems related to the data extraction stage include the need to access many sources that are stored in various formats, the temporary unavailability of some data sources, or the fact that they are outdated.

Data transformation is considered to be the most complex stage of the ETL process. It involves transforming the data into a common format, calculating the necessary aggregates, identifying missing or repeating data. The transformation process is usually carried out using traditional programming languages, scripting languages or SQL (Structured Query Language). When designing transformation procedures, skillful selection of appropriate data processing techniques is very important, which can have a significant impact on the efficiency of the entire ETL process.

In turn, loading data involves supplying a data warehouse with integrated and "cleaned" data. Due to the fact that this process is often associated with switching the system to an off-line mode, it becomes important to minimize the time needed for data transfer at this point.

An analysis of the software market indicates that the ETL tools are functionally quite different. They can be divided into the following categories (Meyer, 2001):

- EtL tools which focus on the processes of data extraction and loading
- eTL or ETl tools which prefer specific types of source data or target data
- eTL tools that perform the data transformation process relatively well, but they are not able to support many typical data formats
- ETL tools with an integrated environment equipped with many solutions supporting the user during the construction of an ETL system.

The most well-known ETL solutions include: SAS Q, DataStage EX, Oracle Warehouse Builder, DataMirror Transformation Server and Microsoft Data Transformation Services. They differ among themselves, *inter alia*, by data access, data processing algorithms, as well as data cleaning and searching components. The choice of a specific ETL tool is an individual matter, largely dependent on the needs of an organization, size, and amount of resources it uses.

Online Analytical Processing

Collected and integrated data in a data warehouse can be the subject of many interesting analyses. OLAP tools support decision-makers in analytical activities such as calculations and modeling, trend testing, and sharing of cross-sectional data. They provide answers to such questions as: *who?, what?, when?, what if?, and why?*. For example, in the field of customer analysis, OLAP tools enable multidimensional segmentation, determining the value of customers during their purchasing activity as well as identifying the most profitable and non-profit customers, determining customer loyalty, identifying the shopping basket for specific customer groups, and testing customer response to advertising campaigns.

The roots of OLAP tools are derived from databases and advanced mathematical models. Conceptually, the OLAP model can be presented as a hypercube that has measures inside, while dimensions are its edges. All data analyses most often relate to different levels of detail, which is why the dimensions have an internal structure that facilitates the transition from general to detail. Dimensions in the OLAP model can describe key aspects of organization's operation, such as time, product, service, customer, distribution channels, personnel, fixed assets, etc. On the other hand, measures are usually numerical values that are the subject of analysis such as sales, number of items, number of failures, number of complaints, etc. Operations supporting multidimensional data analysis usually include mining down, mining up, mining across, and mining around.

The analysis of the IT market shows that various specialized tools are used to create multidimensional analyses, e.g., SAS OLAP Cube Studio, Oracle Warehouse Builder, and Microsoft SQL Server 2000 with Analysis Services.

Data Extraction

While a data warehouse with multidimensional analysis allows for aggregated data to be processed and grouped according to various analysis criteria, data extraction goes a step further and allows discovering new knowledge. Discovered knowledge can be valuable in predicting future events, e.g., customer behavior or opportunities to enter new markets. Such knowledge can be represented in the form of rules, correlations, exceptions, and trends and can mainly be used to describe and forecast the future.

Data extraction techniques allow discoveries of relationships that cannot be found using traditional data analysis methods. Generally speaking, data extraction means discovering various types of patterns, generalizations, regularities, properties, rules in the available data resources, and thus something that constitutes new knowledge. Gartner Group defines data extraction as a process of discovering important relationships (correlations), patterns, and trends by searching large amounts of data stored in data repositories. Nowadays, data extraction uses achievements in various fields, in particular statistics, databases and data warehouses, machine learning, data visualization, and decision making.

Knowledge resulting from data extraction can be used to predict or describe reality. Forecasting involves using known variable values to predict the future. For example, the forecasting model helps, based on data from previous periods, estimate revenues within individual product groups or customer groups. In turn, the description of reality with the help of data extraction techniques consists in creating a human readable and understandable representation of knowledge extracted from the data in the form of charts, formulas, rules, and tables. Generated knowledge, e.g., on customer purchases, can be used to support price policy decisions (Moss & Alert, 2003).

Data extraction techniques of particular interest and usefulness in the decision-making process include:

- association analysis, which consists in recognizing certain events and processes and relating them. Information about association rules is used in making decisions about preparing promotions for specific customer groups or product shelf-stacking;
- time dependency analysis, identifying time relationships between events. This type of data mining raises high interest, *inter alia*, among telecommunications service operators (e.g., discovering knowledge about telecommunications alerts);
- classification (the most widely known technique of data extraction), consisting in assigning objects (with specific attributes) to predefined classes. The classification technique can be used to skillfully conduct advertising campaigns, identify business fraud, and determine the level of risk;
- cluster analysis, involving the allocation of objects to specific groups in such a way that the objects in one group are more similar to each other than to any object assigned to another group. Such algorithms are suitable for use in customer segmentation, product grouping, etc. Another method is the discovery of exceptions and anomalies (e.g., particularly demanding customers, expensive products); and
- forecasting, the purpose of which is to predict the value of output attributes based on known input attribute values. Forecasting usually uses historical, statistical, and repeatable data. Prediction techniques are used, among others, for forecasting traffic in telecommunications networks, sales volume, and employee turnover.

When discussing the issue of data extraction, it should be noted that it is increasingly related to online resources. This type of data extraction is called Web mining. Web mining can mean (Kantardzic, 2002; Thuraisingham, 2003)

- discovering new information and knowledge based on data contained in documents and directly on websites (Web Content Mining) (Rasmussen, Goldy, & Solli, 2002; Wells & Hess, 2004;);
- discovering the structure of websites and links to other websites (Web Structure Mining) (Poul & Gautman, & Balint, 2003; Perkowitz & Etzioni, 1999); and
- discovering user behaviors and interactions on websites (Web Usage Mining).

Visualization and Dashboards

Even the most advanced data analysis may be considered of little use if its results are not properly presented to the user. Dashboards are tools for data visualization in the form of graphic indicators, charts, and tables. They are most often available through web browsers, which means that the way to reach data is intuitive and does not require specialized IT knowledge. Dashboards are often treated as a type of interface designed to provide users with information, e.g., on firm's condition and market trends. Based on key KPIs and relevant reports, managers can better assess and understand the firm's situation.

Models of Business Intelligence Systems

Practice shows that organizations can develop different BI models, characterized by different functionality, range of impact, scope of decision support, and techniques used.

The development of BI systems can be illustrated by the example of the so-called five BI styles proposed by MicroStrategy (Figure 2.4, MicroStrategy, 2004):

- Corporate reporting – consisting in creating standard reports for the needs of analysts, individual specialists and the firm's management board.
- Simple analysis (Cube Analysis) – using single OLAP cubes.
- *Ad hoc* queries and multidimensional analysis – allowing in-depth data analysis and formulation of *ad hoc* queries.

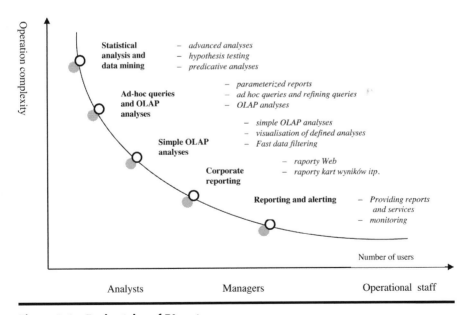

Figure 2.4   Basic styles of BI systems.

Source: Elaborated on (MicroStrategy, 2004).

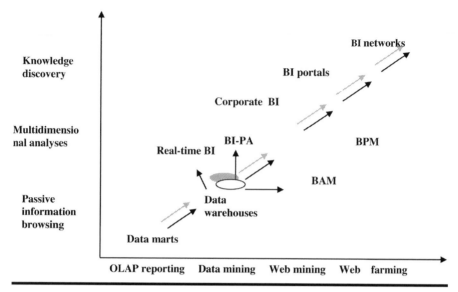

Figure 2.5 Development map of the most important BI models.

- Statistical analysis and data mining – enabling the use of statistical techniques and data mining algorithms for predictive analysis and discovering correlations between data.
- Reporting and active alerting – providing reports informing about unusual situations, critical conditions, bottlenecks, etc.

Various BI models correspond closely to the listed BI styles, including (a) data marts, (b) global data warehouses, (c) BI-Predictive Analysis (BI-PA), (d) real-time BI systems, (e) BI corporate monitoring and alerting, (f) BI portals, (g) BI networks, and (h) Business Performance Management (BPM) (Figure 2.5).

Data Marts

Many organizations begin their first experience in BI adoption by creating thematic data warehouses, often referred to as a mini-data warehouse (data marts). In such repositories, the scope of collected data is limited to a selected issue (e.g., sales, marketing, and finance). Created analyses and reports usually represent one point of view (e.g., of a given department of an organization). When there are several thematic data warehouses in an organization, they are usually combined together. Due to the fact that thematic data warehouses are often built independently of each other, difficulties may arise in their integration.

A global data warehouse, in contrast to a thematic data warehouse, covers data from many transactional systems (finance, accounting, marketing, human resources, etc.) as well as integrated information systems of the MRP II type. The advantage of such a data repository is the ability to conduct multi-sectional analyses from the perspective of the entire corporation. However, the large amount of data that a global data warehouse should contain requires complex data extraction procedures and query optimization techniques. Experience shows that building a global data warehouse is time-consuming and expensive, although it brings unquestionable benefits for comprehensive analysis of decision-making processes in an organization (Rasmussen, Goldy, & Solli, 2002; Reinschmidt & Francoise, 2000;).

BI–Predictive Analysis

Decision-makers are increasingly interested in solutions enabling them to carry out advanced forecasting by means of Predictive Analysis (PA) that would support them in finding trends hidden in historical data and predicting what will happen in the future. Predictive analytics techniques implemented in BI systems allow tracking of many event scenarios. They have mechanisms of self-control which, based on real data coming from transactional systems, compare them with the produced forecast. BI solutions with predictive analytics, which are referred to as BI-PA, include neural networks, decision trees, basket analysis, hypothesis testing, decision analysis, and text mining. The advantage of this type of a system over a traditional BI is manifested in the fact that they suggest not only what measures must be taken to achieve business goals, but also suggest the time and method of implementation of alternative scenarios. BI-PA systems are usually equipped with self-learning mechanisms (e.g., Sigma Dynamics Oracle). Thus, they enable forecasting the development of the market situation, which, in turn, allows the organization to quickly adapt business activities to changing conditions.

Business Activity Monitoring

While traditional BI systems are used to extrapolate the future and estimate the current state based on historical data, Business Activity Monitoring (BAM) supports the processing of incoming data on an ongoing basis. BAM is primarily addressed to operational managers and is responsible for ongoing monitoring of business activity.

Generalized and past information in a BI system, with a classic data warehouse, is valuable for strategic and tactical decision-makers. Unfortunately, it partially loses its usefulness for the operational level staff. This is due, among other things, to the fact that a data warehouse supply process does not take place on a regular basis, and the data stored in it are aggregated. A key element of a BAM system is the Operational Data Store, which has the features of a transactional processing system. It contains current data, but just like in a data warehouse, they are a thematically oriented data collection illustrating the functioning of an enterprise in a selected segment of reality. BAM systems are used in particular for

(a) ongoing analysis of the volume of incoming orders in relation to the production inventories held and current freight forwarding capacity; (b) sellers' control of indicators describing key customers in real time; (c) supply monitoring; (d) generating automated orders sent electronically if stocks fall below a certain level; (e) notifying, e.g., the bank's management board, when the waiting time for a credit agreement conclusion exceeds the assumed level; (f) notifying about suspicious financial transactions; and (g) sending information to a customer at the end of each stage of a contract.

Real-Time BI

An alternative concept to a traditional data warehouse is real-time BI, which uses a virtual warehouse that integrates corporate data. All queries and analyses are directed to transactional systems. Due to the fact that these solutions refer to current data, they are often referred to as real-time systems. The attractiveness of real-time BI is that there is no need to build an expensive data warehouse and so-called intermediate layer for data storage. Unfortunately, the main drawback of these solutions is the lack of access to many historical data. The quality of data, the load on transactional systems, and their speed of operation are also problematic. However, the implementation of real-time BI is less time consuming and risky than a traditional data warehouse.

Corporate BI

Contemporary organizations need to collect and process information about their stakeholders to cooperate effectively with them. Relationships with business partners largely depend on the knowledge held about them. Corporate BI systems are responsible for collecting, integrating, and analyzing data on markets, customers, and suppliers. Due to the fact that the Internet has significantly influenced their development, they are often referred to as Internet Business Intelligence (IBI). The huge amount of data stored in corporate BI systems, as well as the diverse origin of such data, requires the use of extremely complex mechanisms for extraction, transformation, data loading, and advanced data mining techniques (Meyer, 2001).

BI Portals

A BI portal is a place of integration of various information resources, applications, and web services. In addition to knowledge about business partners, it also stores information on stock exchange quotations and the financial situation in the region and the country. A BI portal is a combination of BI ideas, teamwork, decision–making, and content management. Such an integrated environment provides the opportunity, *inter alia*, to initiate various economic scenarios, conduct a comprehensive analysis of critical factors of the organization's success, support intra-organizational cooperation, create training programs, as well as access schedules of individual employees, their tasks, and skills.

BI Networks

BI networks refer to the concept of social network, understood as the new architecture of organization and economic order. The logic of a BI network is to generate new relationships between organizations, customers, suppliers, and shareholders, and meeting different people in such a network is to lead to the emergence of collective intelligence. Recently, the development of social media has had an enormous impact on the development of this type of BI model. BI networks focus on building expert networks, communities of practices, knowledge sharing, developing good practices, business patterns, and competence centers (Simmers, 2004). A crucial role in this BI model is played by data exploration techniques, enabling the mining of data generated by mobile devices, discussion groups, and online chats. Techniques for the systematic delivery and improvement of information sources on the web, and advanced techniques for content and documentation management are also helpful. It is believed that BI networks are an important step toward the development of network management and social capital.

BI-Business Performance Management

An interesting area of BI system application is process management, where the key to continuous process improvement is constant monitoring of previously defined measures and measurement of the level of implementation of previously set goals. Process-oriented systems, modeling plans and company performance management are referred to as Business Performance Management – BPM. Not only do they allow identifying deviations from the assumed plans and performance, but also determining the reasons for their existence. It is assumed that a BPM system consists of three components (Hurbean & Fotache, 2006): (a) a measurement system that allows the user to immediately evaluate the achieved results against the intended goals; (b) a communication system – which is the key in business analytics and is based on efficient mechanisms for the exchange of information between users; and (c) an implementation system – permanently reminding about the adopted operational strategy.

A BPM system combines business strategy with business planning, forecasting, and capacity modeling. It includes predefined reports, alerts, dashboards, analytical tools, and KPI to monitor and improve business processes that are set based on corporate strategic goals. BPM uses various methods, e.g., Balanced Score Card (BSC) and Activity-Based Costing (ABC). Therefore, BPM creates a closed process loop, which begins with creating the highest level of corporate goals and defining appropriate

KPIs, by measuring current results, comparing them with, e.g., a balanced score-card, and ends with correcting processes in the next cycle. Many BPM systems have an operational character, although the latest solutions in this field allow conducting predictive analyses.

BPM systems are difficult to be considered as typical BI solutions. While tradi-tional BI systems aid understanding of business trends, dependencies, and behav-ior, BPM systems additionally operationalize all analyses. BPMs must use various integrated data contained in typical BI systems. BI systems usually enable users to answer the questions: *what happened?*, *why did it happen?*, or *what will happen?*. In contrast, BPM systems also permit modeling of organization's strategy and man-agement of its performance. In other words, they allow defining "what do we want to happen" scenarios.

BPMs are based on BI achievements, though the way information is used is much broader. Unlike BI, BPM has more built-in functions for conducting anal-yses. They particularly concern budgeting and planning, financial consolidation and reporting in various layouts and perspectives, managerial dashboards, forecast-ing as well as modeling of many business scenarios and various Key Performance Indicators.

It is easy to see that the wide functionality of BPM systems causes that a tradi-tional data warehouse turns out to be insufficient for them. BPM systems require a repository that combines the features of a traditional data warehouse and an opera-tional data store. Today, active data warehouses provide such possibilities. They are suitable for supporting both strategic and operational activities.

The comparison of the most important BI models is presented in Table 2.3.

Finally, it is worth mentioning that each BI model, regardless of the scope and function it performs, should have the following properties:

- Simplicity – meaning ease of use of the system, thanks to which users can quickly understand the essence of BI. The user should be able to build their own reports and analyses without knowing the complicated data structures and query languages.
- Compliance – meaning taking action in accordance with the organization's strategy. BI solutions should provide mechanisms that would control whether the decisions taken lead an organization in a desired direction. As an exam-ple, "dashboards" presenting key indicators in relation to the assumed stra-tegic plans, e.g., in the form of a balanced scorecard or electronic control cards, monitoring the quality of processes in accordance with the Six-Sigma methodology.
- Trust – a decision-maker should be able to verify data, i.e., check where the data came from, presented in sets, and what calculations they covered.
- Creativity – BI systems should encourage users to search for new decision problems, create new business models, as well as innovative products and services.

Table 2.3   Comparison of the Most Important BI Models

BI Type	Functions	Impact Range	Type of Decision Support	Applied Techniques and Tools
Thematic data warehouses	*Ad hoc* analyses, comparative lists	Narrow, limited to a department (e.g., sales)	Operational, structured	Reporting, OLAP
Global data warehouses	Multi-sectional analyses	Entire firm	Operational, tactical, strategic	OLAP, data mining
BI with advanced analytics	Forecasting event scenarios	Narrow, limited to a selected part of the firm's activity	Operational, tactical, strategic	OLAP, PA
Business Activity Monitoring	Ongoing monitoring and alerting	Current processes and organizational activities	Operational	Operational Data Store
Real-time BI	Current activity monitoring, interference detection	Narrow, limited to a selected part of the firm's activity	Operational, structured	EII
Corporate BI	Corporate management, creating a loyalty policy	Value chain partners	Operational, tactical, strategic	ETL, data mining
BI portals	Content and documentation management, teamwork	Dedicated communities	Operational, tactical, strategic	Internet, Web mining, CMS, group work techniques, personalization
BI networks	Building expert networks, social capital management	Global, various communities	Operational, tactical, strategic	Web mining, Web farming
BI-Business Performance Management	Strategy modeling, performance management, KPI calculation	Entire organization	Operational, tactical, strategic	Alerts, dashboards

Development of Business Intelligence Systems

The development of a BI system is a difficult and complex undertaking, which consists of many stages. It involves in-depth and continuous research for information needs of an organization (present and future), authentic cooperation of users (i.e., decision-makers, operational staff) with IT departments and the knowledge management center in an organization, information sharing, ability to interpret analyses, and their proper use in management as well as competences in the use of various IT tools.

This section presents a general model of BI system development that can be compared to the BI life cycle. The model is a set of guidelines and a kind of beacon for an organization on how to approach the issue of building BI. There are two main phases in the model: creation and "consumption" (Dresner et al., 2002).

Creating a BI system consists of many stages, in particular

- defining the venture, i.e., BI vision and strategy,
- identification and preparation of data,
- selection of BI tools,
- BI design, implementation and training, and
- discovering and exploring new knowledge (new information needs, new BI applications and practices, etc.).

The first stage related to the creation of BI involves determining the overall vision, strategy and motives for developing BI in an organization (i.e., potential benefits) as well as certain threats and limitations associated with their use. This stage requires, above all, the recognition of information needs in an organization, identification of key business processes as well as future BI users, i.e., decision-makers, managers, and specialists from the IT department. Identified information needs and key business processes enable the development of indicators and measures that are crucial during the implementation of business strategy and its relationship with the BI system. In other words, the goal of this stage is to define the overall business needs and processes that require support from BI systems.

The second stage is related to the identification and preparation of data that will be the source for conducting analyses using a BI system, relevant from the point of management processes and supporting key business processes. This requires identification of both internal sources (intellectual resources of an organization, knowledge resources, internal knowledge bases and databases, reports, files, etc.) as well as external resources (concerning customers, suppliers, shareholders, etc.). This stage requires recognition of what kind of processing and analysis will be carried out on this type of data. The implementation of this stage requires significant help from decision-makers, operational staff, IT departments, knowledge management departments, as well as strategic customers. This stage is closely related to the construction of a future data warehouse, which means, among other things, the need to create procedures responsible for supplying a data warehouse, creating OLAP cubes and various reports.

Selection of tools to develop a BI system can be a difficult task. Currently, there is a whole range of proposals on offer for firms, starting with simple reporting technologies and ending with extended BI platforms. When choosing tools for BI construction, the following criteria, as in the case of purchasing other IT products, should be taken into account: functionality, comprehensiveness of the solution, compatibility, etc. It should not be overlooked that the information needs of an organization will evolve. Therefore, the BI construction tool should be sufficiently up-to-date to meet applicable standards for software and hardware.

Companies that set BI standards and development directions include:

- Business Objects – proposes the development of BI systems with the participation of, e.g., WEBINTELLIGENCE.
- Cognos, Microstrategy – offers integrated applications: Cognos Impromptu, CognosPowerPlay, Cognos Scenario, Cognos 4Thought, Cognos Decision Stream.
- Hogarti Mineral Midrange – dedicated BI solutions based on the systems of leading software producers, e.g., Baan, Oracle, JD Edwards, Symfonia, IFS, etc.
- IBM – IBM's offer includes, among others, the integrated Visual Warehouse business package.
- Information Builders – the firm offers the following modules: WebFOCUS, WebFOCUS for ERP, components for designing and building data warehouse solutions, FOCUS (programming language for building reporting systems and analyzing information from firm's IT resources), WorldMart (application for reporting and analyzing data together with data supply system).
- Microsoft – integrated BI system consisting of Microsoft Data Transformation Services, Microsoft SQL Server 2000 and 2005, Microsoft Analysis Services, Microsoft Excel, Internet Explorer, DataAnalyze.
- Microstrategy – integrated applications: MicroStrategy Server, MicroStrategy Architect, MicroStrategy Administrator, MicroStrategy Agent, MicroStrategy Web, MicroStrategyInfoCenter, MicroStrategy Broadcaster, MicroStrategy Objects.
- Oracle – Appication Server product, consisting of such modules as Oracle Application Server Discoverer (a tool for constructing ad-hoc queries, generating reports, analyses and publishing on websites), Oracle Application Server Personalization (possibility to be tailored to customer requirements), Oracle Application Server Portal (used to create and implement e-business portals), Oracle Business Intelligence Beans (to create own applications and business analyses).
- SAP – SAP Knowledge Management, mySAP Business Intelligence and SAP Business Intelligence applications – provide data warehouse functions, tools for creating reports and conducting analyses, best practice models, applications for analyzing business activities and administrative resources.

■ SAS – the firm offers many solutions, e.g., SAS Enterprise Business Intelligence Server, SAS Web Report Studio. SAS Enterprise Business Intelligence Server is an open and integrated architecture that enables delivery of information across the entire corporation. In turn, SAS Web Report Studio is an intuitive application that enables asking questions and creating reports. It was designed for business users who want to view and share reports on the World Wide Web.

The next stage that makes up the BI creation cycle is the design and implementation of a BI system. The scale of work at this stage can be very different. It depends primarily on the complexity of a planned BI system, i.e., types of analyses, reporting, number of users of a future BI system, etc. Generally, creating a fully personalized BI application requires a lot of time. This involves the design of, e.g., data warehouses, mini data warehouses, reports, dashboards, and individual user interfaces. At this stage, care should be taken to ensure consistency and logic in the entire BI application. This stage is also associated with numerous user training sessions and familiarizing users with the capabilities of a BI system.

The exploration and discovery stage is critical throughout the BI building cycle. The implemented BI environment shows in a new, previously unknown light the weight of a wide variety of information, analyses, and new knowledge discovered. Naturally, at this stage new information needs arise and new ways of information management are created. They should be the basis for the evaluation of a current BI system and its improvement, and modification in the future. This stage requires significant cooperation of IT department representatives with the knowledge management center and end users.

The "consumption" phase is primarily associated with the end user and reveals their crucial role in using the analyses carried out and applying them in decision-making, improving decision-making processes, as well as creating new business models.

Depending on the tasks that the users of a BI system have to perform, the process of using various data repositories, prepared analyses, comparing and interpreting them begins. At this stage, a considerable involvement of users is required, who, depending on the emerging needs, should create proprietary analyses and reports, and demonstrate competence in sharing knowledge.

Analyses carried out, new knowledge discovered may indicate alternative ways of solving specific tasks and possibilities of optimization of many activities. It involves the cooperation and communication of all people participating in the decision-making process.

Working with information and tools for data analysis and exploration often shows the possibility of fundamental changes in an organization, e.g., introduction of new forms of cooperation, outsourcing, entering new markets, and creating new alliances with partners.

The end of the last stage of the BI system life cycle does not mean the end of work with BI. As already noted, the cycle is interactive and a kind of loop that requires, each time, to re-analyze information needs, re-evaluate existing solutions, modify them, and optimize and adapt to new needs of the environment.

Business Intelligence Competence Center

BI systems can be classified as highly complex and interdisciplinary, requiring the involvement and work of many people. Increasingly, organizations are not able to properly coordinate them through traditional IT departments. There are opinions that complex IT projects, such as BI systems, should be entrusted to specialized entities. In this case, BI competence center may be such a cell (Dresner et al., 2002). In principle, a BI competence center takes over information management, ranging from identifying the source of its creation and ending with its effective use. It is responsible for coordinating and adjusting BI initiatives to the firm's goals, in particular

- developing a coherent analytical approach throughout an entire organization;
- coordinating various analytical initiatives in an organization;
- conducting complex analyses in cooperation with management staff;
- introduction of standards in defining models, data architectures, and common business terms;
- setting standards for BI tools; and
- user training in the independent use of BI tools, data access mechanisms and their operation.

It is assumed that a BI competence center should gather experts in the fields of business, data analysis, and computer science who would support the management in making intelligent decisions.

Developing business skills within a BI competence center means primarily

- understanding the nature and needs of individual departments of an organization, such as finance, sales and marketing, human resources, logistics;
- ability to communicate with the management and combine BI initiatives with the firm's strategic goals; and
- supporting the management in analyzing and creating various business cases.

In particular, analytical competences include:

- studying business problems and creating models that enable their analysis;
- data mining, discovering patterns, relationships, anomalies, and trends;
- cooperation with the IT department to identify data for the needs of specific analyses or applications;

- effective utilization of various techniques ranging from simple data aggregation to statistical analysis and complicated data mining;
- liquidity development and maintenance in the use of analytical tools;
- extraction of new information and knowledge and creating appropriate recommendations for their utilization; and
- user training in the use of data.

Business analysts gathered around a BI center should be responsible for providing valuable knowledge and substantive care from the perspective of the end user and business entities, while creating good relationships with individual departments of an organization. They should also help in the transformation of data to a data warehouse (for the needs of future analyses) and preparation of training for users (in the use of BI data and tools).

As part of the BI competence center, it is recommended to develop IT knowledge and skills which is mainly associated with

- access to relevant data sources and skills to manage them,
- BI tools and technologies and data administration, and
- implication of BI infrastructure on the functioning of an organization.

It is believed that fitting a BI competence center within organizational structures can be different and depends on the sector and its characteristics. Sometimes, the current IT department turns out to be the right place – provided that information technologies are treated as strategic tools for an organization. It may also be beneficial to place it next to the financial department – but mainly in a situation where it has evolved from a financial control function to management control. A BI competence center cannot focus on the business discipline chosen only. Therefore, placing it within one department makes sense when organizational policy does not limit cooperation between individual departments of an enterprise, on the contrary, it encourages it.

References

Adelman, S., & Moss, L. (2000). *Data warehouse project management*. Upper Saddle River, NJ: Addison-Wesley.

Albescu, F., Pugna, I., & Paraschiv, D. (2008). Business intelligence & knowledge management – Technological support for strategic management in the knowledge based economy. *RevistaInformatica Economică, 4*(48), 5–12.

Alter, A. (2004). A work system view of DSS in its fourth decade. *Decision Support System, 38*(3), 319–327.

Anandarajan, M. A., & Srinivasan, C. A. (2004). *Business Intelligence Techniques – A Perspective from Accounting and Finance*. Berlin: Springer.

Baaras, H., & Kemper, H. G. (2008). Management support with structured and unstructured data—an integrated Business Intelligence framework. *Information Systems Management*, *25*(2), 132–148.

Bui, T. (2000). Decision support systems for sustainable development. In G. E. Kersten, Z. Mikolajuk, & A. Gar-on Yeh (Eds.), *Decision support systems for sustainable development. A resource book of methods and applications*. New York: Kluwer Academic Publishers.

Business Objects (2007). About Business Intelligence. Retrieved from http://www.businessobjects.com/businessintelligence/default.asp?intcmp=ip_company2.

Carlsson, C., & Turban, E. (2002). DSS: Directions for the next decade. *Decision Support Systems*, *33*(2), 105–110.

Chen, H., Chiang, R. H. L, & Storey, V.C. (2012). Business Intelligence and Analytics: from Big Data to Big Impact. *MIS Quarterly*, *36*(4), 1–24.

Chung, W. Chen, H., & Nunamaker, J. F. (2005). A visual framework for knowledge discovery on the web: An empirical study of business intelligence exploration. *Journal of Management Information Systems*, *21*(4), 57–84.

Cognos (2007). Cognos 8 Business Intelligence: What Is Business Intelligence? Cognos Corporation. Retrieved July, 2007 from http://www.cognos.com/products/cognos-8businessintelligence/businessvalue/whatis-business-intelligence.html.

Davenport, T. H., & Harris, J. G. (2007). *Competing on analytics. The New Science on Winning*. Boston Massachusetts: Harvard Business School Press.

Davenport, T. H., Harris, J. G., & Morison, R. (2010). *Analytics at work: Smarter decisions, better results*. Cambridge: Harvard Business Press.

Dresner, H. J., Buytendijk, F., Linden, A., Friedman, T., Strange, K. H., Knox, M., & Camn, M. (2002). The Business Intelligence Center: An Essential Business Strategy. Gartner Research.

Eckerson, W. W. (2005). The keys to enterprise business intelligence: Critical success factors. The Data Warehousing Institute. Retrieved from http://download.101com.com/pub/TDWI/Files/TDWIMonograph2-BO.pdf.

Gangadharan, G. R., & Swamy, N. S. (2004). Business intelligence systems: Design *and* implementation strategies. *Proceedings of 26th International Conference on Information Technology Interfaces*. Cavtat, Croatia.

Glancy, F. H., & Yadav S. B. (2011). Business intelligence conceptual model. *International Journal of Business Intelligence Research*, *2*(2), 48–66.

Gratton, S.J. BI 3.0 (2012). *The journey to business intelligence. What does it mean?* Retrieved from http://www.capgemini.com.technology.

Gray, P., & Watson H. (1998). *Decision support in the data warehouse*. New York: Prentice Hall.

Gray, P. (2003). Business intelligence: A new name or the future of DSS. In T. Bui, H. Sroka, S. Stanek, & J. Gołuchowski (Eds.), *DSS in the Uncertainty of the Internet Age*. Katowice: Wydawnictwo Akademii Ekonomicznej w Katowicach.

Gurjar, Y.S., & Rathore, V.S. (2013). Cloud business intelligence – Is what business need today. *International Journal of Recent Technology and Engineering*, *1*(6), 81–86.

Hannula, M., & Pirttimaki, V. (2003). Business intelligence empirical study on the top 50 Finnish companies. *Journal of American Academy of Business*, *2*(2), 593–599.

Hostmann, B. (2007). Business intelligence scenario. Gartner Business Intelligence Summit. London: Gartner Research.

Hurbean, L., & Forach, D. (2006). Improve business insight with business performance management. *Economy Informatics*, 1–4.

Inmon, W. H. (1996). *Building the data warehouse*. New York: John Wiley & Sons.

Inmon, W.H., Strauss, D., & Neushloss, G. (2008). *DW 2.0: The architecture for the next generation of data warehousing*. Amsterdam: Elsevier Science.

Isik, O., Jones, M. C., & Sidorova, A. (2011). Business intelligence (BI) success and the role of BI capabilities. *Intelligent Systems in Accounting, Finance and Management, 18*, 161–176.

Jourdan, Z., Rainer, R. K., & Marschall, T. (2008). Business intelligence: An analysis of the literature. *Information Systems Management, 25*(2), 121–131.

Kalakota, R., & Robinson, M. (1999). *E-business roadmap for success*. New York: Addison-Wesley.

Kantardzic, M. (2002). Data mining: Concepts. *Models, methods and algorithms*. New York: John Wiley & Sons.

Kulkarni, J., & King R. (1997). *Business intelligence systems and data mining*. SAS Institute.

Laudon, K., & Laudon, J. (2004). *Management information systems. Managing the digital firm*. New York: Prentice Hall.

Laudon, K.C., & Laudon, J. P. (2018). *Management information systems. Managing the digital firm* (15th ed.). Harlow, England: Pearson.

Liautaud, B., & Hammond M. (2001). *E-Business intelligence. Turning information into knowledge into profit*. New York: McGraw-Hill.

Lonnqvist, A., & Pirttimaki, V.(2006). The measurement of business intelligence. *Business Intelligence, 23*(1), 32–40.

Luhn, H. P. (1958). A business intelligence systems. *IBM Journal of Research and Development, 2*(4), 314–319.

Markarian, J., Brobst, S., Bedell, J.(2007). Critical success factors deploying pervasive BI. *Informatica*. Teradata, Microstrategy.

Menon, L., & Rehani, B. (2014). Business intelligence on the cloud – Overview and use case. Retrieved from http://www.tcs.com/SiteCollectionDocuments/White%20Papers/HighTech_Whitepaper_Business_Intelligence_Cloud_0412-1.pdf.

Meyer, S. R. (2001). Which ETL tool is right for you?, *DM Review Magazine*, 1, Brookfield.

MicroStrategy (2004). *The 5 Styles of Business Intelligence. Industrial Strength Business Intelligence*. A White Paper Prepared by Micro Strategy.

Moss, L. T., & Alert, S. (2003). *Business intelligence roadmap – The complete project lifecycle for decision support applications*. New York: Addison-Wesley.

Moss, L., & Hoberman, S. (2004). *The importance of data modeling as a foundation for business insight*. Teradata.

Negash, S. (2004). Business intelligence. *Communications of Association for Information Systems*, 13, 177–195.

Negash, S., & Gray, P. (2008). Business intelligence. In F. Burstein & C. W. Holsapple (Eds.), *Decision support systems* (pp. 175–193). Berlin: Springer.

Nemec, R. (2012). The application of business intelligence 3.0 concept in the management of small and medium enterprises. In M. Tvrdikova, J. Minster, & P. Rozenhal (Eds.), *IT for practice* (pp. 84–89). Ostrava: Economicka Faculta, VSB-TU.

O'Brien, J.A., & Marakas, G.M. (2007). *Introduction to information systems* (13th ed.). New York: McGraw-Hill.

Olszak, C.M., & Ziemba, E. (2006). Business intelligence systems in the holistic infrastructure development supporting decision-making in organizations. *Interdisciplinary Journal of Information, Knowledge and Management*, 1, 47–58.

Olszak, C. M. (2016). Toward better understanding and use of business intelligence in organizations. *Information Systems Management, 33*(2), 105–123.

Oracle (2007). Oracle Business Intelligence and Enterprise Performance Management. Retrieved from http://www.oracle.com/solutions/business_intelligence/indx.html.

Ouf, S. & Nasr, M. (2011). The cloud computing: The future of BI in the cloud. *International Journal of Computer Theory and Engineering, 3*(6), 750.

Perkowitz, M., & Etzioni, O. (1999). Adaptive web sites: Conceptual cluster mining. *Proceedings of the 16th Joint National Conference on AI.*

Poul, S., Gautman, N., & Balint, R. (2003). *Preparing and data mining with Microsoft SQL Server 2000 and Analysis Services.* New York: Addison-Wesley.

Rasmussen, N., Goldy, P. S., & Solli, P. O. (2002). *Financial business intelligence: trends, technology, software selection, and implementation.* New York: Wiley & Sons.

Reinschmidt, J., & Francoise, A. (2000). *Business intelligence certification guide.* IBM, International Technical Support Organization.

SAS (2011). Information evaluation model. Retrieved from http://www.sas.com/software/iem.

Sauter, V.L. (2010). *Decision support systems for business intelligence.* New Jersey: Wiley.

Schmarzo, B. (2013). *Big data. Understanding how data powers big business.* New York: Wiley.

Simmers, C. A. (2004). A stakeholder model of business intelligence. *Proceedings of the 37th Hawaii International Conference on System Sciences,* Hawaii.

Tamer, Ch., Kiley, M., Ashrafi, N., & Kuilbar, J. (2013). Risk and benefits of business intelligence in the Cloud. *Northeast Decision Sciences Institute Annual Meeting Proceedings,* 86–95.

Thuraisingham, B. (2003). *Web data mining and applications in business intelligence and counter-terrorism.* New York: CRC Press.

Turban, R., Sharada, R., Delen, D., & King, D., (2014). *Business intelligence. A managerial approach.* London, England: Pearson.

Watson, H. J. (2010). *SME performance: Separating myth from reality.* Cheltenham: Edward Elgar Publishing.

Watson, H. J., Fuller, C., & Ariyachandra, T. (2004). Data warehouse governance: Best practices at Blue Cross and Blue Shield of North Carolina. *Decision Support Systems, 38*(3), 435–450.

Watson, H. J., & Wixom, B. (2007). Enterprise agility and mature BI capabilities. *Business Intelligence Journal, 12*(3), 4–6.

Wells, J. D., & Hess, T. J. (2004). Understanding decision-making in data warehousing and related decision support systems. An explanatory study of a customer relationship management ppplication. In M. Raisinghani (Ed.), *Business intelligence in the digital economy.* London: Idea Group Publishing.

Wells, D. (2008). Business analytics – Getting the point. Retrieved from http://b-eye-network.com/view/7133.

White, C. (2004). Now is the right time for real-time BI. Information Management Magazine. Retrieved from http://www.dmreview.com.

Whitehorn, M., & Whitehorn, M. (1999). *Business intelligence: The IBM solution dataware housing and OLAP.* London: Springer.

Williams, S., & Williams, N. (2007). *The profit impact of business intelligence.* San Francisco: Morgan Kaufmann.

Chapter 3

Big Data for Business Intelligence

Era of Data-intensive Computing

Estimations indicate that today, about 98% of all information is stored in a digital form; while in 2000, the share of digital data in global information resources was only 25% (Xu, Frankwick, & Ramirez, 2016). It is asserted that currently, the data is increasing 40 times faster than the population. To illustrate the scale of data surge, it is enough to account for the fact that Twitter, a social networking site, alone generates 12 terabytes of data daily. Oracle Company (2014) contends that the Internet is expanding at the rate of more than 40% from year to year. Today, it has more than 6 zettabytes of data and in 2020 its size, in all probability, will reach to 45 zettabytes. In 2012, Google processed 24 petabytes of information per day. In turn, Facebook every hour received about 10 million photographs for publication and about 3 billion likes and comments during the day (Mayer-Schoenberger & Cukier, 2013). People using the Internet through various types of services, portals, applications, stationary and mobile devices are a kind of data generators. They leave behind a digital trail, expressed in: the sequence of websites visited, IP addresses, GPS geolocation data, data from cellular networks, electronic payments, blog entries, forums, social networking sites, and purchases made (Paharia, 2014).

Recently, the Internet of Things (IoT) has also become an important data source. The main idea of IoT is communication between objects without human intervention, which is to monitor and manage these objects. In 2014, according to the International Data Corporation (IDC) report, the number of computerizable items worldwide was estimated at 200 billion, of which 14 billion was already connected to the Internet. These are items of everyday and unusual use – both cars and toys, jet planes, dishwashers, etc.… They relate to opinions on products, services, shopping preferences, labor market, and job satisfaction.

Big Data, originating mainly from the Internet, social media, various government portals, distributed databases, as well as from mobile devices, are treated as a new form of capital. Big Data are considered to have high business value (Chen & Zhang, 2014). They can provide valuable knowledge about customer behaviors and opinions, competition activities, the labor market, emerging ecological and environmental threats, trends in the economy, the popularity of various products and services, as well as social and political moods (Olszak & Zurada, 2019). According to some analysts, the value of the Big Data global market is expected to increase from around $18 billion in 2014 to around $92 billion in 2026 (Connick, 2017).

Aspects related to Big Data have become extremely interesting for representatives of the world of science as well as business and governments of various countries. This is evidenced by some facts (Wang & Yuang, 2014).

In some prestigious journals and publishing houses, scientific papers and reports have started to appear for some time, referring to the subject of Big Data and its importance for business, economy and the whole society. For example, in July 2008, a monograph entitled *Beautiful Data* was published by O'Reilly Media. In September, *Nature* had a special issue on *Big data* and *The Fourth Paradigm-Data Intensive Scientific Discovery* book was brought out. February 2011 brought the special issue on *Dealing with Data* by *Science* and the journal launched a joined discussion of its sub-journals as *Science: Signaling, Science: Translational Medicine and Science: Careers* on the importance of data for scientific research. The *Wall Street Journal* announced a big-data era of information technology and pointed out that Big Data, smart manufacturing, and the wireless revolution would be the components of the coming tech-led boom (Mills & Ottino, 2012). In April 2012, *Nature Biotechnology* published an article entitled *Finding correlations in big data* in which eight biologists were invited to evaluate a paper in *Science* entitled *Detecting Novel Associations in Large Data Sets* (Reshef et al., 2011).

Many research projects devoted to Big Data have been implemented in recent years. In May 2009, the project *Global Pulse* under the agenda of the United Nations launched *Big Data for Development: Challenges & Opportunities* for promoting the innovating ways to rapidly collect and analyze digital data (United Nations Global Pulse, 2012). In 2011, McKinsey Global Institute (Maniaka et al., 2011) began research in the potential application of Big Data in different industries, conducting analyses from the economic and commercial dimensions, and outlined the development policy on how the decision-makers handled Big Data in governmental and industrial organizations.

The giants of IT industry are beginning to develop software and entire Big Data processing technologies. In 2011, Microsoft launched Hadoop-based Big Data Solution compatible with Windows, as a component of SQL Server 2012.

IBM presented InfoSphere BigInsights, integrated with the DB2 with non-SQL (NoSQL) database and carried out a series of acquisitions. In 2007, IBM took over Cognos—a vendor of business intelligence software. Year 2009 witnessed further expansion of the company which bought the database analysis software vendor Netezza, business rules management software vendor ILOG, and data analysis and statistical software vendor SPSS. A year later, IBM took over web analytics software vendor Coremetrics. In 2009, Amazon Elastic MapReduce launched a hosted Hadoop framework in which the load can be adjusted to suit user's needs for the data-intensive distributed programs to work. Oracle integrated the NoSQL Database and Big Data Appliance, which enabled a direct dealing with unstructured massive data by customers.

Interestingly, the governments of various countries have become focused on Big Data issues. For example, in March 2012, the United States government launched *Big Data Research and Development Initiative* which promoted the development and application of Big Data from business enterprises to the national deployment strategy to enhance the capability of extracting knowledge from large and complex data sets to aid the nation in solving some of the most crucial challenges (Office of Science and Technology Policy, 2012a, 2012b). A national research Center for Visual and Decision Informatics (CVDI) was established by the U.S. National Science Foundation. The center's research interests focused on data mining, decision-making, and visualization which resulted in bringing together the National Science Foundation, industry, government agencies, and universities.

In March 2012, China's Ministry of Science and Technology announced the *Twelve-Five 2013 annual national science and technology alternative project solicitation Guide*, which brought into focus the Big Data research.

The issue of Big Data has also become a key priority for the European Union. This thesis is evidenced by the first programs and initiatives, such as (Buchholtz, Bukowski, & Śniegocki, 2014) *The Big Data Europe (BDE) Project* and *European Big Data Value Partnership: Strategic Research and Innovation Agenda (SRIA)*, which set out the main objectives and tasks for the use of large-scale data in Europe until 2020. These initiatives indicated the areas and sectors in which Big Data should be used in the near future, namely: health, transport and logistics, energy, food, security, climate, sales, trade, services, public administration, and spatial planning. The resources of Big Data are perceived as a profitable opportunity for Europe as well as a tool for creating more innovative products and services improving productivity of all economic sectors, increasing innovation, reducing costs by creating a more personalized service, and boosting efficiency in the public sector. According to IDC report (Catteneo, 2014), 30% of West European countries will soon start to exploit the potential offered by large-scale data. Other countries, in order to be more innovative and competitive, will have to take immediate action to utilize large-scale data in their business models.

Eventually, there are the first reports on the use of Big Data in business. In July 2012, Gartner incorporation released the first data survey report *Hype Cycle for Big data, 2012*, which thought deeply about Big Data (Lapkin, 2012). Fortune 1000 conducted research on the use of Big Data in the period of 2012–2017. The obtained results confirmed that the number of enterprises benefiting from investments in Big Data systems is growing. In 2017, CEO and managers of over 80% of the largest American firms rated Big Data investments as successful and nearly 50% of them indicated specific, measurable effects from Big Data (Bean, 2017). Furthermore, research conducted by Forrester Research indicates that about 75% of American enterprises recognize the importance of Big Data for their business, although only less than 30% of them admit that they are able to fully take advantage of the knowledge provided by Big Data. One of the barriers to effective Big Data utilization is considered to be an insufficient development level of skills and analytical capabilities of organizations (Hopkins, 2016).

Big Data Term – Interpretation

Although the term *Big Data* has gained in considerable popularity in recent years, there is no consensus how to interpret it. According to Devey (2014), Big Data refers to a technological phenomenon which rose in the mid-1980s due to the enhancement of computers, and growing storage and processing capacities. These have offered new and improved ways of sifting through the infinite quantities of data available. Pence (2014) described Big Data not only by the amount of information but also by its variety and complexity as well as the speed at which the data have to be analyzed or delivered. The term Big Data is frequently understood as databases which, due to their massive size, are difficult to manage using conventional software (Manyika et al., 2011). According to Hassan (2014), Big Data are data sets whose rate of growth is exponentially high over a time interval. Typical data mining tools do not serve their analysis. Such data sets result from daily capture of stock exchange, any credit card user's timely usage trends, insurance cross line capture, health care services, etc. In real time, these data sets go on increasing and create complex scenarios over time.

Cox and Ellsworth (1997) while discussing the concept of Big Data pointed out to two different meanings of this concept: Big Data collections and Big Data objects. However, they argued that for processing such huge collections and objects it becomes necessary to use nonstandard algorithms and software. SaaS defines Big Data as a popular term used to describe the quick growth and availability of data, structured, unstructured, and semi-structured. Structured data consist of sets with a defined structure like databases. They comprise data tables with defined columns and rows intertwined (database relationships). Structured data come from records of people's or other objects' behavior (transactions, clicks, likes, logins, etc.) and from sensors/detectors referred to as part of the IoT. Unstructured data do not have specified structure. These are data generated by people in the form of spoken language, video files, or images. Semi-structured data are similar to structured data but can be extended with some unstructured data. Data stored in XML, RSS, or JSON format constitute this category.

Many authors associate Big Data with the Internet and social media as a new social phenomenon (Hsu, Chang, & Hsu, 2017). According to them, Big Data are a new generation of technologies and architectures which are designed to economically extract value from very large volumes of a wide variety of data, by enabling high velocity capture, discovery and analysis (Halaweh & Massry, 2015). It is said that Big Data are a technological innovation where complex unstructured and structured data are parallelly distributed, stored and direct queries could be applied to those data stored (Puschamann, Burges, 2014). Through Big Data services, organizations could better monitor the acceptance of products in the marketplace and understand its business environment, potentially fueling competitive advantages. Lu, Li and Zhang (2015) posit that Big Data analytics applications are a new type of software applications that process large-scale data utilizing large parallel processing framework to obtain hidden value.

Schamrzo (2013) points out that Big Data are not about technology but about business transformation—transforming organizations from retrospective, batch, data-constrained structures that monitor the business environment into predictive, real-time, data hungry structures that optimize the business environment. Chen & Zhang (2014) classified Big Data as one of five "critical technical areas" contributing to Business Intelligence and analytics, the others being text analytics, web analytics, network analytics, and mobile analytics. They view Big Data as a subset of Business Intelligence. They stated that Business Intelligence could be seen as an umbrella term that includes applications and tools that enable access and analysis of Big Data and information in order to improve business performance, competitive advantage, and create business value. Many authors argue that Big Data mean new ways of running a business, of decision-making, and of understanding the customers, suppliers, and other stakeholders of organizations (McAfee & Brynjolfsson, 2012; Schmarzo, 2013). It is stated that Big Data enables the creation of innovative business models, products, and services. It gives organizations a way to outperform the competition. This kind of data may be used to achieve a better understanding of an organization's customers, employees, partners, and operations.

Big Data V Model

The essence of *"Big Data"* is often described with the so-called V model referring to important attributes of Big Data resources. In the first model, attention was paid to three basic attributes (3V): Volume, Velocity, and Variety. Today, Big Data is usually described in terms of the 7V model, including: Volume, Velocity, Variety, Veracity, Visualization, Variability, and Value (Figure 3.1; Erl, Khattak, & Buhler, 2015; Manyika et al., 2011).

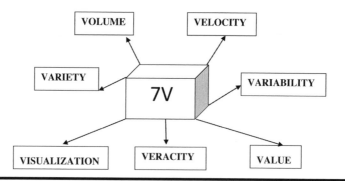

Figure 3.1 7 V model.

Volume

The amount of data collected today is counted in tera and petabytes. Such data mainly come from the Internet, streaming portals, various sensors, and mobile devices. For example, it is estimated that 300 hours of video are uploaded to YouTube every minute. An estimated 1.1 trillion photos were taken in 2016, and the number is projected to rise by 9% in 2017. As the same photo usually has multiple instantiations stored across different devices, photo or document sharing services as well as social media services, the total number of photos stored is also expected to grow from 3.9 trillion in 2016 to 4.7 trillion in 2017. In 2016, the estimated global mobile traffic amounted was 6.2 exabytes per month. That is equal to 6.2 billion gigabytes.

Most organizations do not have the infrastructure to store such enormous volumes of data. Thanks to distributed system technology that allows data collection and storage in different places, organizations have the chance to utilize large data sets.

Velocity

Velocity mainly refers to the speed at which data are generated, produced, created, and refreshed. Interestingly, Google alone processes on average more than "40,000 search queries every second," which roughly translates into more than 3.5 billion searches per day. Velocity requires different processing algorithms generated in real mode. Currently, technologies are emerging that allow data analysis while generating them, without entering them into a traditional database.

Variety

Big Data are identified not only with huge amounts of incoming data but also with their diverse nature. Variety means that the data can be textual, numerical, graphic (images), multimedia (movies), and sound; and that they can come from a variety of sources (e.g., social networking sites), sensors, and devices. Much of the data are weak or unstructured data, i.e., data that cannot be saved and stored in traditional relational database management systems (RDBMS). NoSQL databases are most often used to record such data.

Veracity

The veracity feature refers to the accuracy and integrity of data. The data to be subject of data analysis must contain true information as well as uniform and consistent descriptions of the value of individual data fields.

Visualization

Results obtained after Big Data processing should be presented in a readily accessible and understandable form. Sometimes dashboards are treated as an easy to read, often single page, real-time user interface showing a graphical presentation of the current status and historical trends of organization's key performance indicators to enable instantaneous and informed decisions to be made at a glance. They extend static reporting with analytical elements. They aggregate and sensitize data using such methodologies as: BSC, Six Sigma, and Economic Value Added. Therefore, they enable managers to better assess operational and strategic information and better understand business.

Variability

Variability in Big Data context refers to a number of different things (Firican, 2017). One is the number of inconsistencies in the data. These need to be found by anomaly and outlier detection methods in order for any meaningful analytics to take place. Big Data are also variable because of the multitude of data dimensions resulting from multiple disparate data types and sources. Variability can also refer to the inconsistent speed at which Big Data are loaded into different databases.

Value

This feature draws attention to the fact that Big Data resources have great business potential and provide opportunities to generate profits, thanks to information extracted from data. It is believed that Big Data analyzed together with traditional data enable organizations not only to better understand their business but to change it also and have new sources of revenues, stronger competitive position, and greater innovation.

Techniques for Big Data Analyzing

The complex nature of Big Data resources requires the use of advanced techniques for processing and analyzing them. These techniques are data mining, text mining, web mining, graph mining, network analysis, machine learning, deep learning, neural networks, genetic algorithms (GAs), spatial analysis, and search-based application (Table 3.1). These techniques impact on the functionality and possibilities of Big Data applications and consequently on the quality of decision-making, personalization of products and services, as well as the enhancement of business processes and customer relationship management (Chen, Chiang, & Storey, 2012; Olszak, 2016).

Table 3.1   Techniques for Big Data Analyzing

Technique for BD Analyzing	Description
Data mining	An interactive process aimed at the analysis of large databases, with the purpose of extracting information and knowledge that may prove accurate and potentially useful for knowledge workers engaged in decision-making and problem-solving. The main purpose of the data mining analysis is interpretation and prediction. Different mathematical models and methods can be used in data mining. Most important include regression, time series, classification, association rules, and clustering.
Text mining	Text mining offers the discovery of dominant patterns of word use and patterns of relationships between words or documents that come from various sources: mail communication, Internet documents as well as data coming from social networks. Text mining is used, *inter alia*, in: identifying relationships, detecting subjectivity and generating abstracts. Text analytics techniques have been actively pursued in several emerging areas, including information extraction, topic models, question answering, event detection, and opinion mining.
Web mining	Web mining is used to process and analyze unstructured web contents based on XML, Internet protocol (HTTP, SMTP), and application programming interface (API). It enables developers to integrate diverse content from different web-enabled systems. Web mining may include: (1) content mining that involves analyzing documents published on the Internet and websites; (2) user mining that relates to the analysis of user behaviors, consisting in the analysis of network traffic and ways users behave; and (3) structure mining where the subject of analyses is interrelationships between various objects in the network (e.g., websites).

Table 3.1   Continued

Technique for BD Analyzing	Description
Graph mining	Graph mining is a set of methods for facilitating the detection of interesting associations within the analyzed graph structure. Graph mining techniques have been categorized into three main groups: graph clustering, graph classification, and subgraph mining. Graph mining techniques may be based on different algorithms. They include mainly: D-Walks, multilevel kernel k-means, genetic algorithm (GA), CFFTree, coring method, bipartite graph co-clustering, clique matrix, SSHGCA, K-NN, HSG, and distributed algorithm.
Network analysis	One of the most known network analysis is social media mining (SMM). SMM is the process of representing, analyzing, and extracting actionable patterns from social media data. SMM introduces basic concepts and principal algorithms suitable for investigating massive social media data. Network analysis can provide consumers' behavior and preference information for the business as well as express the change of the public mood and even predict the trend of stock market. It can also identify target audience groups through brand influence based on customer big data on the social media platform and support location-based personalized messaging services.
Machine learning	Machine learning is the process of using computers to imitate a person to acquire skills through learning. Machine learning is trained through extensive data and algorithms that allow machines to own the ability to predict management trends and make decisions in the process of analyzing and optimizing operating management of Big Data. Machine learning can build models from mass data or discover various relationships implied in the observed data according to the specific needs of users.
Deep learning	Deep learning is a nonlinear combination of Multi-layer Representation Learning method. Representation Learning means learning representation (or feature) from data in order to extract useful information from the data when categorizing and predicting. Deep learning begins with raw data and transforms each representation (or feature) layer into higher and more abstract representation, thereby discovering the intricate structure in high-dimensional data.

(Continued)

Table 3.1 Continued

Technique for BD Analyzing	Description
Neural networks	Neural networks are the most advanced methods of artificial intelligence. They are used especially for pattern recognition and prediction. The most important types of neural networks include: Multilayer Perceptron, Radial Basis Function Network, Support Vector Machine, Generalized Regression Neural Network, and Self-Organizing Map.
Genetic algorithms	GA is applied over the problem domain where the outcome is very unpredictable and the process of outcome contains complex interrelated modules. GA is used to obtain optimized solutions from a number of candidate solutions. GA is inspired by evolutionary theory: weak and unit species are faced with extinction by natural selection and the strong ones have greater opportunity to pass their genes to future generations via reproduction.
Spatial analysis	Spatial data mining is the process of discovering interesting and previously unknown, but potentially useful, patterns from large spatial data sets. The content of spatial data can be the value of point height, road length, polygon area, building volume and imagery pixel, also the string of geographical name and annotation, and further the graphics, images, multimedia, relationships, and autocorrelation. Compared with the general data, spatial data are distinct, e.g., geographic location, temporal change, multidimensional massive volume, complex relationships, and so on.
Search-based applications	Search-based application is a category of application that enables users to find information from any source and in any format. The user can enter anything he knows about the customer or product and the search engine will try to find those customers or products that resemble the keywords entered by the user.

Data Mining

Data mining activities constitute an interactive process aimed at analyzing large databases, with the purpose of extracting information and knowledge that may prove accurate and potentially useful for knowledge workers involved in decision-making and problem-solving (Vercellis, 2009). Data mining activities can be sub-divided into two major investigation streams, according to the main purpose of the analysis, that are interpretation and prediction (Poul, Gautman & Balint, 2003).

The purpose of interpretation is to identify regular patterns in the data and express them through rules and criteria that can be easily understood by experts in the application domain. The purpose of prediction is to anticipate the value that a random variable will assume in the future or estimate the likelihood of the future events. Different mathematical models and methods are used in such advanced data mining. The most important procedures include: regression, time series, classification, association rules, and clustering (Han, Kamber & Pei, 2011; Larose, 2005; Vercellis, 2009).

Regression Models

The purpose of regression models is to identify a functional relationship between a target variable and a subset of remaining attributes contained in a data set (Vercellis, 2009). The aim of regression models is twofold. Regression models can serve to highlight and interpret the dependency of the target variable on other variables. They can also be used to predict the future value of the target attributes, based upon the functional relationship identified and the future value of the explanatory attributes (Tan, Steinbach, & Kumar, 2005). Therefore, the development of regression models allows knowledge workers to acquire a deeper understanding of the phenomenon analyzed and evaluate the effects determined on the target variable by different combinations of values assigned to the remaining attributes (Vercellis, 2009). Regression models may refer to: (a) simple linear regression representing the most widely known family of regression models that are based on a class of hypothesis consisting of linear functions; and (b) multiple linear regression illustrating how to derive the regression coefficient in the general case. In other words, multiple linear regression attempts to model the relationship between two or more explanatory variables and a response variable by fitting a linear equation to observed data.

Time Series Model

The time series model refers to the data sets in which the target attribute is time dependent. It is a statistical method of analyzing data from repeated observations on a single unit or individual at regular intervals over a large number of observations. The aim is to find any regular pattern of observations relative to the past, with the purpose of making predictions for future periods (Larose, 2005). There are two main goals of time series analysis: (a) identifying the nature of the phenomenon represented by the sequence of observations and (b) forecasting (predicting future values of the time series variable). Both of these goals require that the pattern of observed time series data is identified and more or less formally described. Time series analysis can be viewed as an example of longitudinal designs. Classic time series analysis methods focus on decomposing series changes and building forecasting models. The most widely employed approach is based on the class of models known as Autoregressive Integrated Moving Average (ARIMA) models. ARIMA models can address several major classes of research questions, including an analysis of basic processes, intervention analysis, and analysis of the pattern of treatment effects over time. Time series analysis has many applications in business, financial, socioeconomic, environmental, and industrial domains. Depending on the specific application, predictions may refer to future sales of products and services, trends in economic and financial indicators, or sequences of measurements relative to ecosystems.

Classification

Classification is to assign a new object to the correct class. The allocation of objects to a given class is determined on the basis of the characteristics of the values that particular attributes of a given object take. The purpose of classification is, therefore, to find a relationship between the classification of objects and their characteristics. Classification requires defining classes, i.e., dividing the set into mutually exclusive groups in such a way that the objects included in one class are close to each other, while the groups are maximally distant. There are two main stages of the classification. The first stage consists of building a certain model based on historical data, used to implement the function whose values are class indexes, and variable attributes of objects. In turn, the second stage is determining the classes for new data. Modeling is mainly about setting classes and boundaries between them. Various techniques and algorithms are used here, among which the most popular are decision trees and the nearest neighbor algorithm.

Decision trees are one of the most popular techniques for setting boundaries between classes. Each branch of a tree is a classification question and tree leaves form an appropriately classified data group. In the process of building a tree, a question is searched for each branch of the tree that delimits the data as much as possible. The process of splitting data is carried out until a segment of data with identical characteristics is achieved or when making further splitting does not bring relevant information. The most commonly used tree building techniques include Classification and Regression Trees (CART) and Chi Squared Automatic Interaction Detection (CHAID). The first technique divides the set into halves. The second one is similar to the first, but thanks to setting the Chi-square test, it allows the division of sets into many subsets.

According to the nearest neighbor algorithm, in order to classify a new object described by several features, it is necessary to analyze of the objects nearest (most similar) to it. It is necessary to specify a measure of similarity for the input variables and then assign a new object to the class to which the most of the examined objects (neighbors) belong. The algorithm is based on the assumption that objects that are similar to the input variables also have similar values of the resulting variable (they belong to the same category).

Association Rules

The main aim of association rules is to select regular patterns and recurrences within a large set of transactions. Rules have the form of an *if* implication (set of conditions) **then** (set of facts). Probabilistic rules are the modified form of association rules. They take the form of **if** A **then** B with probability p. Conditional probability p is called the "accuracy" or "confidence" of the rule. The rule "accuracy" means the probability that B is true provided that A is true. The associative rule is also combined with the concept of "support" (or frequency) and a frequent set. Frequency defines this part of all objects to which the rule applies (i.e., how often a given rule applies). The frequent set is, in turn, a simple pattern that says that variables in this set often occur together, where "often" means that they occur at least as often as "support" defines. Association rules are fairly simple and intuitive and are frequently used to investigate sales transactions in a market basket analysis, navigation paths within websites, as well as fraud detection and purchases with a credit card (Vercellis, 2009).

Clustering

Clustering is a popular technique used for classifying a data set into groups (Jain et al., 1999). Data points under particular group share similar features. The purpose of clustering is to find homogeneous groups of records called clusters. Cluster analysis seeks to identify natural subgroups in data with closer resemblance between items within a subgroup than between items in different subgroups. It represents a form of unsupervised learning, where the algorithm is not provided with known examples from the number of prespecified classes or other information on the nature of the classes. Instead, the classes and their profiles are derived from data without additional guidance. The grouping into clusters of a set of multidimensional observations represented as data points scattered through an N-dimensional data space is a fundamental procedure which has been used in a wide variety of scientific and engineering applications.

Data clustering can take place using various algorithms (Kanungo et al., 2002; Senthilnath, Omkar, & Mani, 2011). The most common are hierarchical (i.e., hierarchical grouping) or nonhierarchical (i.e., split-based) algorithms. In the first case, a cluster hierarchy is created in which each cluster consists of more specific subclusters. The top-level cluster contains all elements of the analyzed file (all database records) and the lowest-level clusters are identical elements of the set. The hierarchical clustering algorithm works without user intervention. It only requires an indication of whether the grouping should be done by the *top-down* or *bottom-up* method. In the *top-down* method, the top-level cluster is determined first and then it is divided until elementary clusters are obtained. In the *bottom-up* method, elementary clusters with homogeneous content are established first and then they are merged at the subsequent levels of the hierarchy.

In contrast, in the case of nonhierarchical algorithms, the cooperation of the user is necessary to specify the target number of clusters or a similarity condition whereby two records should be included in one cluster. The algorithm begins by creating the desired number of clusters at random and then "shuffle" the data on every iteration until the best breakdown is achieved. The goal is to divide the data set into disjoint subsets so that the elements of each subset are as homogeneous as possible.

Shekhar et al. (2005) distinguished, in addition to hierarchical clustering methods, other groups of clustering algorithms. They included: partitional clustering algorithms, density-based clustering algorithms, and grid-based clustering algorithms.

Partitional clustering algorithms start with each pattern as a single cluster and iteratively reallocate data points to each cluster until a stopping criterion is met. These methods tend to find clusters of spherical shape. K-means and K-medoids are commonly used partitional algorithms. The squared error is the most frequently used a criterion function in partitional clustering. The recent algorithms in this category include partitioning around medoids, clustering large applications, clustering large applications based on randomized search, and expectation maximization.

In turn, density-based clustering algorithms try to find clusters based on the density of data points in a region. These algorithms treat clusters as dense regions of objects in the data space. The density-based clustering algorithms include density-based spatial clustering of applications with noise, ordering points to identify clustering structure, and density-based clustering.

Then, grid-based clustering algorithms first quantize the clustering space into a finite number of cells and then perform the required operations on the quantized space. Cells that contain more than a certain number of points are treated as dense. The dense cells are connected to form the clusters. Grid-based clustering algorithms are primarily developed for analyzing large spatial data sets. The grid-based clustering algorithms include the statistical information grid-based method, WaveCluster, BANG-clustering, and clustering-in-quest.

In some applications, the clusters generated may provide a meaningful interpretation of the phenomenon of interest. For example, grouping customers on their purchase behaviors may reveal the existence of a cluster corresponding to a market niche to which it might be appropriate to address specific marketing actions for promotional purpose (Han, Kamber, & Pei, 2011).

Text Mining

Text mining is used to discover the dominant patterns of word usage and patterns of relationships between words or documents that come from various sources: mail communication, Internet documents as well as data coming from social networks (Chen et al., 2012; O'Connor, Bamman, & Smith, 2011). In particular, text mining is used for (Blake, 2011) following processes:

■ Relationship identification: Keywords in a specific field are marked in the source texts. Next, phrases characterized by frequent occurrence in the vicinity of given keywords are identified. The pairs of phrases identified this way are candidates for consideration as association compounds.

- Detecting subjectivity: In this application, the analysis of the text is aimed at detecting characteristic phrases indicating the speculation, guesses or expressing private opinions carried out by the author. Such assessment has a significant impact on determining the reliability of the analyzed source.
- Generating abstracts: The essence of the problem in this case is the algorithmic execution of a short text summarizing the content of the analyzed source. The analyzed source can be both a single document and their entire collection.
- Information synthesis: The application is based on the identification of relationships between scientific publications. These relationships are identified based on the content of the entire publication, not just titles, keyword lists, and abstracts. This is to allow for the emergence of previously unknown interactions between the studied phenomena and to indicate new research directions not yet realized by the authors.

Text mining may refer to: (1) data processing: preprocessing of the data to the needed format; (2) concept extraction: extraction of important concepts and terms through initial text analysis; (3) narrative analysis: writing a narrative analysis to identify patterns and co-occurrences of identified concepts; (4) automatic categorization: developing an automated solution; and (5) ontology building: building ontology for future analysis.

Leveraging the power of Big Data and statistical natural language processing (NLP), text analytics techniques have been actively pursued in several emerging areas including information extraction, topic models, question answering (Q/A), event detection, and opinion mining.

Information extraction aims at automatic extraction of specific kinds of structured information from documents. As a building block of information extraction, named entity recognition (NER) is a process that identifies atomic elements in a text and classifies them into predefined categories. NER techniques have been successfully developed for news analysis and biomedical applications (Witten et al., 2011).

Q/A systems rely on techniques from NLP, informational retrieval, and human–computer interaction. Primarily designed to answer factual questions (who, what, when, and where kinds of questions), Q/A systems involve different techniques for question analysis, source retrieval, answer extraction, and answer presentation (Maybury, 2004).

Event detection focuses on identifying information about events, such as type, time, place, participants, and date of the event. Examples of a business event appearing in a newspaper could be a company establishing a new production facility or releasing a new product. Event detection process consists of three steps: event topic reasoning, event property extracting, and similarity comparison. The event topic reasoning step includes: representing the input text by a feature set pertaining to each event topic (e.g., when, who, where, and what) and classifying the text into an appropriate event topic based on the event categorization patterns. Event property extraction refers to extracting the event properties (e.g., names of participating companies, dates, time, and place of the event) based on event ontology. Event similarity comparison refers to the process of determining whether a new input document discusses a new or a previously known event.

Opinion mining, also known as sentiment analysis, is intended to analyze people's opinions, sentiments, evaluations, appraisals, attitudes, and emotions toward entities, such as products, services, organizations, individuals, issues, events, topics, and their attributes. It refers to the computational techniques for extraction, classifying, understanding, and assessing the opinions expressed in various online news sources, social media comments, and other user-generated content (Chen, Chiang, & Storey, 2012; Newman, 2010). It attempts to automatically measure human opinions from a text written in a natural language. Sentiment analysis uses NLP techniques to read and attribute meaning to textual information, such as whether the author felt positive, negative, or neutral. It can provide broad insights into public reactions to a particular event in ways that have not previously been possible. There are two main approaches used in sentiment analysis. The first approach is called the list or corpus approach, where software is used to search for particular words that are considered to have positive or negative meanings. This is the quickest and least labor-intensive approach. The second approach refers to the machine learning approach, which builds on the list approach using machine learning algorithms. This involves a human analyst manually indicating how the program should interpret the use of specific terms or phrases in different contexts using text samples. This requires more human input, but produces more accurate results, for example, by detecting humor or irony.

Finally, an interesting application of text mining in social research can be mentioned which was used to create a contextual sarcasm detector—a model built on Twitter entries (Baumman & Smith, 2015). Google translator is also a very popular tool and constantly improved, thanks to text mining. Elements of text mining are also an important part of the well-known Google Flu Trends project. It provided estimates of influenza activity for more than 25 countries. By aggregating Google Search queries, it attempted to make accurate predictions about flu activity. This project was first launched in 2008 by Google.org to help predict outbreaks of flu.

Web Mining

The analysis of data obtained from the World Wide Web is called web mining (Fürnkranz, 2010). Web mining is used to process and analyze unstructured web contents, based on XML, Internet protocol (HTTP, SMTP), and application programming interface (API). It enables developers to integrate diverse content from different web-enabled systems. Web mining may comprise (Chang et al., 2001):

- content mining which concerns the analysis of documents published on the web and websites;
- user mining which concerns the analysis of user behaviors consisting of analyzing network traffic and ways the users behave; and
- structure mining in which the subject of analyses are interrelationships between various objects on the web (e.g., websites).

Content mining is the field most closely connected to text mining. In this case, the source of data for analysis is not only files containing typical text but mainly the content of websites (written in HTML) and the content of XML files (Chen & Chau, 2004).

The goal of user mining is to identify patterns of user behaviors on the web (Kumar & Gosul, 2011). The sources of data are primarily user entry registers stored on servers, history of transactions carried out in online stores and online banking as well as information about downloaded, and saved files. At this point it should be noted that this way of collecting information about users often raises a lot of controversy. It is sometimes treated as a breach of privacy and security of personal data protection. However, it is also believed that among others, this way of obtaining data allows better understanding of customer preferences and the use of increasingly effective methods of personalizing products and services.

The purpose of structure mining is to determine the interrelationships between resources operating in the network. This issue mainly concerns the identification of relationships between individual websites (Chang et al., 2001). This is especially important for building search algorithms (Kumar & Gosul, 2011).

A major component in web analytics is cloud computing which includes applications, systems software, and hardware delivered as services over the Internet (Chen, Chiang, & Storey, 2012; Newman, 2010; Riad & Hassan, 2008).

Graph Mining

Graph mining can be defined as a set of methods facilitating the detection of interesting associations within the analyzed graph structure. A graph is a pair of sets $G = (V,E)$. V is the set of vertices and the number of vertices $n = |V|$ is the order of the graph (Rehman, Khan, & Fong, 2012). The set E contains the edges of the graph. In an undirected graph, each edge is an unordered pair $\{v, w\}$. In a directed graph, edges are ordered pairs. The verticals v and w are named the endpoints of the edge. The graphical representation of graph is a usually a set of circles representing the nodes connected with lines representing the edges (Jensen, 2010).

According to Rehman, Khan and Fong (2012), graph mining techniques have been categorized into three main groups: graph clustering, graph classification, and subgraph mining. The main task of graph clustering is grouping of verticals of the graph into clusters taking into consideration the edge structure of the graph in such a way that there should be many edges within each cluster and relatively few between clusters. The graph clusters are formed on the basis of some similarities in the underlying structured data graph. In turn, graph classification is based on supervised/semi-supervised learning technique in which the classes of the data are defined in prior. A subgraph is a graph whose verticals and edges are subset of another graph. The subgraph mining problem is to produce the set of subgraphs occurring in at least some given threshold of the given *n* input sample graphs (Ketkar, Holder, & Cook, 2009).

It is emphasized that graph mining techniques may be based on different algorithms (Rehman, Khan & Fong, 2012). They include mainly: D-walks (Callut et al., 2008), multilevel kernel k-means (Kashima & Inokuchi, 2002), GA (Dias & Ochi, 2003), CFFTree (Zhao & Yu, 2007), coring method (Le, Kulikowski, & Muchnik, 2008), bipartite graph co-clustering (Chen & Fonseca, 2004), clique matrix (Barber, 2008), SSHGCA (Kraus, Palm & Kestler, 2007), K-NN (Schenker et al., 2003), HSG (Ozaki & Ohkawa, 2008), and distributed algorithm (Fatat & Borthold, 2005).

An interesting algorithm with advanced visualization software is ForceAtlas2. This algorithm is developed by the Gephi team as an all-around solution to Gephi users' typical networks (scale-free, 10–10,000 nodes) (Bastian, Heymann, & Jacomy, 2009). Gephi is a network visualization software used in various disciplines (social network analysis, biology, genomics etc.). One of its key features is the ability to display the spatialization process, aiming at transforming the network into a map. ForceAtlas2 is a force-directed layout close to other algorithms used for network spatialization. According to Jacomy et al. (2014), ForceAtlas2 is a force-directed layout. The principle of the ForceAtlas2 algorithm is based on the physical aspects. The key concepts used to describe the algorithm are the attracting and repulsive forces. A repulsive force occurs between each pair of connected nodes v_1 and v_2. It is analogous to the interaction between like electrical charges.

The most important features of the ForceAtlas2 algorithm can be summarized as (Jacomy et al., 2014): (a) algorithm stop condition is to exceed the set number of iterations; (b) the result of the algorithm is mapping the neighborhood of the analyzed objects by the proximity of the nodes on the visualized graph; and (c) in the interpretation of the resulting graph, one should concentrate on the mutual position of the nodes.

A typical use case of ForceAtlas2 is the social network. A common feature of this type of network is the presence of many "leaves" (nodes that have only one neighbor). This is due to the power law distribution of degrees that characterizes many real-world data. The forests of "leaves" surrounding the few highly connected nodes are one of the principal sources of visual cluttering.

Graph mining finds its application in various problem domains, including scientific data mining (Raymond & Belbin, 2006), software engineering (Eichinger & Boehm, 2010), bioinformatics, chemical reactions, program flow structures, computer networks (Rehman, Khan, & Fong, 2012), consumer behavior analysis (Yada et al., 2004), video image analysis (Koga et el., 2010), decision support systems (Omar & Salleh, 2012), social network analysis (Bezerianos et al. 2010), Big Data analysis (Aridhi & Nguifi, 2016), and creativity support systems design (Olszak, Bartus, & Lorek, 2017). All these examples of applications are based on the analysis of nonstructural data but with clearly emphasized relational nature.

Network Analysis

One of the best known network analysis is social media mining (SMM). SMM is the process of representing, analyzing, and extracting actionable patterns from social media data. SMM introduces basic concepts and principal algorithms suitable for investigating massive social media data. It discusses theories and methodologies from different disciplines such as computer science, data mining, machine learning, social network analysis, network science, sociology, ethnography, statistics, optimization, and mathematics. It encompasses the tools to formally represent, measure, model, and mine meaningful patterns from large-scale social media data (Zagarani, Abbasi, & Liu, 2014). Network analysis can provide consumers' behavior and preference information for the business as well as express the change of the public mood and even predict the trend of stock market (Bollen et al., 2011). It can also identify target audience groups through brand influence based on customer Big Data on the social media platform (Zhang et al., 2016) and support location-based personalized messaging services (Wang Kai et al., 2015).

Machine Learning

Machine learning is a process of using computers to imitate a person to acquire skills through learning. Machine learning is trained through extensive data and algorithms that allow machines to own the ability to predict management trends and make decisions in the process of analyzing and optimizing operating management of Big Data. Machine learning can build models from mass data or discover various relationships implied in the observed data according to the specific needs of users. The mainstream machine learning algorithms in Big Data environments include: large-scale data classification, Big Data cluster learning, Big Data correlation analysis algorithms, and Big Data parallel algorithms, such as Bayesian network, decision tree, and support vector machine Big Data classification model, K-means and K-mediods Big Data cluster algorithm, big data correlation analysis method based on MapReduce parallel processing model, etc.

Deep Learning

Deep learning has evolved from machine learning and Multilayer Perceptron Architecture, and it is the frontier of current research and analysis of Big Data. The key problem of processing Big Data is how to communicate, interpret, and learn from the data effectively, whatever it is in image, sound, or textual form.

Deep learning is essentially a nonlinear combination of Multilayer Representation Learning method. Representation Learning means learning representation (or feature) from data in order to extract useful information in the data when categorizing and predicting. Deep learning begins with raw data and transforms each representation (or feature) layer into higher and more abstract representation, thereby discovering the intricate structure in high-dimensional data. The key technologies of Google's AI Robot AlphaGo and AlphaGo 2.0 are deep learning and intensive learning of convolutional neural networks (CNN) structures. Deep learning methods are also used in areas such as computer image recognition, speech recognition, NLP, and information retrieval. Krizhevsky, who works in Google, and his mentor Hinton use deep CNNs to recognize and classify social network images. Collobert et al. trained a deep neural network containing a convolutional layer to solve the multiple NLP problems simultaneously using learned intermediate expressions. The study of deep learning in the future will be evolved to more complex problems of deep structure and deep learning algorithm, especially the combination of deep neural networks (DNN) and recurrent neural networks (RNN) which make the use of reinforcement, expecting to learn visual initiative of human being.

Neural Networks

Neural networks are among the most advanced methods of artificial intelligence. In particular, they are used for (Osowski, 2006) the following:

■ pattern recognition that concerns recognizing by the neural network characteristic features that determine if a classified pattern belongs to a particular class; and
■ predictions, where the forecast value y_{t+1} is determined based on past values $y_{t-1} \ldots y_{t-n}$.

Neural networks are a very effective method for dealing with (Cios et al., 2000):

■ cluster analysis, which is a search for the characteristics of the classes to which processed patterns belong (a particularly important issue in data mining and compression);
■ associative memory that allows reproduction of the full form of the pattern based on incomplete, noisy, or distorted data (relevant process in the case of data transmission).

The most frequently mentioned advantages of neural networks include (Kordon, 2010):

■ Extraction of features from source data: The neural network does not require making any assumptions about the source data. It is possible to discover potentially previously unknown patterns in the data related to the studied phenomenon. The learning process is relatively fast, and the correct and effective operation of the neural network is not determined by knowledge of the nature of the studied problem;

■ High approximation capacity: The neural network is able to approximate any continuous and nonlinear relationship between specific factors. The only essential requirement is that the approximated relationship should be deterministic. If such a relationship exists, it can be discovered and successfully approximated; and

■ Speed of development: Algorithms for training neural networks are characterized by relatively good performance. However, access to the right amount of learning data may be an important limitation. Too few learning samples can lead to an insufficient level of network modeling of the relationships or to a discrepancy in the learning algorithm.

Furthermore, there is a comprehensive set of learning algorithms and a large variety of network types. The selection of the learning algorithm is partly determined by the type of network used. The most important types of neural networks include: *Multilayer Perceptron, Radial Basis Function Network, Support Vector Machine, Generalized Regression Neural Network*, and self-organizing feature map (*Self-Organizing Map*). Choosing the type of network for a particular application usually involves the need for experimental verification. Performing experiments involves a fairly large amount of work as well as the demand for the right amount of source data needed to be used as learning data (Lorek, 2017).

Genetic Algorithms

GA is applied over the problem domain where the outcome is very unpredictable and the process of outcome contains complex interrelated modules (Hassan, 2014). GA is used to obtain optimized solutions from a number of candidate solutions (Mitchel, 1998). GA is inspired by evolutionary theory: weak and unit species are faced with extinction by natural selection and the strong ones have greater opportunity to pass their genes to future generations via reproduction (Konak, Coit, & Smith, 2006). Compared with other classic or optimization methods, GAs have their specific advantages in terms of their broad applicability, ease of use, and global perspective (Deb, 1999; Lu, Li, & Zhang, 2015; Thede, 2004;).

GA is also very apt for such class of problems where problem specification is very difficult to formulate. The whole process of GA is based on the idea of natural evolution and selection. This knowledge of evolution and selection is encoded in a chromosome and can be analyzed with conditional or random probability.

Using GA over data mining creates great robust, computationally efficient, and adaptive systems. In the past, there were several researches focused on data mining using statistical techniques. The statistics that have heavily contributed are the ANOVA, ANCOVA, Poisson's Distribution, and Random Indicator Variables etc.

The biggest drawback of any statistical tactics lies in its tuning. With exponential explosion of data, this tuning goes on taking more time and inversely affects the throughput. Also, due to their static nature, often complex hidden patterns are left out. The idea here is to use genes to mine out data with great efficiency (Hasan, 2014).

Spatial Analysis

In Big Data, spatial data specifically account for the vast majority. About 80% of data are associated with the spatial position (Grossner, Goodchild, & Clarke, 2008). Any kind of object or structure may be related to a geospatial location such as buildings, roads, places, bridges, or rivers. The content of spatial data can be the value of point height, road length, polygon area, building volume and imagery pixel, also the string of geographical name and annotation, and further the graphics, images, multimedia, relationships, and autocorrelation (Shekhar, & Chawla, 2003).

Spatial data mining is a process of discovering interesting and previously unknown, but potentially useful, patterns from large spatial data sets. Extracting interesting and useful patterns from spatial data sets is more difficult than extracting the corresponding patterns from traditional numeric and categorical data due to the complexity of spatial data types, spatial relationships, and spatial autocorrelation (Shekhar et al., 2005).

Specific features of geographical data that preclude the use of general purpose data mining algorithms are (Shekhar et al., 2005): (a) spatial relationships among the variables; (b) spatial structure of errors; (c) mixed distributions as opposed to commonly assumed normal distributions; (d) observations that are not independent; (e) spatial autocorrelation among the features; and (f) nonlinear interaction in feature space.

The complexity of spatial data and intrinsic spatial relationships limit the usefulness of conventional data mining techniques for extracting spatial patterns. Efficient tools for extracting information from geospatial data are crucial to organizations which make decisions based on large spatial data sets, including NASA, the National Imagery and Mapping Agency, the National Cancer Institute, and the United States Department of Transportation. These organizations are spread across many application domains, including: ecology and environmental management, public safety, transportation, Earth science, epidemiology, and climatology (Shekhar et al., 2005).

Search-Based Application

Search-based application is a category of application that enables users to find information from any source and in any format. The users can enter anything they know about the customer or product and the search engine will try to find those customers or products that resemble the keywords entered by the user. According to Capgemini (2013), there are different reasons for using search engines: (a) they are very flexible in handling any format and type of information, be it structured, unstructured, or external; (b) they are able to cope with continuously evolving data structures. Indexing both existing and new data does not require extensive data-modeling; (c) search engines enable content-driven dimensional navigation. At each step of navigation search engines propose different possibilities to filter results according to the content of the data sets that are being indexed and analyzed in near real time; (4) search engines, unlike solutions based on RDBMS, are able to analyze data without the need to know the various data types; (5) end users are now quite familiar with the "Google" interface. As a consequence, they are much more independent from IT departments if they can access decision support data through a search engine; (6) when external and unstructured data are needed to support decision-making, traditional data warehouse architectures are limited and search engines can help to fill the gap; (7) search engines include functionality to automatically generate categories and clusters, hence improve the contextualization and meaning of data; and (8) search engines can work with existing information systems (e.g., data warehouses, data marts, production systems, etc.) and provide a uniform view of data without compromising performance.

Big Data Technologies

Nowadays there are a growing number of technologies used to aggregate, manipulate, manage, and analyze Big Data. These include mainly: NoSQL, Big Table, Apache Cassandra, Google File System (GFS), Apache Hadoop, MapReduce, and Mashup (Table 3.2).

NoSQL

The acronym NoSQL comes from the words "non SQL," although it is often said "not only SQL." NoSQL is a technology that enables the collection and use of nonstructured data. Data in such databases are modeled in a different way than tabular (used in relational databases). Non-relational databases perfectly fit into the Big Data trend. Unlike classic databases, they allow quick analysis of unstructured data and study of correlations between them. In the traditional database, the pattern and relationships are imposed from above. We can use structural SQL queries to provide structural answers within the framework described earlier. The latest trends show that it is worth collecting a variety of data, often unstructured, which may initially seem irrelevant but ultimately provide valuable business information. NoSQL enables users to transfer any data for later analysis without first preparing a data schema. These data can be used for various analyses and to discover potential correlations.

Table 3.2 Examples of Big Data Technologies

Technology	Description
NoSQL	NoSQl is a technology that, unlike classic databases, allows quick analysis of unstructured data and testing the correlation between them. NoSQL facilitates transfer of any data for later analysis without first preparing a data schema.
Big Table	Big Table is a compressed, high performance, proprietary data storage system built on Google File System (GFS), Chubby Lock Service, SSTable (log-structured storage like LevelDB), and a few other Google technologies. The database was designed to be deployed on clustered systems and uses a simple data model that Google has described as "a sparse, distributed, persistent multidimensional sorted map." Data are assembled in order by row key, and indexing of the map is arranged according to row, column keys, and timestamps. Different compression algorithms help achieve high capacity.
Apache Cassandra	Apache Cassandra is a highly scalable, high-performance distributed database designed to handle large amounts of data across many commodity servers, providing high availability with no single point of failure. It is a type of NoSQL database. At the moment, Apache Cassandra is the most efficient NoSQL database of the "widerow" class while maintaining full scalability on any class equipment.
Google File System	GFS is a scalable distributed file system created by Google Inc. and developed to accommodate Google's expanding data processing requirements. GFS provides fault tolerance, reliability, scalability, availability, and performance to large networks and connected nodes. The GFS node cluster is a single master with multiple chunk servers that are continuously accessed by different client systems. Chunk servers store data as Linux files on local disks. Stored data is divided into large chunks which are replicated in the network a minimum of three times. The large chunk size reduces network overhead.

Table 3.2   Continued

Technology	Description
Apache Hadoop	An open-source software framework for processing huge data sets on certain kinds of problems on a distributed system. Open-source software is being developed within Apache™ Hadoop R project. It enables the processing of distributed large data sets in computer clusters using simple programming models. The Appache™ Hadoop project includes various modules such as: Hadoop Common, Hadoop Distributed File System, Hadoop YARN, and Hadoop MapReduce.
MapReduce	A software framework introduced by Google for processing huge data sets on certain kinds of problems on a distributed system. It allows parallel processing. The basic assumption of this model is to divide the problem into two main stages called mapping and reduction. The distributed file system from MapReduce enables data to be processed at the place of storage.
Mashup	An application that uses and combines data presentation or functionality from two or more sources to create new services. Mashup approach allows users to build ad hoc applications by combining several different data sources and services from across the web.

However, high data availability in NoSQL databases is obtained at the expense of data consistency. Information gathered in different clusters may differ from each other. MapReduce, Hadoop, Cassandra or Hypertable are the examples of platforms that provide mechanisms for ad hoc and on-time extraction, parsing, processing, indexing, and analytics in a scalable and distributed environment (Chen, Chiang, & Storey, 2012).

Big Table

Big Table is a compressed, high performance, proprietary data storage system built on GFS, Chubby Lock Service, SSTable (log-structured storage like LevelDB), and a few other Google technologies. Big Table development began in 2004 and is now used by a number of Google applications such as web indexing, MapReduce, which is often used for generating and modifying data stored in Big Table, Google Maps, Google Book Search, Google Earth, Blogger.com, Google Code hosting, YouTube, and Gmail. Big Table was designed to support applications requiring massive scalability. From its first iteration, the technology was intended to be used with petabytes of data. The database was designed to be deployed on clustered systems and uses a simple data model that Google has described as "a sparse, distributed, persistent multidimensional sorted map." Data are assembled in order by row key, and indexing of the map is arranged according to row, column keys, and timestamps. Different compression algorithms help achieve high capacity.

Big Table has had a large impact on NoSQL database design. Google software developers publicly disclosed Big Table details in a technical paper presented at the USENIX Symposium on Operating Systems and Design Implementation in 2006. Google's thorough description of Big Table's inner workings has allowed other organizations and open-source development teams to create Big Table derivatives, including the Apache HBase database, which is built to run on top of the Hadoop Distributed File System (HDFS). Other examples include Cassandra, which originated at Facebook Inc., and Hypertable, an open-source technology that is marketed in a commercial version as an alternative to HBase. (Google Big Table, from: https://searchdatamanagement.techtarget.com/definition/Google-BigTable).

Apache Cassandra

Apache Cassandra is a highly scalable, high-performance distributed database designed to handle large amounts of data across many commodity servers, providing high availability with no single point of failure. It is a type of NoSQL database. Apache Cassandra was created in 2008 by Facebook engineers. The rapidly growing number of users showed that traditional, relational database solutions are not able to provide adequate performance in data processing. Apache Cassandra is now the most efficient NoSQL database of the "widerow" class, while maintaining full scalability on any class equipment.

Apart from Cassandra, there are other NoSQL databases as well. The most well-known are Apache HBase and MongoDB. Apache HBase is an open source, non-relational, distributed database modeled after Google's Big Table and is written in Java. It is developed as a part of Apache Hadoop project and runs on top of HDFS, providing Big Table-like capabilities for Hadoop. Then, MongoDB is a cross-platform document-oriented database system that avoids using the traditional table-based relational database structure in favor of JSON-like documents with dynamic schemas making the integration of data in certain types of applications easier and faster.

Google File System

GFS is a scalable distributed file system created by Google Inc. and developed to accommodate Google's expanding data processing requirements. GFS provides fault tolerance, reliability, scalability, availability, and performance to large networks and connected nodes (Ghemawat, Gobioff, & Leung, 2003). GFS was designed to meet the rapidly growing demands of Google's data processing needs. GFS grew out of an earlier Google effort, "BigFiles", developed by Larry Page and Sergey Brin in the early days of Google. Files are divided into fixed-size chunks of 64 megabytes, similar to clusters or sectors in regular file systems, which are only extremely rarely overwritten or shrunk. GFS shares many of the same goals as previous distributed file systems, i.e., performance, scalability, reliability, and availability.

GFS is made up of several storage systems built from low-cost commodity hardware components. It is optimized to accommodate Google's different data use and storage needs, such as its search engine, which generates huge amounts of data that must be stored.

The GFS capitalized on the strength of off-the-shelf servers while minimizing hardware weaknesses. The GFS node cluster is a single master with multiple chunk servers that are continuously accessed by different client systems. Chunk servers store data as Linux files on local disks. Stored data are divided into large chunks which are replicated in the network a minimum of three times. The large chunk size reduces network overhead. GFS is designed to accommodate Google's large cluster requirements without burdening applications. Files are stored in hierarchical directories identified by path names. Metadata such as namespace, access control data, and mapping information are controlled by the master, which interacts with and monitors the status updates of each chunk server through timed heartbeat messages (retrieved from https://www.techopedia.com/definition/26906/google-file-system-gfs).

Apache Hadoop

Apache Hadoop is an open-source software framework for processing huge data sets on certain kinds of problems on a distributed system. Open-source software being developed within the Apache™ Hadoop R project enables the processing of distributed large data sets in computer clusters using simple programming models. It has been designed to scale from one server to thousands of computers, offering the possibility of calculations and data storage. The Apache Hadoop software library is fault tolerant, designed to detect and handle faults in the application layer. The Apache Hadoop project includes various modules. These are: (a) Hadoop Common—common tools that support other Hadoop modules; (b) HDFS—distributed file system that provides access to high-bandwidth application data; (c) Hadoop YARN—programming platform (Framework) for work planning and cluster resource management; and (d) Hadoop MapReduce—YARN-based system designed for parallel processing of large data sets.

MapReduce

MapReduce is a software framework introduced by Google for processing huge data sets on certain kinds of problems on a distributed system. It enables parallel processing. The basic assumption of this model is to divide the problem into two main stages called mapping and reduction. The distributed file system from MapReduce allows data to be processed at the place of storage. Thanks to this solution, there is no need to send information from computers that store data to servers. Instead of sending large amounts of data, MapReduce is sent with a size of several kilobytes. With this solution, users can gain time that is lost if data were sent.

Mashup

Mashup is an application that uses and combines data presentation or functionality from two or more sources to create new services. Mashup approach allows users to build ad hoc applications by combining several different data sources and services from across the web.

Big Data Management

The complex nature of Big Data resources requires not only the use of various techniques to process them, but also to organize the entire process of managing such data. There are five identified phases in Big Data analysis system which include (Agrawal et al., 2011): (a) acquisition/recording; (b) extraction/cleaning/ annotation; (c) integration/aggregation/representation; (d) analysis/modeling; and (e) interpretation.

The data acquisition stage is a particularly important because the quality of the results of the analysis depends on its performance. The main difficulty at this stage is to reach relevant and reliable data sources. NoSQL databases are frequently used to acquire and store Big Data. Such systems just extract all data and do not categorize them or parse them by designing a schema. There exists a big challenge to generate right metadata to make a description of all data that are recorded, and the ways in which they are recorded and measured.

The second phase refers to cleaning and extracting the information that has already been received. It is necessary to change the format of the distributed data and prepare it for further analysis. The information that can be extracted from the data depends on its quality. It means that poor-quality data will almost always lead to poor results ("garbage in, garbage out"). Therefore, data cleaning (or scrubbing) is highlighted as one of the most important steps that should taken before data analysis is conducted. This often involves significant costs as the whole process can take from 50 to 80% of a data analyst's time together with the actual data collection costs (Reimsbach-Kounatze, 2015).

The next step involves preparing and processing the data by using specific programs and programming languages, in other words organizing data. All data must be comprehensible for the computers. It has to be noticed that there is more than one way to store the information, which means that depending on the purpose the data can be presented differently in a more effective way.

The step of analysis/modeling refers to the use of different data mining techniques (Schmarzo, 2013; Zhao, 2015). They include mainly (Chen et al., 2012) clustering, classification and prediction, outlier detection, association rules, sequence analysis, time series analysis, text mining, and also some new techniques such as social network analysis and sentiment analysis. Every data mining model relies on machine learning—supervised or unsupervised.

At the last stage, a critical assessment of the results obtained should be made. First of all, it should be decided whether the results obtained can be considered reliable, taking into account the scope of the sources analyzed. If the results obtained do not raise any doubts, they can be proceeded to their descriptive formulation and conclusions can be drawn which is the basic goal of the whole process.

The management of Big Data would not be successful if it was not for an appropriate environment that could support Big Data in dealing with storage, analytics, reporting, and applications. The environment must include all considerations of hardware, infrastructure software, operational software, management software, well-defined application programming interfaces, and even software developer tools (Hurwitz et al., 2013). The appropriate employment of Big Data algorithms to the analysis of the data of sufficient quality can provide numerous opportunities for improvements in the whole society. In addition to the market-wide benefits such as defining a more effective way of matching products and services to consumers, Big Data can also create opportunities for low-income and underserved communities (Ramirez et al., 2016).

References

Agrawal, D. et al. (2011). Challenges and opportunities with Big data 2011-1. Purdue University Labraries: Purdue e-Pubs. Retrieved from http://docs.lib.purdue.edu/cgi/viewcontent.cgi?article=1000&context=cctech.

Aridhi, S., & Nguifo, E. (2016). Big graph mining: Frameworks and techniques. *Big Data Research*, 6, 1–10.

Barber, D. (2008). Clique matrices for statistical graph decomposition and parame-nite matrics. Proceedings of the Twenty-Fourth Conference on Uncertainty in Artificial Intelligence. AUAI Press, 26–33.

Bastian, M., Heymann, S., & Jacomy, M. (2009). Gephi: An open source software for exploring and manipulating networks. Proceedings of the Third International Conference on Weblogs and Social Media, ICWSM, 361–362.

Baumman, D., & Smith, N.A. (2015). Contextualization sarcasm detection on Twitter. International AAAI Conference on Web and Social Media, North America, 574–577. Retrieved from https://www.aaai.org/ocs/index.php/ICWSM/ICWSM15/paper/view/10538/10445.

Bean, R. (2017). How Companies Say They're Using Big Data. Retrieved from https://hbr.org/2017/04/how-companies-say-theyre-using-big-data.

Bezerianos, A., Chevalier, F., Elmqvist, N., & Fekete, J.D. (2010). GraphDice: A system for exploring multivariate social networks. *Computer Graphics Forum*, 29, 863–872.

Blake, C. (2011). Text mining. *Annual Review of Information Science and Technology*, 45(10), 121–155.

Bollen, J., Mao, H., & Zeng, X. (2011). Twitter mood predicts the stock market. *Journal of Computational Science*, 2(1), 1–8.

Buchholtz, S., Bukowski, M., & Śniegocki, A. (2014). *Worldwide Big Data Technology and Services 2013–2017 Forecast*, report, IDC, December 2013, *Big and open data in Europe. A growth engine or a missed opportunity?* Warsaw Institute for Economic Studies, report commissioned by demosEUROPA, 2014.

Callut, J., Francoisse, K., Saerens, M., & Dupont, P. (2008). Semi-supervised classification from discriminative random walks. *Lecture Notes in Artificial Intelligence*, 5211, 162–177. Berlin Heidelberg: Springer.

Capgemini (2013). Consulting. Technology. Outsourcing. Retrieved from http://www.capgemini.com/sites/default/files/resource/pdf/Search-Based_BI.pdf.

Catteneo, G. (2014). *The European Data Market*, raport IDC, presentation given at the NESSI summit in Brussels on 27 May 2014. Retrieved from http://www.nessi-europe.eu/?Page=nessi_summit_2014.

Chang, G., Healey, M., McHugh, J.A.M., & Wang, T.L. (2001). *Mining the world wide web. An Information Search Approach*. Springer.

Chen, C., & Zhang, C. Y. (2014). Data-intensive applications, challenges, techniques and technologies: A survey on Big Data. *Information Science*, 275, 314–347.

Chen, H., & Chau, M. (2004). Web mining: Machine learning for web applications. *Annual Review of Information Science and Technology*, 38, 289–329.

Chen, H., Chiang, R. H. L., & Storey, V. C. (2012). Business Intelligence and analytics: from Big Data to big impact. *MIS Quarterly*, 36(4), 1–24.

Chen, Y., & Fonseca, F. (2004). A Bipartite Graph Co-Clustering Approach to Ontology Mapping. Retrieved from http://yiling.seas.harvard.edu/wp-content/uploads/ISWC03.pdf.

Cios, K. J., Pedrycz, W., & Swiniarski, R. W. (2000). *Data mining methods for knowledge discovery*. New York: Springer.

Connick, H. (2017). Turning Big Data into Big Insights. Retrieved from https://www.ama.org/marketing-news/turning-big-data-into-big-insights.

Cox, M., & Ellsworth D. (1997). Managing Big Data for Scietific Visualization. Retrieved from https://www.researchgate.net/publication/238704525_Managing_big_data_for_scientific_visualization.

Davenport, T. H., Barth, P., & Bean, R. (2012). How big data is different. *MIT Sloan Management Review*, 54(1), 22–24.

Davenport, T. H., & Harris, J. G. (2007). *Competing on analytics. The new science on winning*. Boston Massachusetts, MA: Harvard Business School Press.

Deb, K. (1999). An introduction to genetic algorithms. *Sadhana*, 24(4-5), 293–315.

Dewey, J.P. (2014). Big Data. Salem Press Encyclopedia.

Dias, C. R., & Ochi, L. S. (2003). Efficient evolutionary algorithms for the clustering problem in directed graphs. *Proceedings of the 2003 IEEE Congress on Evolutionary Computation*, 1, 983–988.

Eichinger, F., & Boehm, K. (2010). Software-bug localization with graph mining. In C. C. Aggarwal, H. Wang (Eds.), *Managing and Mining Graph Data, Advances in Database Systems*, vol. 40, 515–546. New York Dordrecht Heidelberg London: Springer.

Erl, T., Khattak, W., & Buhler, P. (2015). *Big Data fundamentals: concepts, drivers & techniques*. Boston: Prentice Hall.

Fatat, G.D., & Berthold, M.R. (2005). High performance subgraph mining in molecular compounds. *HPCC*, 866–877.

Firican,G. (2017). The 10 Vs of Big Data. TDWI. Retrieved from https://tdwi.org/articles/2017/02/08/10-vs-of-big-data.aspx.

Fürnkranz, J. (2010). Web mining. In: O. Maimon, L. Rokach (Eds.), *Data Mining and Knowledge Discovery Handbook*. Springer.

Ghemawat, S., Gobioff, H., & Leung, S.T. (2003). The Google File System, SOSP'03, October 19–22, Bolton Landing, New York, USA. Retrieved from https://storage.googleapis.com/pub-tools-public-publication-data/pdf/035fc972c796d33122033a06 14bc94cff1527999.pdf.

Ghemawat, S.,Gobioff, H., & Leung, S.T. (2003). Proceedings of the 19th ACM symposium on operating systems principles. Bolton Landing, NY: ACM, 20–43.

Grossner, K. E., Goodchild, M. F., & Clarke, F. C. (2008). Defining a digital earth system. *Transactions in GIS*, 12(1), 145–160.

Halaweh, M., & Massry, A. E. (2015). Conceptual model for successful implementation of Big Data in organizations. *Journal of International Technology and Information Management*, 24(2), 21–29.

Han, J., Kamber, M., & Pei, J. (2011). *Data mining: Concept and techniques*. New York: Morgan Kaufmann.

Hassan, A.K. (2014). *Big Data: Techniques and technologies in geoinformatics*. Boca Raton: CRC Press. Taylor and Francis.

Himmi, K., Arcondara, J., Guan, P., & Zhou, W. (2017). Value oriented Big data strategy: analysis & case study. Proceedings of 50th Hawaii International Conference on System Sciences. Hawaii.

Hopikins, B. (2016). Think you want to be "data-driven". Insights in the new data. Retrieved from https://go.forrester.com/blogs/16-03-09-think_you_want_to_be_data_driven_insight_is_the_new_data/.

Hsu, H. H., Chang, C. Y., & Hsu, C. H. (2017). *Big data analytics for sensor-network collected intelligence*. Academic Press.

Hurwitz, J., Nugent, A., Halper, F., & Kaufman, M. (2013). *Big data for dummies*. New Jersey, Hoboken: John Wiley & Sons, Inc.

Jacomy, M., Venturini, T., Heymann, S., & Bastian, M. (2014). ForceAtlas2, A Continous Graph Layout Algorithm for Handy Network Visualisation for the Gephi Software, *PLoS ONE*,9(6). Retrieved from http://journals.plos.org/plosone/article?id=10.1371/journal.pone.0098679.

Jensen, T. R. (2010). Graphs. In: C. Sammut, G. I. Webb (Eds.), *Encyclopedia of Machine Learning*, 479–482. Berlin Heidenberg: Springer.

Kanungo, T., Mount, D. M., Netanyahu, N. S., Piatko, C. D., Silverman, R., & Wu, A. Y. (2002). An efficient k-means clustering algorithm: Analysis and implementation. *Pattern Analysis and Machine Intelligence*. IEEE Transactions. 24(7), 881–892.

Kashima, H., & Inokuchi, A. (2002). *Kernels for graph classification*. In: Proceedings of the *ICDM Workshop on Active Mining*, 31–36. Maebashi, Japan.

Ketkar, N.S., Holder, L.B., & Cook, D.J. (2009). Empirical Comparison of graph classification algorithms. IEEE. Symposium on Computational Intelligence and Data Mining. Washington State University. Retrieved from https://www.eecs.wsu.edu/~cook/pubs/cidm09.2.pdf.

Koga, H., Tomokazu, T., Yokoyama, T., & Wanatabe, T. (2010). New application of graph mining to video analysis. In: C. Fyfe, P. Tino, D. Charles, C. Garcia-Osorio, H. Yin (Eds), *Intelligent Data Engineering and Automated Learning – IDEAL 2010*. Lecture Notes in Computer Science, *6283*, 86–93. Berlin-Heidelberg: Springer.

Konak, D. Coit, W., & Smith, A. E. (2006). Multi-objective optimization using genetic algorithms: a tutorial. *Reliability Engineering & System Safety, 91*(9), 992–1007.

Kordon, A. (2010). *Applying computational intelligence:How to create value*. Berlin-Heidelberg: Springer.

Kraus, J. M., Palm, G., & Kestler, H. A. (2007). On the robustness of semi-supervised hierarchical graph clustering in functional genomics. 5th International Workshop on Mining and Learning with *Graphs*, 147–150. Italy, Florenz.

Kumar, G.D., & Gosul, M. (2011). Web mining research and future directions. In: D. C. Wyld, M. Wozniak, N. Chaki, N. Meghanathan, D. Nagamalai. (Eds.), *Advances in Network Security and Applications*. CNSA 2011. Communications in Computer and Information Science, 196. Berlin, Heidelberg: Springer.

Lapkin, A. (2012). *Hype cycle for big data*. Gartner, Inc. Retrieved from https://www.gartner.com/en/documents/2100215/hype-cycle-for-big-data-2012.

Larose, D. T. (2005). *Discovering knowledge in data: An introduction to data Mining*. New York: John Wiley & Sons, Inc.

LaValle, S., Lesser, E., Shockley, R., Hopkins, M., & Kruschwitz, N. (2011). Big data, analytics and the path from insights to value. *MIT Sloan Management Review, 52*(2), 21–31.

Le, T. V., Kulikowski, C. A., & Muchnik, I. B. (2008). *Coring methods for clustering a graph*. In: 19th International Conference on Pattern Recognition (ICPR *2008*), December *2008*, 1–4. New York: IEEE.

Lorek, P. (2017). Metody i narzędzia do projektowania systemów wspomagania twórczości organizacyjnej. In: C. M. Olszak (Eds.), *Twórcza organizacja. Komputerowe wspomaganie twórczości organizacyjnej*. Warszawa: CH. Beck.

Lu, Q., Shanshan Li, S., & Zhang, W. (2015).Genetic algorithm based job scheduling for Big data analytics. 2 015 International Conference on Identification, Information, and Knowledge in the Internet of Things. Beijing, China: IEEE, 33–38. Retrieved from https://www.researchgate.net/publication/300408982_Genetic_Algorithm_Based_Job_Scheduling_for_Big_Data_Analytics.

Manyika, J., Chui, M., Brown, B., Bughin, J., Dobbs, R., Roxburgh, C., & Byers, A. H. (2011). *Big data: The next frontier for innovation, competition, and productivity*. KY: McKinsey Global Institute.

Maybury, M. (2004). *New directions in question answering*. Cambridge. US: MIT Press.

Mayer-Schönberger, V., & Cukier, K. (2013). *Big data: A revolution that will transform how we live, work, and think*. Boston: Houghton Mifflin Harcourt.

McAfee, A., & Brynjolfsson, E. (2012). Big data: The management revolution. *Harvard Business Review*, October, 59–69.

Mills, M. P., & Ottino, J. M. (2012).*The coming tech-led boom*. Retrieved from www.wsj.com.

Mitchell, M. (1998). *An introduction to genetic algorithms*. MIT Press.

Newman, M. E. J. (2010). *Networks: An introduction*. Oxford: Oxford University Press.

O'Connor, B., Bamman, D., & Smith, N. A. (2011). Computational Text Analysis for Social Sciences: Model Complexity and Assumptions. Second Workshop on Computational Social Scienceand Wisdom of the Crowds (NIPS 2011).Retrieved from http://brenocon.com/oconnor+bamman+smith.nips2011css.text_analysis.pdf.

O'Driscoll, T. (2014). Can big Data deliver added value. *Training, 51*(2), 51.

Office of Science and Technology Policy, Executive Office of the President (2012a). *Fact sheet: Big dataacross the federal government.* Retrieved from www. WhiteHouse.gov/ OSTP.

Office of Science and Technology Policy, Executive Office of the President (2012b). *Obama Administration Unveils "Big data" Initiative: Announces $200 Million in New R&D Investments.* Retrieved from www. WhiteHouse.gov/OSTP.

Olszak, C. M. (2016). Toward better understanding and use of Business Intelligence in organizations. *Information Systems Management, 33*(2), 105–123.

Olszak, C. M., Bartuś, T., & Lorek, P. (2017). A comprehensive framework of information system design to provide organizational creativity support. *Information & Management, 55*, 94–108.

Olszak, C. M., & Zurada, J. (2019). Big Data-driven Value Creation for Organizations, Proceedings of Hawaii International Conference on System Sciences (HICSS-52). University of Hawai'i at Mānoa, Scholar Space for the University of Hawai'i at Mānoa, January, 8-11. pp 164–173, DOI: http://hdl.handle.net/10125/59457.

Omar, A. H., & Salleh, M. N. M. (2012). Integrating spatial decision support system with graph mining technique. In: V. Khachidze, T. Wang, S. Siddiqui, V. Liu, S. Cappucio, & A. Lim (Eds.), *Contemporary Research on E-business Technology and Strategy.* Communications in Computer and Information Science, *332*, 15–24. Berlin-Heidelberg: Springer.

Oracle (2014). *Information Management and Big Data. A Reference Architecture.* Retrieved from http://www.oracle.com/technetwork/database/bigdata-appliance/overview/ bigdatarefarchitecture-2297765.pdf.

Osowski, S. (2006). *Sieci neuronowe do przetwarzania informacji.* Warszawa: Oficyna Wydawnicza Politechniki Warszawskiej.

Ozaki, T., & Ohkawa, T. (2008). Mining correlated Subgraphs in Graph Databases. *Proceedings of 12th Pacific-Asia Conference.* Japan, Osaka: PAKDD.

Paharia, R. (2014). Lojalność 3.0: jak zrewolucjonizować zaangażowanie klientów i pracowników dzięki big data i rywalizacji. Tłum. D. Gasper, Warszawa: MT biznes Ltd.

Parise, S., Iyer, B., & Vesset, D. (2012). Four strategies to capture and crate value from big data. *Ivey Business Journal,* Issue July 2012. Retrieved from http://iveybusinessjournal.com/publication/four-strategies-to-capture-and-createhttp://iveybusinessjournal.com/publication/four-strategies-to-capture-and-create-value-from-big-data/ value-from-big-data/.

Pence, H. E. (2014). What is Big data and why it is important. *Journal of Education Technology Systems, 43*(2), 159–171.

Poul, S., Gautman, N., & Balint, R. (2003). *Preparing and data mining with Microsoft SQL Server 2000 and Analysis Services.* New York: Addison-Wesley.

Ramirez, E., Brill, J., Ohlhausen, M., & McSweeny, T. (2016). Big Data: A tool for inclusion or exclusion? Understanding the issues. Federal Trade Commission. Retrieved from: https://www.ftc.gov/system/files/documents/reports/big-data-tool-inclusion-or-exclusion-understanding-issues/160106big-data-rpt.pdf.

Raymond, B., & Belbin, L. (2006). Visualization and exploration of scientific data using graphs. In: G. J. Williams, S. J. Simoff (Eds.), *Data Mining, Lecture Notes in Computer Science, 3755*, 14–27. Berlin – Heidelberg: Springer.

Rehman, S.U., Khan, A. Ul., & Fong, S. (2012). Graph mining: A survey of graph mining technique. Seventh International Conference on Digital Information Management (ICDIM), IEEE, 88–92. Retrieved from https://www.researchgate.net/ publication/233801707_Graph_mining_A_survey_of_graph_mining_techniques.

Reimsbach-Kounatze, C. (2015). The proliferation of Big data and implications for official statistics and statistical agencies. *OECD Digital Economy Papers*, 245, Paris: OECD Publishing.

Reshef, D. N., Reshef, Y. A., Finucane, Hilary K., Grossman, S. R., McVean, G. Turnbaugh, P.J., Lander, E. S., Mitzenmacher, M., & Sabeti, P. C. (2011). Detecting novel associations in large data sets. *Science*, 334(6062), 1518–1524.

Riad, A., & Hassan, Q. (2008). Service oriented-architecture: A new alternative to traditional integration methods in b2b applications. *Journal of Convergence Information Technology*, 3(1), 41.

Schenker, A., Last, M., Bonke, H., & Kandel, A. (2003). Classification of Web Documents Using a Ggraph Mode. Proceedings of the Seventh International Conference on Document Analysis and Recognition, 1–5. IEEE.

Schmarzo, B. (2013). *Big data: Understanding how data powers big business.* Indianapolis: John Wiley and Sons.

Senthilnath, J. S., Omkar, N., & Mani, V. (2011). Clustering using firefly algorithm: performance study. *Swarm and Evolutionary Computation1*, 3, 164–171.

Shekhar, S., Zhang, P., Huang,Y., & Vatsavai, R.R. (2005). Spatial data mining. In: Maimon, O., Rokach, L. (Eds.), *The Data Mining and Knowledge Discovery Handbook.* Heidelberg: Springer.

Tan, P. N., Steinbach, M., & Kumar, V. (2005). *Introduction to data mining.* New York: Addison-Wesley.

Thede, S. M. (2004). An introduction to genetic algorithms. *Journal of Computing Sciences in Colleges*, 20(1), 115–123.

United Nations Global Pulse. (2012). Big data for development: Challenges & opportunities. UN Global Pulse. Retrieved from https://www.unglobalpulse.org/document/ big-data-for-development-opportunities-and-challenges-white-paper/.

Vercellis, C. (2009). *Business Intelligence.* Chichester: Wiley.

Wang, K., Yu, W., Yang, S., Wu, M., Hu, Y.H., & Li, S.J. (2015). A Method of estimating online social media location in Big data environment. *Journal of Software*, 26(11), 2951–2963.

Witten, I. H., & Frank, E. (2005). *Data mining: Practical machine learning tools and techniques.* San Francisco, US: Morgan-Kaufland.

Xu, Z., Frankowick, G. L., & Ramirez, E. (2016). Effects of big data analytics and traditional marketing analytics on a new product success: a knowledge fusion perspective. *Journal of Business Research*, 69(5), 1562–1566.

Yada, K., Motoda, H., Washio, T., & Miyawaki, A. (2004). Consumer behavior analysis by graph mining technique. In: M. G. Negoita, J. R. Howlett, L. C. Jain (Eds.), *Knowledge-Based Intelligent Information and Engineering Systems – KES 2004.* Lecture Notes in Computer Science, *3214*, 800–806. Berlin-Heidelberg: Springer.

Zhang, K., Bhattacharyya, S., & Ram, S. (2016). Large-scale network analysis for online social brand advertising. *MIS Quarterly, 40*(4), 849–868.

Zhao, P., & Yu, J.X. (2007). Mining closed frequent free trees in graph databases. *Proceedings of Databases Systems for Advance Application*, 91–102.

Zhao, Y. (2015). R and data mining: Examples and case studies. Academic Press, Elsevier. Retrieved from: http://www.rdatamining.com/docs/RDataMining-book.pdf.

Chapter 4

Analysis of Business Intelligence and Big Data Adoption in Organizations

Areas of Business Intelligence and Big Data Utilization in Organizations

The role and impact of analytical systems on an organization and its environment have changed over time. From simple and static applications, they have evolved into solutions that can be utilized in forecasting economic and social phenomena, predicting and modeling customer behaviors, and analyzing product profitability. Various organizations and industries, e.g., marketing, sales, production, banking, finance, controlling, telecommunications, insurance, administration, health care sector, and education have become beneficiaries of analytical systems based on Business Intelligence and Big Data (BI&BD). It can even be said that it would be difficult to provide examples of organizations that could not benefit from BI&BD. Both large corporations and the small and medium enterprises sector seek many advantages in these solutions.

According to Goodhue, Wixom and Watson (2010), we can distinguish three goals that organizations achieve by implementing BI&BD. These are as follows:

- Improving the work of individual departments, e.g., marketing, sales, etc. controlling. Organizations usually create mini-data warehouses supporting specific tasks in such cases, e.g., management of advertising campaigns, analysis of specific product profitability, and Internet user behaviors.
- Creating a comprehensive information infrastructure that ensures effective collection and filtering of data (from various places and devices), their integration, and analysis in various systems and perspectives.
- Conducting transformation in an organization, i.e., introduction of new business models focused on change management, knowledge management, and customer relationship management (CRM). Typically, this involves investing in a variety of data repositories (databases, data warehouses), streaming computing, cloud computing, and the Internet of Things, which enable the support of organization's strategic goals.

The analysis of various case studies confirms that BI&BD can be used in organizations, above all, for the following (Chaudhary, 2004; Davenport, Harris, & Morison, 2010; Hawking, Foster, &, Stein, 2008; Olszak, 2016):

- Improving the effectiveness of strategic, tactical, and operational planning, in particular: (a) modeling various options of the firm's development; (b) informing about the implementation of the strategy, goals, and tasks of an organization; (c) providing information on the results of making changes to business processes and the implementation of plans; (d) identifying bottlenecks; (e) providing analyses of the "best" and "worst" product, region; and (f) providing information on the organization's environment.
- Creating and improving customer relationships, mainly by (a) providing sales people with knowledge about customers so that they can respond quickly to their needs; (b) tracking the level of customer satisfaction related to the achieved efficiency; and (c) identifying market trends.
- Analyzing and improving business processes and operational efficiency of an organization by (a) providing knowledge and expertise regarding the development and launch of new products onto the market; (b) providing knowledge of key business processes; and (c) exchanging knowledge between teams and individual departments.

The most spectacular effects of using BI&BD were observed during the creation of advertising campaigns, anticipation of sales and customer behaviors, development of loyalty policy as well as research on anomalies and embezzlement.

The most important areas of BI&BD application are presented in Table 4.1.

Table 4.1 Selected Areas of BI&BD Adoption in Organizations

Application Area	Description
Relational marketing	Customer satisfaction survey, forecasting customer behaviors, customer segmentation and profiling, and effectiveness analysis of advertising campaigns
Customer relationship management	Improvement of customer relations, communication with clients, need anticipation, customer segmentation and profiling, and customer value analysis
Sales and distribution	Sales dynamics and structure analysis, deployment of sales departments, analysis of the degree of implementation of sales plans, sales network analysis and contact management, analysis of customer transactions, analysis of distribution channels, estimation of sales margins, analysis of sales results in various cross sections
Insurance	Agent and sales network management, improvement of actuarial efficiency, risk assessment and insurance policy preparation, claim settlement, fraud and error detection as well as assessment of the level of claims, insurance risk level analysis
Production	Analysis of technical manufacturing costs, estimation of production profitability, and analysis of cost centers
Telecommunications	Effective add-on and supplementary sales of various packages and services, analysis of customer profitability, their loyalty, probability of migration to competition, retention of valuable customers, management of marketing campaigns
Energy sector	Energy demand management and forecasting customer behaviors, monitoring energy networks
Finance and controlling	Planning and budgeting, cost analysis (structure and amount of costs), revenue and profitability analysis, income statement and balance sheet analysis, financial market analysis, financial risk analysis, profitability and customer loyalty analysis, analysis of financial indicators, and reporting

(*Continued*)

Table 4.1 Continued

Application Area	Description
Logistics	Optimization of the supply chain as well as the parameters of a given process, and factors affecting the end product
Health care	Improving the quality of medical services, quick access to medical information, reducing the risk of making mistakes when completing medical records, improving patient safety, analyzing hospital costs, allocating free places in hospitals, monitoring citizens' health status and epidemiological threats
Human resources management	Human resources analysis and reports, intellectual capital allocation, training and employee career path planning
Public administration	Analysis of allocation, costs, and profitability of investments in regions, analysis of the labor market structure, unemployment analysis, traffic intensity analysis, and customization of public services
Education/school systems	Individualization of access to knowledge resources, monitoring of students' work progress, monitoring of staff's work efficiency, quick access to collective information, e.g., from grade books, analysis of profitability of introducing education services, analysis of education costs

Source: own elaboration.

Business Intelligence and Big Data in Relational Marketing

The difference between classic and modern marketing, i.e., relational marketing, is expressed in a different approach to building relationships with customers. In the traditional approach, the emphasis was on acquiring the largest number of buyers and the volume of transactions. In relational marketing, however, special attention is given to creating lasting relationships with customers, in-depth knowledge of their changing needs, and their satisfaction through the intensive and diverse use of marketing instruments. In other words, the relational marketing strategy aims at initiating, strengthening, intensifying, and preserving over time the relationships between a company and its stakeholders, represented primarily by its customers, and involves the analysis, planning, execution, and evaluation of the actives carried out to pursue these objectives (Vercellis, 2009).

The development of information and communications technologies (ICTs) and the Internet has contributed to the popularization of the concept of relational marketing. Universal access to the Internet means that information processes have a "many-to-many" dimension and are both collective and individual. There is a departure from the one-way marketing message in favor of dialog implemented, inter alia, through multifunctional customer contact centers. Communication, in addition to anticipating the needs and quality of service, is perceived as one of the factors having the greatest impact on customer loyalty. From the customer's point of view, the development of new technologies also enables the abolition of information asymmetry between the customer and the organization.

According to Xu et al. (2016), the basic possibilities of using BI&BD in marketing are market forecasting; profiling target buyers; quantifying the needs of buyers and their purchase motives; identifying the perception, purchase, and use of products; identifying brand success factors; designing innovations; introducing new products; optimizing marketing and production activities; and CRM.

It is asserted that BI&BD enables better than before forecasting of demand in domestic and foreign markets based not only on geographical and demographic criteria but on behavioral criteria also. It offers completely new possibilities in identifying target groups and tracking customer behaviors. It enables multidimensional statistical analysis of server logs and behavioral analyses. Organizations can more effectively allocate their resources and identify buyer characteristics, purchasing behavior patterns, and their relationships with products, brands, and firms (Vriens & Kidd, 2014). By accessing numerous real-time data sources, organizations using Big Data analytics can continuously monitor buyers' and competitors' behaviors, buyers' responses to new goods and services, and obtain detailed knowledge about their relationship to product features, prices, and sales methods (Xu et al., 2016). In addition to creating ideas for new products, accelerating the innovation process, reducing the risk of price changes, and modifying the market offer, BI&BD analyses can be useful in efficiency programs, serving cost, and revenue optimization (Vriens & Kidd, 2014; Bean, 2017).

Analysis of Websites

Websites have become an important marketing tool for many organizations. They provide important information about potential customers, suppliers and competitors, news about market opportunities, technological trends, as well as about the development of the global economy. Websites play the role of a platform for conducting new ways of communication, business, advertising, and the development of new consumer behaviors. In this situation, analysis and evaluation of the operation of websites are extremely important tasks of each organization. Thanks to this analysis, the basic knowledge about who, when, why, and how uses the website can be obtained (Thuraisingham, 2003; Linoff & Berry, 2002). The use of advanced classification, grouping, matching, and regression models in relation to data on the operation of the website and its users, business data, and data on the experiences of users with the website enable the identification of customers and their preferences. The analysis and assessment of the operation of websites is mainly reduced to discovering and analyzing information collected on the website, discovering and analyzing patterns of website use by users, and analyzing the structure of the website.

The source of useful data that contribute to the improvement of online operations on websites are, among others, web logs files. They usually contain the following information:

- Website navigation: This is an analysis of a typical path followed by a user while browsing a website. In addition, analyses of the most popular pages of the website are available. Such an analysis helps in website optimization by transforming the website into a more user-friendly one.
- Referral analysis: There are specified sites that generate user traffic by referring users.
- Error analysis: These analyses show which errors the user faces when navigating the site. They prove to be very helpful in solving problems of the current operation of the website and in creating a more friendly way of browsing it.
- Keyword analysis: These are analyses of the most popular keywords used in search engines that enable finding a website of a given company.

Through the methods of analyzing and evaluating the operation of websites, a valuable knowledge is gained about the attractiveness of the firm's offer and the way it is shaped to suit the individual needs of customers. Such knowledge is used to personalize the website, automate navigation, shape pricing and promotional strategy, and develop smart business.

Google is the most popular search engine for browsing websites. Data from the search engine can be used, inter alia, for the construction of (a) the index of public agenda setting; (b) issue salience barometer; and (c) search queries as indicators of public opinion. In the construction of these and other Internet data-based indicators, it is assumed that the more queries are inserted into the search engine, the more important a given problem in the studied population is.

Designing and Analyzing Marketing Campaigns

BI&BD tools are suitable for assessing the effectiveness of marketing and promotional campaigns. The effects of individual campaigns in the area of sales of the promoted product can be tracked using basket, sequences, and connections analysis. Thanks to them, it is possible to search for products or services that are selected by a given group of customers at the same time. Often, an increase in sales of a promoted product may result in a decrease in the sales of other product. In such a case, analytical tools help identify such relationships. Data on individual campaigns are stored in central repositories (data warehouses, databases) and can be used to predict the effectiveness of similar campaigns in the future.

The most well-known analytical tools that are used for marketing research are Google Analytics and Google Adwords. Google Analytics is one of the leading tools for analyzing website traffic. First of all, Google Analytics provides two types of information: about website users and traffic sources. Google Analytics is a web analytics tool that shows how users find the site, what actions they take on it, and when they become customers. Google Analytics enables to increase the effectiveness of online activities by offering analysis tools for advertisers, publishers, and website owners. Examples of data that Google Analytics collects about users during website traffic analysis are: how did they hit our website (whether through a search engine, by sending them back from another page, or by manually entering the page address in the browser), where were they physically present (country, city), what software do they use (operating system, browser, type of device), how did they behave on the website (how long they stayed on a particular subpage, how many subpages they visited). All this information, properly analyzed and interpreted, can help improve the website and better adapt its content to the needs of the recipients.

Google Analytics can work with the Google Adwords tool to automatically generate reports showing the effectiveness of individual advertising campaigns, groups of advertisements, and keywords. This combination provides new possibilities in tracking sales and conversion rates, measuring goal achievement according to defined criteria, tracking e-mail campaigns, banner ads, offline ads, optimizing Adwords system performance, and identifying the best sources of revenue. The main functionality of Google Analytics is the possibility of compiling reports that help design effective landing pages, and choosing the right keywords and advertisements for them. Reports with advanced segmentation enable visualization and analysis of data according to many different factors. The tips obtained can be used to streamline the processes that lead to conversions by removing the elements most often causing the conversion path to be abandoned. Google Analytics reports include advanced segmentation, custom user-defined reports, advanced analysis, and data visualization.

Recommender Systems

Recommender systems are listed among many tools for developing relational marketing and meeting customer needs. The goal of recommender systems is to offer the customer products/services that are most suited to their needs from a set of many possibilities. These systems operate on the principle of filtering data in terms of the needs of the developed personalized user (customer) profile.

Many firms use recommender systems today. An example would be Amazon. com. From the very beginning, the company wanted to increase sales of books by recommending customers new and interesting titles. Initially, these instructions were written by teams of high-class literary critics and were posted on Amazon.com (Mayer-Schönberger & Cukier, 2013). Over time, it turned out that these recommendations were superficial, because only randomly selected representative data samples were tested. In connection with the aforementioned, all collected data began to be examined, and connections were sought not only among customers but primarily among products. It is worth noting that no hypotheses were made and only statistical relationships among all books were examined. The resulting algorithm works in real mode, displaying recommendations to the customer on the store's website (Żulicki, 2017). It turned out that this method has contributed to a multiple increase in book sales compared with critic reviews. Currently, on this basis, Amazon.com sells its other products, such as films, electronic equipment, sports equipment, and various accessories. A similar strategy is used by many other firms, e.g., Netflix, where approximately 75% of new orders are generated due to recommender systems (Mayer-Schönberger & Cukier, 2013; Żulicki, 2017). However, it is noted that recommender systems only identify relationships among products, without explaining the reasons behind customers' purchasing choices in any way.

Price Comparison Websites

Price comparison websites (PCWs) are considered one of the most important channels of reaching a customer with the offer. This is due to the fact that many customers start purchasing by comparing prices through price comparison websites. PCWs are a catalog that is also a bulletin board on which sellers publish their offers. PCWs usually offer their customers the following options: (a) familiarizing with the offer of a specific product 24 hours a day; (b) comparing the products offered without having to physically go to the store; (c) product price comparison; (d) securely carrying out the purchase transaction; (e) prechecking the availability of the product on the market (in a specific location—city, store); (f) comparing opinions about products and stores offering them; and (g) checking the opinions of other customers.

Based on the results displayed by PCWs, customers can choose the best offer (price, location, awareness of a shop brand, opinions, etc.). In this case, PCWs provide the seller with the opportunity to increase revenues while maintaining high sales conversion.

Google and Amazon are among the most well-known players on the search engine market. Virtually every product can be found with their search engines. They integrate many sellers in one place. However, both solutions are not typical PCWs. One of many classic price comparison engines known in the world is, Shopping.com, which belongs to one of the e-commerce giants—eBay. The portal covers France, Germany, and the United Kingdom. Pricegrabber is another commercial solution, which is mainly popular in the United States, Canada, and the United Kingdom. Currently, this price comparison site has over 100 million products and offers that come from over 4000 sellers. Monthly, this price comparison site is visited by 26 million unique buyers, and the average value of the cart is around $200. Other, though less popular, solutions are Nextag, Shopzilla, Twenga, and a number of local price comparison websites in given countries.

Group Shopping

The concept of group shopping also fits into the concept of relational marketing. The online form of group purchases appeared in 2008, and its founder was A. Mason, who was the first to propose a group shopping portal—Groupon. The group shopping website cooperates with firms which want to offer their products/services in the form of group purchases. Then, the subject of the sale is determined and the date of issue of the announcement informs about the promotion. When a group of volunteers gather, the product is sold with agreed discounts. Factors that prompt users to make group purchases include, above all, group activities—confirming the legitimacy of purchases and obtaining significant discounts for a given product/service. BI&BD tools enable the assessment of the effectiveness of such group purchases, sharing knowledge and shopping experience, and quickly connect customers into groups.

Customer Relationship Management Systems

The origins of CRM are strongly associated with the management concept of relational marketing (Olszak & Bartuś, 2013). The relational marketing orientation focuses on building, developing, and maintaining long-term relationships with customers and other stakeholders (Gummesson, 2002; Grönroos, 2000). It is an integrated effort to identify, build up, and maintain a network with individual customers for the mutual benefit of both sides (Shani & Chalasani, 1992). The key for acquiring and maintaining customers is to understand their preferences and to prepare a customized offer (McKenn, 1991; Peppers, Rogers & Dorf, 1999). In turn, CRM is a connection between relational marketing and management theories and approaches (Gummesson, 2002). It concerns managing relationships between a firm and its customers with its all various contacts, interactive processes, and communication elements (Grönroos, 2000).

Although the roots and the CRM idea come from relational marketing, CRM has had a very technical connotation (Fjermestad & Romano, 2003; Xu, et al., 2002). Data warehouses, online analytical processing (OLAP) techniques, and data mining techniques belong to the key technologies that are used to build CRM systems. Employment of the aforementioned techniques in CRM systems can facilitate customer data collection, thus supporting customer service, sales, and marketing by providing up-to-date customer information and knowledge. The systems are also implemented to reduce the power of some staff groups, particularly sales staff and sales agents (Roscoe, 2001). The adoption of CRM systems leads to redesigning customer-oriented processes, similar to the effect that enterprise resource planning systems have had on production-oriented processes (Alt & Puschmann, 2004).

Three different types of CRM systems are distinguished (Peppers & Rogers, 2011; Shanmugasundaram, 2010; Tuzhilin, 2012; Wilde, 2011;): operational, analytical, and collaborative. Recently, a concept of social CRM system has emerged.

An operational CRM system, called a front office CRM system (Wilde, 2011), functions at the customer interface by collecting customer data (Minna & Aino, 2005). It supports marketing, sales, and service departments through (Buttle, 2009) (a) marketing automation, i.e., market segmentation, campaign management, and event-based marketing; (b) sales force automation, i.e., opportunity management, including lead management, contact management, proposal generation, product configuration; and (c) service automation, i.e., contact and call center operations, web-based service, field service.

An analytical CRM system, called a back-office CRM system, structures customer data into customer information (Minna & Aino, 2005). It enables the preparation of business analysis and operational reports (e.g., for sales, marketing research) and forecasts (e.g., of customer behaviors, market). These analyses underpin planning of future sales strategies, marketing campaigns, identification of customer needs and behaviors as well as estimation of costs of retaining and attracting customers (Buttle, 2009; Wilde, 2011). Analytical CRM uses such tools as data warehouses, data mining, marketing and campaign analyses, clustering, and segmentation. Analytical CRM is recognized as an important element in the successful implementation of CRM in firms (Nykamp, 2001).

The main task of collaborative CRM is to improve the process of organization's communication with customers, suppliers, and business partners in order to develop a long-term cooperation. Phones, SMS, e-mail and traditional mail, fax, and voice applications are used to communicate through customer interaction center, partner relationship management, and corporate portals. Collaborative CRM is mainly used for direct communication with customers in the following departments: service (including technical assistance), sales (e.g., customer service center), and marketing (Kracklauer, Mills, & Seifert, 2004; Wilde, 2011).

Some authors also point out strategic CRM (Aurelie & Laid, 2008; Payne & Frow, 2005). This is linked to (or even identified with) the organization's business strategy, which is focused on developing long-term relationships with customers (Buttle, 2009). Connection between different types of CRM systems is presented in Figure 4.1 (Olszak & Bartus, 2013).

Today's customers want to be active players in the market; they wish to maintain an open dialog with various firms, have some impact on sales strategies, and shape public opinion. Social media provide customers with these opportunities (Schaff & Harris, 2012). Social media include such social tools and online services as Facebook, Twitter, LinkedIn, YouTube, blogs, wiki, and traditional and video sites. They enable different people to communicate, create, and share various content, as well as to search and connect with different people of similar interests

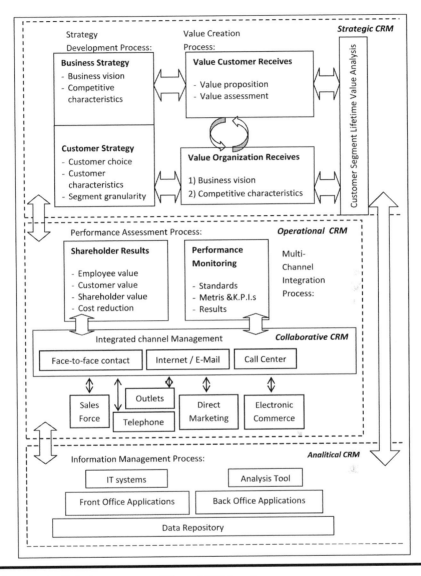

Figure 4.1   Relations among different CRM systems.

Source: Elaborated on (Aurelie & Laid, 2008).

and opinions (Halligan & Shah, 2010; Greenberg, 2010). Popularization of social media means that customers can influence public opinion and share their satisfaction (or dissatisfaction) with products and services purchased. They can also be more effectively involved in the process of planning and designing products and services. This situation creates completely new tasks for marketing and public relations departments (Kostojohn, Johnson, & Paulen, 2011).

The inclusion of social resources in the CRM is called social CRM or CRM 2.0. According to Greenberg (2010), "social CRM is a philosophy and a business strategy, supported by a technology platform, business rules, processes, and social characteristics, designed to engage the customer in a collaborative conversation in order to provide mutually beneficial value in a trusted and transparent business environment." In addition, Deloitte (2011) highlights that "social CRM paradigm adds to the traditional approach the building of the relationship and the knowledge of the customer by analyzing the bidirectional interactions (downwards and upwards) and horizontal, collaborative, community oriented ones, where the essential components are the experiences and emotions of users and communities".

The market offer of CRM systems is very wide in the form of commercial advanced systems offering many functionalities (e.g., SAP, Microsoft, Oracle) as well as open-source solutions (e.g., SugerCRM). Advanced CRM systems are developed primarily for the needs of corporations that mainly strive to achieve a high financial result. However, a solution such as SugarCRM focuses on the needs of actual/most important CRM agents, i.e., the customer and the system user.

Business Intelligence and Big Data–Based Analyses in Customer Relationship Management

The most frequently used analyses in CRM include (Januszewski, 2008; Olszak, 2006; Olszak & Ziemba, 2006) customer profitability, customer value over time, customer segmentation and profiling, market basket analysis, customer loyalty and migration analysis, analysis of customer behaviors, and fraud detection.

Customer Profitability

The high saturation of the market for products and services, high-activity advertising, and promotion mean that customers are acquired with increasing effort and resources. It turns out that it is more important to maintain and increase the profitability of existing customers than constantly acquire new ones. Identifying the most profitable customers is the first step in this direction. Analytical systems provide answers to such questions as: why are some customers profitable and others not? After BI analysis, it may turn out that the customer is unprofitable because the products they use are not suited to their risk profile. Profitability analysis aids developing new products and adapting existing products to the current needs of customers.

Customer Time Value

For many organizations, customer profitability is not the only measure of customer assessment. The customer may have the potential to buy profitable products in the future and be a source of reference about the organization for more profitable customers. The lifetime value (LTV) is regarded as a more useful measure (Kadayam, 2007).

LTV is an analysis of the total value of the customer that takes into account the full history of contacts and benefits expected in the future. As part of this analysis, it is therefore determined not only who is currently the most valuable customer but also how customer value changes over time, and what needs to be done to increase it. Building customer value usually takes place in the following stages: (a) collecting data about customers and their behaviors leading to the purchase; (b) analyzing the collected data to segment customers, identifying behavior patterns, and defining profiles; (c) preparing a personalized offer tailored to the individual needs of customers according to established profiles; (d) presenting the offer to the customer; and (e) handling customer contact as well as possible conclusion and documentation of transactions.

Data mining tools aid modeling customer value in terms of the entire course of their contacts with the organization. This modeling takes into account such elements as the frequency of purchases, the size of a single order, the sum that the customer spends on a given product category, or the estimated time in which they will renew the purchase of a product in the future.

Customer Segmentation and Profiling

A crucial condition for today's organization success is the ability to accurately identify the recipients of the products and services offered and the formulation of the offer in such a way that the customer could feel the personalized approach (Tiwana, 2003). Customer segmentation is one of the basic functions of analytical CRM. It involves identifying customer groups with similar characteristics, behaving in a similar way or buying similar products. Customer segmentation and profiling is based on grouping customers into certain homogeneous groups (segments) that share common attributes. Segments constructed in this way can be treated as separate units and future cooperation with them can be tailored to their needs.

Segmentation can be carried out based on various criteria (Januszewski, 2008) such as type of a customer (e.g., private individual, small company, large company), demographic criteria (gender, occupation, education, income), tastes, preferences, expectations and satisfaction (provided by customers in surveys or collected during other contacts), creditworthiness, willingness to make purchases (paid amount invoiced, frequency of purchases, increasing purchases), value of the customer in the customer's life cycle, and propensity of the customer to exit products or services.

Various methods are used to segment customers, one of them is recency, frequency, monetary (RMF) analysis. It is based on the theory of customer behavior and the simple logic saying that (a) it is more likely that customers who have recently bought something will make the next purchase than those who have not made any purchase for a long time; (b) the next purchase is more likely to be made by customers who shop more frequently than those who rarely make purchases; and

(c) it is more likely that in the future, money will be spent by customers who spent large amounts on purchases in the past than those who spent less.

Analytical systems enable both descriptive and predictive segmentation. As part of the descriptive segmentation, the following are carried out:

- Demographic segmentation: based on such data as customer income, age, gender, education, marital status, ethnic group, religious group, and so on.
- Behavioral segmentation: based on such data as shopping frequency, quantity and type of products purchased, and so on.
- Motivational segmentation: based on variables describing the reasons for which the customer made the purchase (usually the data come from surveys).

In turn, predictive segmentation is used to distinguish between "good" and "bad" customers. At first, the variable describing "good" customers is defined (it can be, e.g., the total of purchases made), and then it is determined for this variable which other variables have the greatest impact on it.

Segmentation is generally the first step in the analysis process. On this basis, a customer profile is established, i.e., a statistical description of the customer of a given type. Profiles can then be used in risk estimation, e.g., whether the customer will not repay the loan or is prone to fraud or leaving to the competition. One of the most important applications of customer profiling is direct marketing. Customer profiles are used in the preparation of personalized promotional campaigns, design of new products, and sales optimization.

Market Basket Analysis

Market basket analysis (MBA) provides knowledge about which services or products should be sold together in sets and which set to recommend to which customer. The MBA enables determining customer preferences, understanding how to choose products, and purposing which products sell best in each store. This information can be used to adapt the range of goods to the requirements of most customers, better shelving of goods, preparation of promotional activities, and advertising campaigns. The MBA scope mainly includes cross-selling and upselling techniques. The former technique consists in developing such sets of offers that may be of interest to specific groups of customers, taking into account their previous purchases and connections between them. The purpose of this technique is, inter alia, to remind the customer about products that may be useful and needed but are forgotten by the customer. This technique increases customer confidence in the firm and reduces the risk of the transition to competition. It is presumed that its use leads to a significant increase in the firm's revenues and the level of customer loyalty. In turn, the latter technique—upselling—offers customer products or services usually at a higher price, higher standard, or with more functions. Often, the customer is not aware that there may be a better version of the product or service they are looking for and would gladly buy it. Another practical application of various MBA techniques is the use of classification models to select the customers most susceptible to a given offer. This allows proper targeting of marketing activities, and consequently, reduction of campaign costs while increasing efficiency. BI&BD-based analyses prove to be helpful in putting in the best offers to customers so that they respond to their current needs as well as in identifying the most receptive customers to a given offer.

Customer Loyalty and Migration Analysis

Customer loyalty is one of the most important issues under strong competitive conditions, small product diversity as well as low costs of switching to another supplier. The ability to predict customer transition to competition (survival time analysis) proves to be very useful. It enables the firm to take preventive measures, forecast sales levels, assess the total value of the customer (i.e., expected revenue generated by the customer throughout the entire period of contact with the firm), or modify the offer accordingly.

The loyalty analysis consists of investigating the time of cooperation with the customer and the customer purchasing power. However, its main goal is to determine the reasons for losing customers and identify those groups of customers who are likely to leave to the competition. As part of the loyalty analysis, various simulations are performed, inter alia, to illustrate how a change in the offer can affect customer loyalty and what action should be taken to prevent customer loss.

Methods of data analysis and data mining can be used to prevent customer migration in many ways and usually relate to four categories: cooperation time, size (value) of cooperation, closeness of cooperation, and quality of cooperation. They are used to describe the distribution of survival times for individuals of a given population, track the strength of the impact of various parameters on the expected survival time, and also enable the comparison of survival distributions in different customer groups. By using these methods, the organization can gain valuable insight into customer behaviors and find ways to extend their loyalty to it. The discovery of factors causing the departure to competition enables the firm to target its activities well. In addition, isolating customer groups with different levels of risk of leaving enables the firm to build effective loyalty programs and to increase focus on the most loyal customers.

Customer Behavior Analysis

The customer behavior analysis allows not only to explain current customer behaviors but also to predict their future response (e.g., to subsequent promotions). It is also used to identify situations that create opportunities for the customer to accept an additional offer (e.g., birthdays, holidays). Typically, the following types of analyses are distinguished (Januszewski, 2008): purchase propensity analysis (knowledge of products which the customer is likely to buy), next purchase (predicting which products or services the customer will buy next), product similarity analysis (knowing which products or services the customer will buy combined with others), and models of price elasticity and dynamic prices (determining the optimal price level for a given product in relation to a given segment).

Fraud Detection

The problem of fraud is present in many industries, especially in banking, insurance, telecommunications, and in companies that use different loyalty systems. It entails significant financial losses, deteriorates the image of the organization, and causes a decrease in customer confidence. Until now, methods based on expert knowledge have been the most popular fraud detection methods. However, the growing number of transactions and ever-changing fraud techniques mean that it has become necessary to support expert knowledge with knowledge obtained using advanced data mining methods. They make it possible to quickly find behavior patterns that suggest fraud (suspicious transfers, orders and other illegal activities directed against the firm), as well as to search for connections between persons involved in dishonest activities (Thuraisingham, 2003).

Fraud detection models can be divided into an application appraisal and a behavioral appraisal. The first type is used to detect suspicious customers at an early stage of signing the contract with the firm and is based on data from a submitted application. On the other hand, behavioral assessment is based on data collected during the customer activity cycle, e.g., transactional data, use of services, or track record.

Fraud detection is often used to prevent credit card fraud (e.g., online fraud, telemarketing, identity theft), computer system security breaches, money laundering, telecommunications fraud, and so on.

Business Intelligence and Big Data in Planning and Budgeting

Planning and budgeting are activities that take place in the context of very complex networks of interconnectedness. For example, on the one hand, we are dealing with management board guidelines for a multiyear development strategy, and on the other, with the need to prepare operational plans for a given year. To ensure maximum efficiency of a planning process, effective communication between all collaborating people is necessary. In practice, due to the lack of appropriate ICT support, the processes of goal distribution and the consolidation of expectations are very often implemented in mutual isolation, and their results are agreed only after the works are completed. BI&BD tools can support modeling and integration of all aspects of this reality. They are primarily used to link the day-to-day and operational activities of all departments, as well as employees with strategic goals. This facilitates the process of translating organization's vision and strategy into measurable goals. OLAP mechanisms efficiently automate plan consolidation processes. Thanks to the use of allocation keys, it becomes possible to quickly map strategic plans onto the operational level and project budgets to subprojects or organizational units. These features combined with the possibilities of working in a group mode enable the firm to get the optimal version of the budget in a short time. In this way, owners and shareholders quickly obtain information on the directions of development and expected profits from the invested capital, and the management has guidelines for optimal refinement of operational plans based on the available resources.

OLAP tools also enable the cost analysis in great detail. Budgeting becomes possible based on the demand and performance indicators as well as effectiveness indicators for the use of individual resources. Models based on data mining tools can also be used to measure the level of exposure of the organization to various risk factors such as change in the structure of shares, instability of stock markets, and so on. The designed models help predict the portfolio effectiveness in various adopted economic scenarios and future demand for current assets.

Business Intelligence and Big Data in Sales and Distribution

Increasingly, sales organizations do not limit their activities to one point-of-sale, one city, or even one region. However, having many sales locations requires knowledge about the allocation of individual goods. Experience shows that good financial results depend to a large extent on whether a given product is in the right place at the right time. Moving goods between stores (e.g., within one network) must often be done very quickly. Products that do not arouse interest in customers in one region may be of interest elsewhere. The possibility of sustainable movement of goods between stores allows the organization to significantly reduce storage costs. In addition, appropriate analyses enable prompt detection of such products, in a whole lot of transactions, on which the firm has, for example, the lowest margins. In other words, BI&BD tools allow the data exploration flowing from various distribution channels and provide information useful for their effective management, namely:

- Distribution of sales departments: By using geographical analysis of the customer base, firms can optimally distribute sales departments in individual locations. This analysis should include information about potential customers and products offered by the firm.
- Sales network development and contact management: BI&BD tools can be used to track the sales results of individual sellers. Such an analysis enables, for example, to identify the best sellers who can later be paid, trained, and so on, according to the merit.

■ Distribution channel analysis: Using BI&BD tools, organizations can compare the results of their activities within individual channels. In the process of assessing the effectiveness of distribution channels, the measurement of the profitability of distribution channels in relation to products sold through them as well as customers acquired and served by those channels deserves special attention.

In the retail industry, many organizations are already using Big Data analytics to improve the accuracy of forecasts, anticipate changes in demand, and then react accordingly. For example, Brooks Brothers, one of the oldest retailers in the United States, introduced business analytics developed by SAS, the US-based business analytics software group, to help improve the stock control. Using analytics to forecast its global stock enabled the store managers to make better decisions around stock levels and pricing.

Business Intelligence and Big Data in Insurance

One of the first industries to start using BI&BD analytics was the insurance industry. Such analytics proved to be beneficial in (Olszak, 2006):

■ identifying relevant customers for marketing activities, and analyzing the reasons for their loss;
■ managing insurance brokers and sales network;
■ improving the effectiveness of actuaries, as well as risk assessment and policy preparation processes;
■ providing critical information necessary for the claim settlement;
■ detecting fraud and errors, and estimating future levels of claim settlement;
■ reducing the insurer's risk level. Using appropriate methods (e.g., ABC methods), BI tools support the process of precise cost and profitability calculation at various levels of detail and identify the places with the greatest potential to increase it.

The actuarial function appears to be vital in the insurance business, and the role of analytical tools is particularly crucial here. It refers to risk estimation in relation to assets that are insured. In the case of "life and health" insurance, it concerns the calculation of the probability of an accident or death, based on different demographic and environmental characteristics. Using appropriate analytical tools, it is possible to determine the following:

■ Risk: Data mining tools are used to identify risk profiles in different customer segments. The most commonly used risk measures are average amount of damage, frequency of damage occurrence, and loss ratio.

- Reinsurance: Estimated models can be built using data mining tools to determine the reinsurance level based on historical compensation data. Models built in this way identify relevant policies that should be reinsured (based on the experience of losses under similar past insurance policies).
- Profitability analysis: Based on historical profitability analyses, actuaries can build more complex estimation models. Using data mining tools, it is possible to estimate demand for new products and identify the most profitable customer segments for these products.

BI&BD tools can significantly improve risk assessment and policy management processes. They prove useful, especially in the following:

- Insurance premium analysis: They enable tracking the effectiveness of premium levels depending on individual products or product lines, economic regions, agencies, individual brokers, and firm branches.
- Loss analysis: They identify the level of profitability and help monitor and protect financial resources.

Institutions around the world (including insurance companies) are looking for technologies that will allow the proper conduct of the claim settlement process. The experience of various organizations shows that without sophisticated analytical techniques, it is difficult to capture the problems of scams, fraud, and inflated compensation amounts. BI&BD tools in the field of claim settlement can be used primarily to the following:

- Damage and compensation analysis: They are the most common applications in the insurance industry. They relate to the analysis of data referring to damages combined with other data sources, such as information on policies and risk assessment. They are mainly used to assess the effectiveness of the claim settlement process that is directly related to customer satisfaction. Damage and compensation analyses are helpful in understanding trends that would otherwise be difficult to see. Data mining tools facilitate fraud detection by analyzing above average payouts through factors such as geographical region, broker, insurance group, and so on.
- Fraud detection: Probable frauds in claim settlement can be detected with complex analyses of compensation data combined with other data, such as payment histories and risk assessment.
- Estimating damage and compensations: The damage assessment impacts on the profitability of an insurance institution. Multidimensional OLAP analyses can be used to predict future compensations. They are used to analyze compensation data through factors, such as customer segment, region, and so on. Data mining tools are used to build advanced compensation estimation models.

Examples of insurance companies that use various BI&BD solutions in their operations include Lemonade, State Farm, Allianz Travel Insurance, John Hancock International, Metro Mile, Safeco, Blue Cross Blue Shield, Vitality, Progressive, Prudential, Nationwide, Aetna, Cigna, Allstate, Geico, Liberty Mutual, Ladder, Root, Haven Life, Amica, and Esurance (https://builtin.com/big-data/big-data-insurance). Their reports state that Big Data significantly facilitates the management and monitoring of insurance company's current operations, as well as predicting behaviors of their customers.

Business Intelligence and Big Data in Credit Risk Assessment

The activities of many organizations are inextricably linked with the existence of risk. Special attention is devoted to the security of lending activities, especially in the financial services sector. Credit scoring can be carried out using a number of methods, such as descriptive methods, expert assessments, and so on. However, solutions using data mining methods are becoming increasingly recognized. They make it possible to determine the financial risk associated with individual customers. Such a process may take place at the time of concluding the contract with the customer and be based on data from their completed application forms.

Credit risk assessment can be carried out according to various models, the right choice of which depends on the purpose of the analysis and the specificity of the data being analyzed. They include the following:

- Application scoring: completed application forms by new customers are the basis for assessing creditworthiness.
- Behavioral scoring: additional information on customer behavior history can be used to forecast customer future behaviors.
- Profit scoring: it takes into account not only the likelihood of a customer paying back the loan but also estimates the profit for the organization associated with cooperation with a given customer. This is a more comprehensive model because it takes into account many additional economic factors.

Thanks to the presented models, it is possible to significantly reduce the number of "bad" credits while increasing the speed of making credit decisions, which can be taken by less experienced staff. Appropriate treatment of customers who have a high risk of cessation of payments enables effective reduction of losses. The possibility of reducing the number of documents required when examining the application is also crucial.

Credit risk assessment models are used both in banking (cash loans, assessment, and delay tolerance in settling receivables), as well as in many other areas related to, e.g., renting or leasing real estate and equipment.

Business Intelligence and Big Data in Engineering and Manufacturing

In engineering and manufacturing, companies are seeking new opportunities to predict maintenance problems, enhance manufacturing quality, and manage costs through the use of BI&BD. Thanks to OLAP analyses and data mining techniques, detailed information about the costs of a technological process can be provided, which enables, among others, quick estimation of margins obtained from the sale of products at many levels of the income statement and a valuable estimation of the profitability of production of individual semifinished products in relation to alternative purchase options on the market. BI&BD analytics also allows the analysis of the actual technical cost of production broken down into production centers, cost centers, and cost carriers (i.e., final products). It facilitates obtaining information about the material composition of products at every stage of the production process. In the same systems, nonmaterial costs allocated to products/semifinished products can be analyzed with accuracy up to the analytical items in the accounting records. The consumption rate can be calculated for individual materials and semifinished products and the unit cost in terms of the physical measure of the product for all the cost items. The BI&BD solution also enables the cost analysis in an extended cost/benefit system. This means that by analyzing the cost of manufacturing a specific product, it is possible, for example, to check what the salary costs were or what the cost of individual raw materials was in the entire multistage process. Such systems make data available for the entire company or for individual production centers. In the latter case, nonmaterial costs (remuneration, purchase, transport) incurred only in a given production center can be analyzed.

BI&BD systems allow performing simulations of the technical cost of manufacturing calculations using input values, such as volume of production, price of raw materials, consumption rate of raw and consumable materials, and value of individual nonmaterial costs that can be incurred in the period. Importantly, such simulations are carried out on the basis of real data.

With regard to product innovation, as McLaren's Formula One cars speed around the track, for example, they send a stream of data back to the team that are processed and analyzed in real time using SAP's Hana in-memory technology. The racing cars are laden with sensors detecting flexing, vibration, load, wear, temperature, and many other measures that impact machine performance. Hana uses sophisticated data compression to store information in random access memory, which is 10,000 times faster than hard disks, enabling the analysis of the data in seconds rather than hours. The real-time analysis of car sensor data is compared with historical data and predictive models, helping the team to develop improved performance, make proactive corrections, and avoid costly, dangerous incidents and, ultimately, win races. These lessons have been extrapolated to many car manufacturers who now embed their vehicles with sensors and microprocessors capturing data for maintenance and repair purposes as well as research and development innovation (Schaeffer, 2014).

Business Intelligence and Big Data in Telecommunications

The telecommunications sector is one of the most competitive markets that is constantly experiencing changes related to the introduction of breakthrough technologies and the emergence of new competitors. Comprehensive knowledge about the customer, attractive price, and the right moment to launch a new product are factors that are essential for gaining competitive advantage in this sector. Analytical tools create a working environment as well as the basis and patterns for making effective decisions in the area of telecommunications. On the example of the SAS Telecommunication Intelligence Solution package, it can be seen that they can support primarily the following:

- Effective add-on and supplementary sales of various packages and services. Acquiring new customers is not the only way to increase the revenues of telecommunications operators. An appropriate offer for new products or their richer versions addressed to current customers usually results in an increase in both the value of these customers and their loyalty. The implemented cross-sell and upsell solutions enable accurate matching of new product offers as well as newer and richer product versions to the customers of the telecommunications operator.
- Management of marketing campaigns: Telecommunication companies have experienced that the strategy of customer relations should be developed in detail, and communication with them carried out in several stages, using a variety of channels (radio, television, direct mail, telemarketing, e-mail, and the Internet). By integrating analytical tools with techniques used to manage marketing campaigns, it becomes possible to effectively plan and coordinate marketing campaigns, monitor their implementation, and analyze the results to maximize their effectiveness.
- Customer profitability analysis: Customer profitability, analyzed from the beginning of the contract, is in-depth knowledge that gives telecommunication operators answers to questions about currently obtained rate of return, expected rate of return, customer value, or customer life cycle. BI&BD tools enable the analysis of customer profitability, thanks to the built-in mechanisms that enable assigning revenues and costs to individual customers/contracts. These tools also allow the analysis of customer profitability in additional perspectives, such as tariff plan, month of activation, marketing promotion, distribution channel, terminal, acquisition, or other defined unitary characteristics of the contract.

■ Retaining valued customers: Competition in the telecommunication market has increased the cost of customer acquisition, making it a standard to identify customers willing to leave. Anticipating this phenomenon and creating strategies to reduce it is a difficult undertaking that requires the analysis of a huge volume of data and the use of advanced data mining techniques. Predefined analytical models created with the use of BI&BD enable operators to quickly learn the factors affecting customers' departure to the competition. Not only do they identify customers willing to leave but also the reasons for this phenomenon (SAS, 2020).

Business Intelligence and Big Data in Energy Sector

Energy demand management and forecasting customer behaviors are becoming the main elements of analyses carried out by energy enterprises. The nature of changes in the energy market as well as the increasing volume and diversity of collected data cause an increase in demand for the use of Big Data technology and various analytical systems. According to SAS (2013), Big Data analysis models in energy enterprises relate to three main areas: business and economic analyses of the enterprise, analyses of the power network operation, and analyses of relations with customers, including those related to behaviors in the area of choosing energy-related services and energy-saving behaviors.

Energy enterprises supply energy through a dedicated infrastructure—the electrical distribution system. Supervision over its proper functioning is of special importance to them. Analytical systems play a key role in managing such an energy network (Pamuła, 2013). They enable, inter alia, the optimization of energy sources work and optimization of the process of connecting new distributed energy sources (Leeds, 2012). They provide extensive and detailed analysis of the smart metering infrastructure, asset management, network management in crisis situations, as well as visualization of network operation using *geospatial intelligence*. Furthermore, they allow the prediction and analysis of failures related not only to the technological process of the network and device operation but also to weather phenomena and cybercrime. They contribute to the reduction of technical and nontechnical losses (preventing theft of electricity) and increase the quality of services provided through the electrical distribution system.

Changing the model of relations with customers becomes the focal point of the reorganization of energy enterprises. In smart electricity networks, consumption, i.e., the demand side, is gaining in importance, which requires the introduction of many new services emerging on the market. *Demand-side management* is one of these basic services. The active participation of the recipient in the energy market forces the supplier to collect and compile a large amount of data and information. Based on these data, BI&BD tools enable building a recipient's energy consumption profile and determine motivations for actions related to effective energy management (Pamuła, 2013). According to the GTM Research report, Greentech Media division (SAS, 2013), the most used analytical tools in 70 energy enterprises in North America are solutions from SAS, IBM, and Opower.

Business Intelligence and Big Data in the Financial and Banking Sector

The financial sector is one of the most data-driven sectors. Data sets have grown immensely in terms of size, type, and complexity and are awkward to work with using traditional database management tools. Many large financial and banking institutions are reaching the upper limits of their existing systems and are now seeking innovative analytics and framework solutions (Deutsche Bank, 2014).

According to Deutsche Bank, the main drivers of Big Data technology adoption in the financial sector are (1) explosive data growth: rapid growth in data from both internal and external sources requires better utilization of existing technologies and new technologies to acquire, organize, integrate, and analyze data; (2) regulation: new regulations require liquidity planning and overall asset and liability management functions to be fundamentally rethought; (3) fraud detection and security; (4) customer insight and marketing analytics given that consumers now have transient relationships with multiple organizations.

Hassani, Huang and Silva (2018) also formulate similar opinions in this regard. The authors argue that the banking sector mainly adopts data mining techniques for the following purposes: (1) security and fraud detection: big secondary data like transaction records are monitored and analyzed to enhance banking security and distinguish the unusual behaviors and patterns indicating fraud, phishing, or money laundering (among others); (2) risk management and investment banking: analysis of in-house credit card data freely accessible for banks enables credit scoring and credit granting, which form part of the most popular tools for risk management and investment evaluation; (3) CRM: data mining techniques have been widely applied in banking for marketing and CRM-related purposes such as customer profiling, customer segmentation, and cross-/upselling. These help the banking sector to have a better understanding of their customers, predict customer behaviors, accurately target potential customers, and further improve customer satisfaction with a strategic service design; (4) other advanced supports: a few less mainstream applications focus on branching strategy, and efficiency and performance assessment, which can substantially assist in achieving strategic branch location and expansion plans.

OLAP analysis support broadly defined reporting and indicator analyses. Financial indicators, such as current liquidity, asset turnover, fixed assets turnover, liabilities, and so on, can be analyzed from the point of various dimensions (time, geographical regions, product types, etc.), and they prompt financial institutions to take corrective action.

Deutsche Bank (2014) understands the transformative potential of Big Data and has been well ahead of the curve, making significant investments across all areas of the bank. Deutsche Bank currently has multiple production Hadoop platforms available through open source, enabling decreasing costs in terms of data processing. Big Data projects have also helped build risk platforms used to mine and process data as well as analyze risk. Examples of risk that can be analyzed with Big Data technologies and the data extracted from the bank's systems include P&L risk, market risk, and Volcker key performance indicators. Big Data technologies have enabled the bank to store over 10 years of proprietary trading data and ensure easy accessibility. Another set of data analytics currently used by the bank is the matching algorithm that enables the business to gain greater visibility on its performance. Other data analytic abilities include profiling of data to identify abnormal information through rule-based algorithms or "teaching" a machine what is abnormal and normal so it can quickly flag errors and minimize false positives, which is mainly applied in activity monitoring and anti-money-laundering processes. In terms of reporting capabilities, reports can now be generated from the data source itself, where the data are stored without the need to create dedicated reporting systems.

JP Morgan Chase & Co.—one of the largest financial holding companies in the world—has turned to counterterrorism technology to spot fraud risk among its own employees. This technology enables the bank to process vast amounts of data to identify individual behaviors that could reveal risks or openings to make money. Other banks have similarly turned to Big Data to identify potential rogue traders who could conceivably bring massive losses. Furthermore, in order to combat credit fraud and security breaches, weblog data from banks' Internet channels and geospatial data from smartphone applications are being retrieved and analyzed along with core operations data.

Business Intelligence and Big Data in Logistics Industry

The logistics industry is complex with critical subareas, such as transportation, inventory, warehousing, material handling, packaging, and security that need to come together for actionable insight. The huge scale of operations makes it increasingly difficult for the logistics service providers to gain visibility across the supply chain and ensure efficient customer service (Fatima, 2018). Powerful data processing and analysis capabilities increase the efficiency of distribution, logistics, and production networks. BI&BD analytics enables companies to share data with partners across the supply chain that results in the development of new services, improved demand forecasting accuracy, and discovery of new demand patterns. For instance, gaining information from unstructured customer data can generate useful insights into product placement, pricing strategies, optimization strategies, layout optimization, operational risk management, and improved product/service delivery.

With BI&BD analytics, the logistics and supply chain companies have an end-to-end visibility for acting promptly on prospective loss of revenues and profits that could occur at various points in the chain. It increases asset uptime and expands throughput and enables preventive maintenance of assets and resource optimization along with conducting near real-time supply planning using dynamic data feeds from production sensors and the Internet of Things. This clear visibility ensures better operational planning, resulting in enhanced service and increased efficiency for their customers.

The logistics industry relies on enormous data to make key decisions. BI&BD provide granular insight. Predictive analysis helps hire and retain talent, forecast staffing needs and improve employee satisfaction. As there seems to be exponential growth in the logistics sector verticals, organizations are abandoning legacy systems and embracing analytics for better transparency.

Finally, with the presence of more variables and more scenarios than ever before, organizations can integrate their analyses with many other interconnected business systems. Analytics on warehouse layout, product inventory, and demand can help optimize operations within the warehouse also enabling alerts on depleted inventory or potential roadblocks. As the number of warehouses gets smaller, the remaining warehouses grow bigger and more efficient. By pooling customer demand across a smaller network of bigger warehouses, the company can decrease the variability of demand and can, therefore, maintain lower levels of inventory.

Big Data can also be used for managing a ship's sensors, and for predictive analysis, which is necessary to avoid delays and increase the industry's overall operational efficiency. In the shipping industry, tracking the cargo properly is very important to maintain the necessary security and privacy. Through the data obtained by tracking shipments properly over the course of a few years, information regarding reasons for losses of ships at sea, losses of containers inside or outside of terminals or warehouses, and other problems related to shipments (e.g., reasons for damaged cargo) can be obtained. This Big Data for the shipping industry can be used for future decision-making to predict and avoid costly problems, and to create more reliable cargo delivery options.

Furthermore, Big Data analysis also plays an important role in vessel operations. Terminal operators and agents can track vessels and make appropriate or even instant decisions about berth and terminal allocation. These immediate decisions can be very crucial for day-to-day vessel operations. They can be made easily using information gathered through global postioning system devices, sensors, or control panels (Tas, 2018).

Another example of SAS technology adoption is its utilization by air traffic controllers at Frankfurt airport in Germany who are able to receive early warnings of storms, and the managers can access an overview of all key performance indicators in near real time, including average times for luggage delivery, delays, and airport security levels. All of this happens on the go—data are refreshed every 5 minutes and both managers and operations experts monitor reports via PCs and mobile devices. US Xpress, the US trucking company, collects 900 data elements from tens of thousands of trucking systems: sensor data for tire wear, fuel consumption, and engine operation; geospatial data for fleet tracking; and complaints posted on trucker blogs. Using Hadoop, a type of open-source database often used for Big Data projects and informatics, US Xpress processes and analyzes this data to optimize fleet usage, saving millions of dollars a year (Deutsche Bank, 2014).

Business Intelligence and Big Data in Health Care

In the health care, there are new opportunities to predict and react more promptly to critical clinical events, allowing better care for patients and more effective cost management. Researchers at the University of Buffalo, New York, are using Big Data analytics to improve the quality of life of multiple sclerosis patients, while the University of Ontario Institute of Technology (UOIT) is using IBM Big Data technology to capture and analyze real-time data from medical monitors, alerting hospital staff of potential health problems before patients manifest clinical signs of infection or other issues (IBM, 2013).

By revealing the genetic origin of illnesses, such as mutations related to cancer, the Human Genome Project, which was completed in 2003, is one project that realizes the promise of Big Data. Consequently, researchers are now embarking on two major efforts, the Human Brain Project and the US BRAIN Initiative, in a quest to construct a supercomputer simulation of the brain's inner workings, in addition to mapping the activity of about 100 billion neurons in the hope of unlocking answers to Alzheimer's and Parkinson's diseases (Michael & Miller, 2013).

Business Intelligence and Big Data in Human Resources Management

The benefits of BI&BD solutions can also be seen in human resources management (Nocker, & Sena, 2019). They enable creating a holistic picture of the employment of staff in a given organization and facilitate the design of employee retention schemes, improving their efficiency and reducing costs.

Big Data tools are suitable for effective monitoring and analyzing of the labor market as well as identifying demand for new competences and skills among employees. Employers, employees, institutions dealing with broadly understood education (high schools, universities, etc.), labor market institutions, and investors are increasingly interested in such research. This issue is becoming increasingly relevant as the number of job seekers online increases.

The most common BI&BD applications in human resources management include the following:

■ Human resources analyses and reports: An integrated overview of data on staff employment becomes possible, especially various analyses regarding their migration and achievements and job separation. Such data may be combined with other information flowing from the labor market, e.g., employment criteria set in a given industry, market demand for specific professional groups.

■ Allocation of workforce: Multidimensional analyses are used to determine the employment level of staff (e.g., in sales departments) in specific regions where demand for specific products and services is expected to increase.

■ Human resources management portal: It is understood as an integrated database of employees, in which information about their competences, salaries, achievements, professional promotions, etc. is stored.

■ Training and career path planning: Precise data on the skills obtained by individual employees can be stored in data warehouses. This is helpful when designing programs to improve their qualifications and planning their career paths (SAS Institute, 2013).

At the end of this chapter, it should be stressed that the use of BI&BD tools requires the organization to operate a specific set of competences combining technical skills with knowledge of information architecture and broad analytical skills. In connection with the aforementioned, there is a need to develop new professions based on classical bibliological and computer science knowledge, extended by highly specialized IT and analytical competences. An example would be professions, such as Big Data analyst, Big Data scientist, or Big Data architect.

References

Alt, R., & Puschmann, T. (2004). Successful practices in customer relationship management. *Proceedings of the 37th Hawaii International Conference on System Science.*

Bean, R. (2017). How companies say they're using big data. *Harvard Business Review*, April. Retrieved from https://hbr.org/2017/04/how-companies-say-theyre-using-big-data

Big Data in insurance (2020). 21 Big Data insurance companies to know. Retrieved from https://builtin.com/big-data/big-data-insurance.

Buttle, F. (2009). *Customer relationship management.* Oxford: Butterworth-Heinemann.

Chaudhary, S. (2004). Management factors for strategic BI success. In: M.S. Raisinghani (Eds.), *Business Intelligence in digital economy. Opportunities, limitations and risks* (pp. 191–206). Hershey: IGI Global.

Davenport, T. H., Harris, J. G., & Morison, R. (2010). *Analytics at work: Smarter decisions, better results.* Cambridge: Harvard Business Press.

Deutsche Bank (2014). Big data. How it can become a differentiator. Passion to perform. Deutsche Bank. Global Transaction Banking. Retrieved from https://cib.db.com/docs_new/GTB_Big_Data_Whitepaper_(DB0324)_v2.pdf.

Fatima, Z. (2018). Big Data and the Logistics Industry. Retrieved from https://www.bbntimes.com/society/big-data-and-the-logistics-industry).

Fjermestad, J., & Romano, N. Jr. (2003). Electronic customer relationship management: Revisiting the general principles of usability and resistance – an integrative implementation framework. *Business Process Management Journal, 9*(5), 572–591.

Greenberg, P. (2010). *CRM at the speed of light. Social CRM Strategies, Tools, and Techniques for Engaging Your Customer.* New York: McGraw-Hill.

Greentech Media Inc., SAS. Retrieved from http://www.sas.com/content/dam/SAS/en_us/doc/whitepaper1/gtmresearch-high-performance-analytics-smart-grid-106115.pdf. 2012.

Grönroos, C. (2000). *Service management and marketing – A customer relationship management approach.* New York: John Wiley & Sons Ltd.

Gummesson, E. (2002). Relationship marketing in the new economy. *Journal of Relationship Marketing, 1*(1), 37–55.

Halligan, B., & Shah, D. (2010). *Inbound marketing get found using google, social media, and blogs.* New Jersey: John Wiley & Sons Ltd.

Hassani, H., Huang, X., & Silva, E. (2018). Digitalisation and Big Data mining in banking. *Big Data in Cognitive Computing, 2*(3) 18; doi:10.3390/bdcc2030018.

Hawking, P., Foster, S., & Stein, A. (2008). The adoption and Use of business intelligence solutions in Australia. *International Journal of Intelligent Systems Technologies and Applications, 4*(1), 327–340.

IBM (2013). Analytics: The real-world use of big data in healthcare and life sciences. How innovative healthcare and life sciences organizations extract value from uncertain data. IBM Global Business Services. Business Analytics and Optimization. Executive Report. Oxford: Saïd Business School at the University of Oxford. Copyright IBM Corporation 2013. Somers, NY: IBMGlobal services. Retrieved from https://www.ibm.com/downloads/cas/KX8N32ZQ.

Januszewski, A. (2008). *Funkcjonalność informatycznych systemów zarządzania. Systemy Business Intelligence.* Tom 2. Warszawa: Wydawnictwo Naukowe PWN.

Kadayam S. (2007). Business Intelligence from Unstructured Data. Real-Time Marketing Intelligence for Agile Enterprises. Intelliseek, www. intelliseek.com.

Kostojohn, S., Johnson, M., & Paulen, B. (2011). *CRM fundamentals.* New York: Apress.

Kracklauer, A., Mills, D., & Seifert, D. (2004). *Collaborative customer relationship management: taking CRM to the next level.* Berlin Heidelberg: Springer-Verlag.

Leeds, D. (2012). *High-performance analytics for the smart grid,* White Paper, 2012,

Levitt, T. (1983). After the sale is over. *Harvard Business Review, 63*(5), 87–93.

Linoff, G. S., & Berry, M. J. A. (2002). *Mining the web: Transforming customer data into customer value.* New York: Wiley.

Mayer-Schönberger, V., & Cukier, K. (2013). *Big data: A revolution that will transform how we live, work, and think.* Boston: Houghton Mifflin Harcourt.

McKenn, R. (1991). *Relationship marketing: Successful strategies for the age of the customer.* Cambridge: MA Perseus Books.

Michael, K., & Miller, K. W. (2013). Big data: New opportunities and new challenges. *IEEE Computer, 46*(6). Retrieved from http://works.bepress.com/kmichael/344/.

Minna, R., & Aino, H. (2005). Customer knowledge management competence: Towards a theoretical framework. *Proceedings of the 38th Hawaii International Conference on System Sciences.*

Nocker, M., & Sena, V. (2019). Big data and human resources management: The rise of talent analytics. *Social Science,8,* 273; doi:10.3390/socsci8100273.

Nykamp, M. (2001). *The customer differential: The complete guide to implementing customer relationship management.* New York: Amacom.

Olszak, C. M. (2016). Toward better understanding and use of business intelligence in organizations. *Information Systems Management, 33*(2), 105–123.

Olszak, C. M. (2006). *Building and using business intelligence systems in a contemporary organization.* Katowice: Publishing House of University of Economics in Katowice.

Olszak C. M., & Bartuś, T. (2013). Multi-agent framework for social customer relationship management systems. *Issues in Informing Science and Information Technology, Informing Science Institute, 10,* 367–387.

Olszak, C. M., & Ziemba, E. (2006). Business intelligence systems in the holistic infrastructure development supporting decision-making in organizations. *Interdisciplinary Journal of Information, Knowledge and Management, 1,* 47–58.

Pamuła, A. (2013). *Zaangażowanie odbiorców z grupy gospodarstw domowych w zarządzaniu popytem na energię.* Łódź: Wydawnictwo Uniwersytetu Łódzkiego.

Payne, A., & Frow, P. (2005). A strategic framework for customer relationship management. *Journal of Marketing, 69*(4), 167–176.

Peppers, D., & Rogers, M. (2011). *Managing customer relationships: A strategic framework.* New Jersey: John Wiley & Sons Ltd.

Roscoe, D. (2001). The customer knowledge journey. *Journal of Database Marketing, 5*(4), 314–318.

SAS (2013). Big Data & Utility Analytics for Smart Grid, The Soft Grid 2013–2020, SAS Research Excerpt, White Paper, Greentech Media Inc, Gtmresearch. Retrieved from http://www.sas.com/content/dam/SAS/en_us/doc/analystreport/soft-grid-2013–2020-big-data-utility-analyticssmart-grid.pdf.

SAS (2020). SAS Telecommunication Solution. Retrieved from https://www.sas.com/en_us/industry/communications.html.

Schaeffer, C. (2014).Big Data + The Internet of Things = Big Manufacturing Opportunity. Retrieved from http://www.crmsearch.com/internetofthings.php.

Schaff, C. &Harris, G. (2012). *7 Secrets to Social media Business Success.* Retrieved from http://www.prnewsonline.com/Assets/File/digitalpr_presentations2012/Clinton_Schaff.pdf.

Shani, D., & Chalasani, S. (1992). Exploiting niches using relationship marketing. *The Journal of Consumer Marketing, 9*(3), 33–42.

Shanmugasundaram, S. (2010). *Customer relationship management: Modern trends and perspectives.* PHI Learning Pvt. Ltd.

Tas, Z. (2018). Big data in the shipping industry. Retrieved from https://www.morethan-shipping.com/big-data-in-the-shipping-industry.

Thuraisingham B. (2003). *Web data mining and applications in business intelligence and counterterrorism.* Boca Raton: Taylor & Francis Group.

Tiwana A. (2003). *Przewodnik po zarządzaniu wiedzą. E-biznes i zastosowania CRM.* Warszawa: Placet.

Tuzhilin, A. (2012). Customer relationship management and web mining: The next frontier. *Data Ming Knowledge Discovery, 24*(3), 584–612.

Vercellis, C. (2009). *Business intelligence.* Chichester: Wiley.

Vriens, M., & Kidd, P. (2014). The big data shift: What every marketer needs to know about advanced analytics. *Marketing Insights*, November/December, 23–29.

Wilde, S. (2011). *Improving customer relationship through knowledge application.* Berlin Heidenberg: Springer-Verlag.

Wixom, B.H., & Watson H.J. (2010). The BI-based organization. *International Journal of Business Intelligence Research*, *1*(1), 13–28.

Xu, Z., Frankowick, G.L., & Ramirez, E. (2016). Effects of big data analytics and traditional marketing analytics on new product success: A knowledge fusion perspective. *Journal of Business Research*, *69*(5), 1562–1566.

Xu, Y., Yen, D., Lin, B., & Chou, D. (2002). Adopting customer relationship management technology. *Industrial Management & Data Systems*, *102*(8), 442–452.

Żulicki, R. (2017). Potecjał big data w badaniach społecznych. *Studia Socjologiczne*, *3*(226), 175–207.

Chapter 5

Measurement and Assessment of Business Intelligence and Big Data Development in Organizations

Maturity Models

Business Intelligence and Big Data (BI&BD) projects are highly complex undertakings both of organizational and technological nature. Such projects are considered to be implemented based on proven research theories and methodologies. Many issues related to the measurement and effective implementation of BI&BD systems in organizations can be explained on the basis of the theory of maturity models, critical success factors (CSFs), as well as the theory of value creation.

The literature describes the term "maturity" as an ideal, perfect, complete state (of individuals, organizations, society) to which one should strive (Lahramnn et al., 2011). Achieving this state is usually associated with going through various stages of development (Fraser, Moultrie, & Gregory, 2002). The maturity model is a structured set of elements describing certain aspects of organization's maturity, which aids the improvement of its functioning as well as passing through the various stages of its evolution. In other words, it is a set of various tools and practices that enable assessing an organization's competencies in management as well as improving key factors that lead to the achievement of objectives pursued (Looy, 2014).

The Object Management Group defines the maturity model as an evolutionary process of implementing key practices in one or several areas of enterprise operation. The maturity model enables a holistic view of an organization and a comprehensive assessment in terms of meeting key expectations set by various requirements (e.g., legal acts, firm's internal arrangements) and its stakeholders (customers, contractors, employees, society, etc.).

Maturity models are regarded to have three basic functions (Becker, Knackstedt, & Poppelbub, 2009; de Bruin et al., 2013; Maier, Moultrie, & Clarkson, 2009; Poppelbub & Roglinger, 2011): (1) descriptive – as descriptive models, being a diagnostic tool, used to determine the current state, e.g., for internal and external reporting; (2) prescriptive – as normative, prescriptive models, used to improve an organization or some its areas by indicating the path to achieve specific organizational states; and (3) comparative – as models enabling internal and/or external benchmarking.

An important category of maturity models includes models related to the assessment of information systems. The first proposals regarding the maturity models of information systems appeared in the 1970s (Gibson & Nolan, 1974). It is estimated that today there are over 100 different variants (Mettler & Rosner, 2009). Many of the existing models refer to the assessment of the information systems design process (de Bruin et al., 2013). The first and one of the best known maturity models was the C.F. Gibson and R. Nolan model, in which the development of electronic data processing was presented in four phases (Gibson & Nolan, 1974).

In the early 1990s, the Capability Maturity Model (CMM) was developed by the Software Engineering Institute in the United States. This model is still popular today and is used to improve software development processes. It consists of five levels of maturity referred to as Initial, Repeatable, Defined, Managed, and Optimizing.

The *Initial* level means that processes are carried out *ad hoc* and in a chaotic manner. Software is usually created without formal procedures. Organizations carrying out projects at the first level are usually characterized by a lack of reliable, proven production, and product maintenance technologies.

The *Repeatable* level is characterized by the fact that software development procedures have been largely defined. Techniques are used to replicate successful projects based on information recorded during previous projects. At this level, team members are required to work more effectively, acquire new skills, learn from their mistakes, as well as develop the ability to document experience gained.

At the *Defined* level, there is a coherent set of definitions and standards relating to both the implementation of a project itself and the organization implementing such a project. Knowledge about how to conduct and organize work on the project becomes the way the firm operates. Standards and procedures are modified as the technological or organizational conditions change. Organizations are starting to modify the way projects are carried out based on their own experience so that they reflect specific characteristics of organizations and products they create.

The *Managed* level means the use of detailed metrics regarding the process itself and product quality. Although the process is managed and measurable, risky places are identified that should be subject to more detailed control. The issue of risk management is a crucial element at this level.

The goal of the *Optimizing* level is optimization and further improvement of the process, increasing its effectiveness (improving results) and efficiency (reducing costs). The organization is already mature enough to identify the strengths and weaknesses of the process. This information is used for further analysis aimed at choosing more effective technologies or organizational solutions.

A standard CMM structure, in the form of division into areas, goals, and assigned practices, as well as a five-grade maturity scale, constituted the basis for its development and increase in its popularity (Kasse, 2008). The model gave the rise to the development of a number of other models in the future.

Currently, the Capability Management Model Integration (CMMI) is one of the best known maturity models in the area of software development management. CMMI is the successor of the CMM. According to the Software Engineering Institute (SEI, 2008), CMMI aids the users to "integrate traditionally separate organizational functions, set process improvement goals and priorities, provide guidance for quality processes, and provide a point of reference for appraising current processes."

Another well-known model is the process maturity framework (PMF), which was described in the ITIL library. PMF is used to assess the maturity of service management – both individual processes and their overall outcome (Lloyd, 2002). The assessment is carried out within five closely related fields on a five-grade maturity scale.

The model to study the maturity of IT service management processes is IT Service Management Maturity Model (ITSM Maturity Model). The structure of the model covers six domain areas to which from three to eight detailed processes have been assigned (www.itsmsolutions.com). In turn, model control objectives for information and related technology were developed by ISACA and IT Governance Institute to collect good practices in the field of IT process management. The assessment is performed within the identified five domains and 37 processes (version COBIT 5.0) on a six-grade maturity scale (ww.isaca.org).

An important characteristic (attributes) of maturity models, irrespective of their purpose, is the concept of maturity, its dimensions and levels, principles of maturity development, and methods of its assessment (Lahrmann et al., 2011) (Table 5.1).

Various research methods can be used to design maturity models, e.g., Delphi studies, case studies, and focus groups (Becker, Knackstedt, & Poppelbuss 2009). Quantitative methods are rarely used. The selection of the appropriate method is driven by the area of application, system stakeholders, and target recipients (Mettler & Rosner, 2009).

Table 5.1   Attributes of Maturity Models

Attributes	Description
Maturity concept	Maturity concepts can refer to: – people, i.e., their knowledge, skills in organizing various business activities, – maturity of processes (their definition, management, measurement, control, and efficiency), – maturity of objects (or technologies) determining their level of development.
Dimension	Dimensions represent specific areas in terms of system capabilities, process support, and system design, which are of interest to an organization. Each dimension is described by different measures (practices, objects, activities).
Level	Levels reflect the state of maturity in different dimensions or areas. Each level has an indicator that illustrates the content of a given level and a detailed description of its characteristics.
Principle (rule)	Maturity can develop in a continuous manner or in stages. The continuous method enables the evaluation of activities at various levels and dimensions. The staged model requires the compilation of all elements subject to evaluation at a given level. They usually specify various goals and key tasks that should be completed to reach the next level of maturity.
Assessment	The assessment may be quantitative or qualitative.

Source: Elaborated on: (Lahrmann et al., 2011).

Maturity Models for Business Intelligence

The assumption is that BI maturity assessment models (MMBI) should provide guidance on how to develop BI systems in an organization to achieve, e.g., competitive advantage and various benefits. It is asserted that MMBI should allow finding answers to questions such as the following:

- *Where* are the reporting and analysis most often used in the organization?
- *Who* uses business reports, analyses, and various organization assessment indicators?
- *What* motivates organizations to use BI systems?
- *Which* BI development strategies are used in the organization?
- *What* added value do BI systems bring to the organization?

The further part of the study presents the characteristics and assessment of selected BI maturity models (Table 5.2).

Table 5.2 Overview of BI Maturity Models

Model	Description
TDWI's Business Intelligence Model – Eckerson's Model Eckerson (2004)	This model mainly focuses on the technical aspect for maturity assessment. It constitutes of six maturity levels and uses a metaphor of human evolution: prenatal, infant, child, teenager, adult, and sage.
Gartner's Maturity Model for BI and PM Burton (2009) and Rayner (2008)	The model is a means to assess the maturity of organization's efforts in BI and PM and how mature these need to become in order to reach business goals. The model recognizes five maturity levels: unaware, tactical, focused, strategic, and pervasive.
AMR Research's Business Intelligence/Performance Management Hagerty (2011)	The model is described by four maturity levels: reacting (where have we been?), anticipating (where are we now?), collaborating (where are we going?), and orchestrating (are we all on the same page?). It is used to assess the organization in the area BI and PM.
Business Information Maturity model Williams (2003)	The model is characterized by three maturity levels. The first level answers the question "what business users want to access," the second "why the information is needed," and the third "how to put information into business use."
Model of Analytical Competition Davenport and Harris (2007)	The model describes the path that an organization can follow from having virtually no analytical capabilities to being a serious analytical competitor. It includes five stages of analytical competition: analytically impaired, localized analytics, analytical aspirations, analytical companies, and analytical competitors.

(*Continued*)

Table 5.2 Continued

Model	Description
Information Evolution Model, SAS SAS (2011)	The model supports organization in assessing how they use information to drive business, e.g., to outline how information is managed and utilized as a corporate asset. It is characterized by five maturity levels: operate, consolidate, integrate, optimize, and innovate.
Model Business Intelligence Maturity Hierarchy Deng (2011)	The model was developed in knowledge management and constitutes of four maturity levels: data, information, knowledge, and wisdom.
Infrastructure Optimization Maturity Model Hribar Rajteric (2010)	The model enables a move from reactive to proactive service management. It aids in assessing different areas comprising firm's infrastructure. The model is described by four maturity levels: basic, standardized, rationalized (advanced), and dynamic.
Lauder of Business Intelligence (LOBI) Cates, Gill, and Zeituny (2005)	The model describes levels of maturity in effectiveness and efficiency of decision-making. IT, processes, and people are assessed from the perspective of six levels: facts, data, information, knowledge, understanding, and enabled intuition.
Hawlett Package Business Maturity Model HP (2011)	The model aims at describing the path forward as companies work toward closer alignment of business and IT organizations. It includes five maturity levels: operation, improvement, alignment, empowerment, and transformation.
Watson's Model Watson, Ariyachandra, and Matyska (2011)	The model is based on the stages of growth concept, a theory describing the observation that many things change over time in sequential, predictable ways. The maturity levels include initiation, growth, and maturity.

Table 5.2   Continued

Model	Description
Teradata's BI and DW MM Miller, Schiller, and Rhone (2011)	Maturity concept is process-centric, stressing the impact of BI on the business processes. The model has five maturity levels: reporting (what happened?), analyzing (why did it happen?), predicting (what will happen?), operationalizing (what is happing?), and activating (make it happen).
Davenport's and Harris' Model (2007)	The model is focused on analytical capability. It distinguishes five stages: analytically impaired, localized analytics, analytical aspiration, analytical companies, and analytical competitors.
Model based on dynamic capabilities BI Olszak (2014)	The model reflects six capabilities areas, such as governance, culture, technology, people, processes, and change management and creativity that can be used to assess BI use in organizations. Each capabilities area is described by various detailed BI capabilities.

Source: Elaborated on: (Olszak, 2016).

TDWI's Business Intelligence Model

TDWI's Business Intelligence Model was developed by Eckerson in 2004 (Eckerson, 2004). It was originally created to assess the maturity of a data warehouse. Over time, along with the dynamic development of BI systems, it was adapted for BI assessment. The discussed model mainly focuses on technical aspects of maturity. The model consists of six stages, defined metaphorically: prenatal, infant, child, teenager, adult, and sage. Maturity evaluation is carried out in eight areas (dimensions): scope, analytic structure, executive perception, types of analytics, stewardship, funding, technology platforms, and change management and administration.

The documentation of the discussed maturity model is consistently modified and supplemented with new elements and can be found on the Internet. The model is particularly useful for assessing the maturity of BI systems from a technical point, but it definitely needs a wider-ranging update of elements related to culture and organization management. TDWI is one of the few firms that provide free questionnaires and evaluation criteria for BI systems.

Gartner's Maturity Model

The Gartner's Maturity Model refers to three key areas (dimensions) of assessment: people, processes, and technology (Burton, 2009). They are evaluated from the perspective of the following levels of maturity: unware, tactical, focused, strategic, and pervasive (Rayner & Schlegel, 2008). Level 1, referred to as *unware*, is characterized by incomplete and inconsistent data and a lack of knowledge in an organization about IT capabilities, especially BI. The second level means that firms are beginning to invest in BI tools and applications. However, there is still a problem of the so-called information silos and shortcomings in the field of efficient reporting and data analysis. Next, the level referred to as *focused* is identified with the creation of data warehouses for selected cells and departments of an organization. However, the problem of data integration and access remains unresolved at this stage. At the succeeding strategic level, organizations use BI to achieve strategic goals, i.e., those related to entering new markets, product placement, creating strategic alliances and supply chains, and HR management. The last level of maturity means comprehensive dissemination of conducted BI analyses as well as using them to create new business models and establish competitive advantage.

This model is particularly suitable for assessing business maturity levels and individual departments. It largely relates to the technical aspects of BI. Compared with TDWIs, it enables the assessment of more elements of business nature. Model documentation is legible and correctly prepared. A series of questionnaires are proposed for BI assessment, although assessment criteria have not been defined in a clear manner. Most of the documentation is payable; only selected parts of it can be obtained on the Internet without paying for a subscription.

AMR Research's Business Intelligence/Performance Management Maturity Model, version 2

AMR Research firm has developed a model to improve maturity in the area of BI and Performance Management (PM). The model refers to three dimensions: technology, processes, and people, which are assessed from a four-level perspective: reacting, anticipating, collaborating, and orchestrating (Hagerty, 2011). The first level means the implementation of projects (tactical), where the goal is to improve access to operational data and their better visualization. At this stage, users have the option of using desktop tools and simple queries for databases. At the second level of maturity, BI projects acquire a more strategic orientation. This is where, inter alia, the use of dashboards becomes important. The third level is to consolidate business goals and resources within an organization. Users have at their disposal dashboards and Key Performance Indicators. The last level of maturity enables the implementation of strategic goals and integration of an organization with its environment, including the use of a balanced scorecard.

Business Information Maturity Model

The Business Information Maturity Model developed by Williams and Williams (2007) brings a new perspective and value to the issue of maturity of BI systems. There are six key areas (dimensions) based on which BI assessment is carried out: (1) BI's strategic position, (2) partnership between individual units and IT, (3) BI portfolio management, (4) quality of information and conducted analyses, (5) business culture, and (6) improvement of decision-making process and technical readiness (BI/DW) (Williams & Williams, 2007). The model consists of three levels of maturity. The first level enables the answer to the question *what* information should be made available for business needs; at the second level, the answers to the questions with *whom, when,* and *where* the information should be shared become important; and at the third level, answers are given on *how* to improve information. The model is well documented and has been equipped with a series of questionnaires to assist the user in self-assessment. The range of assessment ranges from 0 to 5 (0 is the lowest score, 3 is neutral, while 5 is highly mature).

Business Intelligence Maturity Hierarchy

The Business Intelligence Maturity Hierarchy Model is an approach describing the assessment of knowledge management in the organization. The model covers four levels of BI maturity: data, information, knowledge, and wisdom (Deng, 2011). However, the levels are assessed from the technical point of view only. The available documentation is very brief and does not enable a deeper understanding of the concept of the model.

Infrastructure Optimization Maturity Model

The discussed model enables measuring the effectiveness of reporting, data analysis, and data warehouses (Rajteric, 2010). There are four levels: basic, standardized, rationalized (advanced), and dynamic. The model has three classes of infrastructure optimization known as core infrastructure optimization (core IO), business productivity infrastructure optimization (BPIO), and application platform infrastructure optimization (APIO). BI systems only refer to two classes: BPIO and APIO. The BPIO class concerns business processes, business management, and IT management, whereas APIO concerns decision-making. The model is mainly focused on the assessment of technical BI issues. It is relatively poorly documented and does not define, *among others*, criteria for assessing maturity levels.

Business Intelligence Development Model

The Business Intelligence Development Model (BIDM), proposed by Sacu and Spruit (2010), includes six levels of maturity, referred to as (1) predefined reporting, (2) data marts, (3) corporate data warehouse, (4) predictive analysis, (5) operational BI, and (6) PM. The model has three dimensions that consist of people, processes and technology. Model documentation is not available on the Internet. Criteria for assessing maturity levels are also not defined.

Lauder of Business Intelligence

Lauder of Business Intelligence (LOBI) is a model that is suitable for planning and implementing IT in business (Cates, Gill, & Zeituny, 2005). It uses three dimensions: technology, processes, and people, which are considered within six levels of maturity: facts, data, information, knowledge, understanding, and intuition. The model mainly focuses on the IT perspective, not on specific BI components. It is also poorly documented, and maturity criteria have not been defined.

Hewlett Package Business Intelligence Maturity Model

The Hawlett Package Business Maturity Model consists of three dimensions, referred to as business, information technology, and strategy and program management (HP, 2011). The business dimension describes the types of business requirements and problems that are solved with the aid of BI. The dimension of information technology presents solutions that an organization adopts to meet various business needs. The last dimension, however, refers to management skills as a key element in implementing BI. The model is mainly used to assess technical BI issues.

Information Evaluation Model SAS

SAS company proposes a model that is intended to support the assessment of the use and management of information in the business (SAS, 2011). There are four dimensions: people, processes, culture, and infrastructure; five levels of maturity include operate, consolidate, integrate, optimize, and innovative. By understanding and improving the business in these dimensions, firms can maximize their value and the impact of information as a strategic resource on achieving competitive advantage. The concept of the model is not easy to understand, and the assessment is difficult to carry out without the help of SAS specialists.

Watson Model

Watson and his colleagues developed a maturity model for assessing data warehouses (Watson, Ariyachandra, & Matyska, 2011). The model is described from the perspective of three levels (initiation, growth, and maturity) and nine specific dimensions. It is based on solid theoretical foundations and refers to the concept of growth, the theory observation, and change.

The Teradata Maturity Model

The Teradata Model is used to assess the maturity of data warehouses and BI systems. It illustrates the increase in the complexity of BI solutions used in an organization, which include (Miller, Schiller, & Rhone, 2011) reporting, analyzing, predicting, operationalization, and operation in real mode (activating). It consists of six levels of maturity, referred to as operational activities (operate), understand, change, growth, compete, lead, and several dimensions comprising, inter alia, business management, performance management, business analytics, project management, decision support, data management, data acquisition and integration, communication, and training. The concept of maturity in this model is process oriented. The model is relatively poorly documented and difficult to understand without the support of specialists.

Most of the discussed maturity models are oriented toward technical elements. This means that IT components, such as applications, data, and infrastructure, are assessed most often. The so-called soft elements, i.e., information needs, organization structure, staff, organization strategy, and processes, are assessed less frequently.

Business Intelligence Maturity Models Based on Analytical Capabilities

The literature points to the fact that the success of implementing BI systems is largely determined by analytical capabilities of an organization. BI capability means IT-enabled, analytical dynamic capability for improving decision-making and firm's performance (Chae, & Olson, 2013). It is a specific and important type of IS capabilities. Different organizational characteristics and strategic goals may also require the use of different BI capabilities. According to Gartner Group BI, these capabilities relate to information access and analysis of decision-making style within an organization (Isik, Jones, & Sidorova, 2011). Isik, Jones, and Sidorova (2011) delineate information access and analysis capabilities and relate them to the overall BI success. Davenport and Harris (2007) state that analytical capability is a key element of strategy for the business. Wixom, Watson, and Werner (2011) argue that BI capability is "a journey over long periods of time during which foundational competencies are developed."

According to Teece et al. (1997), dynamic capabilities can be divided into three classes of activities, including sensing, seizing, and transformation. In the context of business process management (Ortbach et al., 2012) and also of BI, sensing refers mainly to identification of the need to change organization's business processes, relations with customers and suppliers. Seizing means the exploration and selection of opportunities for change. Transformation involves sociotechnical implementation of redesigned business processes in an organization. Some authors argue that BI capabilities are critical functionalities of BI that aid an organization to improve its adoption to change and its performance (Isik, Jones, & Sidorova, 2011; Wixom, Watson, & Werner, 2011).

It is asserted that organizations may develop two activities to build BI capability. The former activity concerns the widely understood data exploration, whereas the latter refers to data exploitation (Lavie, Stettner, & Tushman, 2010). Data exploration enables an organization to overcome the burden of actual knowledge and its capabilities. This may refer to new technical capabilities, market experience, and new relations with the environment. Furthermore, the exploration is a conscious searching of new knowledge sources, enrichment of existing resources, adoption of new behavioral orientations, and acquisition of new competencies. This all can be achieved through advanced data mining, text mining, web mining, intelligent agents, and search-based application. In turn, data exploitation concerns the utilization of existing knowledge bases. It is limited to actual resources and refers to their detailed analysis.

Model Proposed by Davenport and Harris

The model proposed by Davenport and Harris (2007) is an example of a model in which BI assessment is made mainly from the perspective of BI capabilities. The authors have distinguished in their model five stages of analytical capability called analytically impaired, localized analytics, analytical aspiration, analytical companies, and analytical competitors. The first stage means that "organizations have some desire to become more analytical, but thus far they lack both the will and the skill to do so." They face some substantial barriers – both human and technical. They may also lack the hardware, software, or skills to carry out extensive analysis. The second stage *localized analytics* is characterized by reporting with pockets of analytical activity. Organizations undertake the first analytical activities, but they have no intention of competing on them. BI activities produce economic benefits but not enough to affect a firm's competitive strategy. The third stage called *analytical aspirations* is triggered when BI activities gain management support. Organizations build a plan of utilizing BI. The primary focus in *analytical companies* stage is building word-class analytical capabilities at the enterprise level. Organizations implement the plan developed in a previous stage, making considerable progress toward building the support, culture, skills, strategic insights, data, and technology needed for analytical competition. At the last stage, analytics moves from being a very important capability for an organization to the key to its strategy and competitive advantage. Executive managers trust in BI, and all users are highly educated in BI.

Model Based on Dynamic Capabilities Business Intelligence

The model proposed by Olszak (2014) is a dynamic BI capabilities framework that is strongly combined with the idea of Davenport's and Harris's model. It reflects six capabilities areas, such as governance, culture, technology, people, processes, and change and creativity management that can be used to assess BI use in organizations. Each capability area is described by various detailed BI capabilities (Table 5.3) and mapped on the scale: analytically impaired, localized analytics, analytical aspiration, analytical companies, and analytical competitors.

The first BI capabilities area – governance – is "the mechanism for managing the utilization of BI resources within an organization and for embedding BI initiatives within organizational objectives. It also involves continuous renewal of BI resources and organizational capabilities to respond to changes in dynamic environments and mitigating resistance to change" (Cosic, Shankes, & Maynard, 2012).

Table 5.3 **Dynamic Capabilities BI Framework**

BI Capabilities Area	Detailed BI Capabilities
Governance	Business vision and plan Business analysis planning and monitoring Strategic alignment of BI and business strategy Decision-making rights (operational, tactical, strategic) BI solution assessment and validation
Culture	Executive leadership and support Flexibility and agility Establishing a fact-based and learning culture
Technology	Data management Systems integration and interaction with other systems Flexibility Reporting and visualization technology Advanced BI technology (OLAP, data warehousing, data mining, predictive analysis)
People	Securing and building technology skills Mathematical and statistical skills Organizational skills Organizational knowledge, knowledge sharing Managing analytical people Business interpersonal communication Entrepreneurship and innovation Trustworthiness
Process	Holistic overview of a business process/knowledge processes Business process/knowledge-modeling and orchestration Process redesign and integration
Change & Creativity	Monitoring of competitors, customers, and current trends in the marketplace Introducing new change-oriented business management models, knowledge management, and customer relationship management Generation of new and useful products, services, ideas, procedures, and processes

Source: (Olszak, 2014).

The governance area is described by various detailed capabilities, such as business vision and plan, business analysis planning and monitoring, strategic alignment of BI and business strategy, decision-making rights (operational, tactical, strategic), and BI solution assessment and validation.

The second BI capabilities area refers to a culture of an organization. A culture is described as "personality of an organization" and comprises the assumptions, values, norms, and behavioral signs of organization/s members. They form over time and lead to systematic ways of gathering, analyzing, and disseminating data. Organization's culture influences the way decisions are made and mainly reflects executive leadership and support, flexibility, and agility as well as establishing a fact-based and learning culture.

The next important area in the mentioned model concerns people. People are "all those individuals within an organization who use BI as part of their job function. BI initiatives are considered to be knowledge intensive and require technical, business, managerial, and entrepreneurial skills and knowledge" (Cosic et al., 2012). The model assesses different skills of people, e.g., mathematical and statistical skills, organizational skills, and communication skills.

Technology area refers "to the development and use of hardware, software, and data within BI activities. It includes the management of integrated and high-quality data resources, the seamless integration of BI systems with other organizational information systems, the conversion of data into information through reporting and visualization systems and use of more advanced statistical analysis tools to discover patterns, predict trends, and optimize business process" (Cosic et al., 2012).

The process area consists of activities devoted to gathering, selecting, aggregating, analyzing, and distributing information. Some of these activities are the responsibility of the BI staff, whereas others are the joint responsibility of the BI staff and business units. Processes may be divided into categories of internal and external processes. The first group mainly relates to accounting, finance, manufacturing, and human resources. The second group concerns managing and responding to customer demand and supplier relationships (Davenport & Harris, 2007).

The last area of the proposed model refers to change and creativity management in organizations. Organizations face rapid change like never before. Therefore, the ability to manage and adapt to organizational change is an essential ability required in the workplace today. Change management is an approach to transitioning individuals, teams, and organizations to a desired future state. BI requires permanent development and adaptation to new challenges and expectations of an organization, whereas an organizational creativity is the firm's ability to generate new and useful ideas to address rapidly changing opportunities and threats by making timely and market-oriented decisions and to frame breakthrough changes in its resource base.

The proposed model based on BI capabilities areas was mapped onto the Davenport and Harris model. As a result, a BI capabilities maturity matrix was created (Table 5.4). Such a matrix can be used to assess BI capabilities and competences in selected organizations.

Table 5.4 BI Capabilities Maturity Matrix

BI Capabilities Area	Analytically Impaired	Localized Analytics	Analytical Aspiration	Analytical Companies	Analytical Competitors
Governance	Lack of vision and plan	Businesses plans for limited departments	Integrated business strategy	Have an enterprise BI strategy	BI strategy oriented on customers, suppliers, etc.
Culture	No flexibility and agility	Low support from senior executives	Users are encouraged to collect, process analyze, and share information	Establishing a fact-based and learning culture, skill training in BI	Learning from customers, suppliers, communities of practice, social media
Technology	Missing/poor data Unintegrated systems	Missing important data, isolated BI efforts	Proliferation of BI tools	High quality of data, integrated knowledge repositories	Enterprise-wide BI architecture largely implemented

(Continued)

Table 5.4 Continued

BI Capabilities Area	Analytically Impaired	Localized Analytics	Analytical Aspiration	Analytical Companies	Analytical Competitors
People	Users do not know their own data requirements or how to use them	The users take the first BI initiatives	Users try to optimize the efficiency of individual departments by BI	Users have high BI capabilities but often not aligned with right role	Users have capabilities and time to use BI
Processes	Users do not know business processes	Identification of basic business processes	Standardization of business processes, and building best practices in BI	Business process management based on facts	Broadly supported, process-oriented culture based on facts
Change and Creativity	Fear of change, no creativity	Risk management for selected business process, poor and limited creativity	Building the best practices for change management, individual and team creativity	Integrated risk management, team and organizational creativity	Cooperation with competition, organizational creativity, creative environment

Source: (Olszak, 2014).

Big Data Maturity Models

Big Data Maturity Models (BDMMs) are the next step in creating advanced analytics, which is aimed at better understanding its importance for the development of an organization. The existing BDMMs are largely a continuation and improvement of maturity models developed for the needs of BI. Many of them relate to the assessment and development of processes, analytical capabilities, and their role in the development of new business models, achieving organizational success, and creating a competitive advantage.

According to Braun (2015), BDMMs are the artifacts used to measure BD maturity. These models aid organizations in creating structure around their BD capabilities and in identifying where to start (Halper & Krishnan, 2014). They provide tools that assist organizations in defining goals around their BD program and in communicating their BD vision to an entire organization. BDMMs also provide a methodology to measure and monitor the state of firm's BD capability, the effort required to complete the current stage or phase of maturity and to progress to the next stage. Additionally, BDMMs measure and manage the speed of both the progress and adoption of big data programs in an organization. The goals of BDMMs are (1) to provide a capability assessment tool that generates specific focus on BD in key organizational areas; (2) to help guide development milestones; and (3) to avoid pitfalls in establishing and building BD capabilities.

De Bruin et al. (2005) classify BDMM's as (1) descriptive–assess the "as-is" situation; (2) prescriptive–focus on relationships to business performance and how maturity improvement can positively affect business value; and lastly (3) comparative–enable benchmarking across industries or regions. Mettler and Rosner (2009) identify three factors or aspects in a maturity model, namely, (1) process maturity – to which extent a specific process is explicitly defined, managed, measured, controlled, and effective; (2) object maturity – to which extent a particular object reaches a predefined level of sophistication; and (3) people capability – to which extent the workforce is able to enable knowledge creation and enhance proficiency.

The research literature provides many examples and descriptions of BD maturity models. The most frequently cited and used ones are presented in the following.

The TDWI Big Data Maturity Model

One of the most popular models to measure the maturity level of an organization in the context of BD analytics has been proposed by The Data Warehouse Institute (TDWI). The TDWI BDMM describes the steps that every organization has to follow while undertaking BD initiatives. The model shows how to transform an organization to fully utilize BD. The model consists of five stages (Halper & Krishnan, 2013–2014): (1) nascent, (2) preadoption, (3) early adoption, (4) corporate adoption, and (5) mature/visionary. Each stage is assessed from the perspective of five dimensions: organization, infrastructure, data management, analytics, and governance.

The nascent stage means that an organization has a low awareness of BD or their value. There is little to no executive support for the effort, and only some people in an organization are interested in the potential value of BD. During the preadoption stage, an organization starts taking the first initiatives concerning BD analytics. An organization may have invested in some new technologies, such as Hadoop, in support of BD.

The next stage, called early adoption, is characterized by one or two proofs of concept (POCs) which become more established and production ready. Organizations tend to spend a long time in this stage, often because it is hard to bridge the gap that leads to corporate-wide adoption of BD and BD analytics. Then, corporate adoption stage is the major crossover phase in any organization's BD journey. During corporate adoption, end-users might have started operationalizing BD analytics or changing their decision-making processes. Most organizations would have repeatedly addressed certain gaps in their infrastructure, data management, governance, and analytics. Halper and Krishnan (2013–2014) stress that only a few organizations can be considered as visionary in terms of BD and BD analytics. During this stage organizations are able to execute BD programs and to use highly mature infrastructure. They also have BD governance strategies that are supported by executives. Employees share a level of excitement and energy around BD and BD analytics.

Big Data and Analytics Maturity Model (IBM model)

IBM Institute of Business Value (IBV) proposed Big Data and Analytics Maturity Model (Not, 2015). The model comprises six categories: business strategy, information, analytics, culture and operational execution, architecture, and governance. Each category is described by five levels of maturity: ad hoc, foundational, competitive, differentiating, and breakaway.

According to Not (2015), the first step with any advanced technology capability is to recognize that its use needs to be business-driven. While underpinning technology is needed to acquire data and execute analytics, business expertise is necessary to derive meaningful insight and use it to differentiate outcomes. Differentiation can be achieved by enriching customer engagement and driving operational improvements. It demands the organizational capacity to explore data for new opportunities and an ability to construct quantified business cases. Mature organizations are able to harness available data and apply analytics to it to innovate and create new business models.

The second category in the mentioned model is information. The utilization of data to manage the business is the base capability. However, highly mature organizations recognize that data are a first-class, strategic business asset. Not only is this view based on existing transactional systems – the systems of record – but also on systems that support individual– the systems of engagement – and external data sources. Furthermore, mature organizations provide governed access to data wherever they reside in an organization and are able to provide them with the meaning and context.

Not (2015) stresses that analytics is necessary to understand why something has happened or to predict what is likely to happen. Mature use of analytics optimizes the business. Organizations will already be reporting to show their financial performance and to demonstrate regulatory compliance, but analytics is necessary to understand why something has happened or to predict what is likely to happen. The resulting insight aids the improvement of customer engagement and operational efficiency. Analytics is used to make data-driven decision-making pervasive in an organization, and it requires timely insight into context.

Culture and operational execution reflect the need to engage staff, managers, and top executives in analytics, learning, and sharing knowledge in an organization. Access to data and use of analytics to derive insight builds no business value in and of itself. An organization realizes benefits when its people and systems have a desire to seek out and make use of insight as it operates. Trust in insight is essential, as is an ability to visualize, share, and provide feedback to learn and improve. A mature organization can offer rich data and analytics services that are aligned to and evolve with business priorities.

Advanced analytics based on BD requires coherent architecture and technology. It enables ease of access by end-users, agility in the capabilities required to address current business needs, and a managed approach to accessing required data.

The last category – governance – stresses that information governance is a CSF for BD projects. Policies need to be established and enforced to a degree of confidence in information, and so that resulting insights are understood and reflected in decision-making efforts. Policies also need to include data provenance and accuracy, data quality, master data and metadata, lifecycle management, security, privacy, and ethical use.

Dell Data Maturity Model

The Dell Data Maturity Model defines four levels of maturity (Dell, 2016): data aware, data proficient, data savvy, and data driven. The first level of maturity is referred to as *data aware*. Firms at this level are aware of the importance of the data they have and of the fact that they can gain immediate benefits. However, most of the work associated with the creation of reports and the acquisition of data from various systems and information sources is done manually.

At the second level, *data proficient* are firms that despite the incomplete integration of all data, sources have already achieved a fairly high level of standardization in reporting. Such firms are more aware of how data are collected and stored. They seek to standardize reports and automate the measurement of key indicators for a given area.

Data savvy is the third level of maturity in the approach to data. Firms at this level experience real business effects resulting from the utilization of BD. This has a visible impact on their operational activities as well as results in noticeable savings and acceleration of the decision-making process. It is argued that it is only at this stage that information held by an organization begins to be used to achieve a real competitive advantage.

The full utilization of collected data occurs in organizations at the fourth level, known as *data driven*. These are organizations in which relevant indicators have been defined for all key business processes and are analyzed on an ongoing basis. The information obtained is used to analyze trends and optimize, predict, and create new values. These organizations are well aware that BD enable them not only to measure but above all to analyze and draw conclusions, because such analytics makes it easier to run the business and increase the competitive advantage.

Big Data Business Model Maturity Index

Schmarzo (2013) proposed the Big Data Business Model Maturity Index as a tool for assessing the maturity of a business model in the context of BD utilization. As Schmarzo claims, organizations may use this index to (1) get information on the stage of utilizing advanced BD analytics, on their value creation process, and on business models – that is, get information on current state and (2) identify desired target state.

Schmarzo's model is composed of five levels (stages): business monitoring, business insights, business optimization, data monetization, and business metamorphosis. The first three levels focus on the organization itself and on optimizing its internal business processes. The last two levels focus on organization's environment – its customers and markets.

The Hortonworks Big Data Maturity Model

The Hortonworks Big Data Maturity Model assesses organization's BD capabilities across five domains: (1) data sponsorship, (2) data and analytics practices, (3) technology and infrastructure, (4) organization and skills, and (5) process management. Each domain is described by four different components. Data sponsorship domain refers to vision and strategy, funding, advocacy, and business case. The second domain concerns data collection, storage, processing, and analysis. Domain of technology and infrastructure is assessed by hosting, functionality, tools, and integrations. The next domain is characterized by analytic and development skills, talent strategy, leadership, and collaboration models. The last domain, called process management, is assessed by planning and budget, operations, security and governance, program measurement, and investment focus.

Critical Success Factors for Implementing Business Intelligence and Big Data in Organizations

The utilization of BI&BD systems in organizations is inseparably associated with seeking answers to such questions as: what elements (factors) decide and determine the effective implementation of BI, what is the main barrier to their use, and what is the relationship of BI with organizational success. The theory of CSFs assists in answering many questions in this area.

CSFs are defined in the research literature as elements that affect the success of a given venture and the achievement of the set goal. For the first time, the definition of CSFs was presented by D. Ronald Daniel (1961) in 1960; however, John F. Rockart (1979) contributed to the popularization of this concept in the 1970s. CSFs were to serve as a tool for the business, facilitating the implementation of various projects and strategies. According to Rockart (1979), CSFs represent the areas of enterprise activity in which obtaining satisfactory results guarantees good performance and competitiveness of the entire organization. In other words, it is a certain (limited) number of key areas of the firm's operations in which achieving good results is necessary for the results of the entire organization to be satisfactory. If the effects of key areas are not satisfactory, then the results of the entire organization are below expectations. Rockart (1979) defined four sources of CSFs. They are related to (1) organization – own specific conditions defined by the field of organization's activity, e.g., product characteristics, product demand, implemented technology, etc.; (2) the environment of an organization, customer preferences, economic and political factors in the state; (3) current organizational factors whose significance depends on the situation, e.g., lack of specific skills among employees; and (4) organization's position.

As early as the 1980s, Bullen and Rockart (1981) emphasized the need to refer to CSF's theory in the context of the development of Management Information Systems (MIS). It was noticed that many MIS projects fail; i.e., they do not end within the time schedule envisaged, significantly exceed the planned budget, and do not implement all the assumed (planned) functionalities. The "iron triangle" principle was then disseminated, referring to the three basic resources (restrictions) of each project: time, budget, and scope, and stating that any change in at least one of them affects the others. For example, if a project for which the scope has been increased is to be carried out within the same time schedule, the budget of that project should be increased. Kerzner (2009) also noted that the success of the project does not only mean carrying out work within the limits of time, budget, and scope but also meeting customer expectations. Shenhar and Dvir (2007) proposed that the assessment of a project should be performed in the short and long term and be based on five basic groups of measures: achievement of the planned objective, impact on the customer, impact on the team, business success, and direct and long-term benefits of project. The assessment of a project from the customer's and project team's point of view is also stressed by Rad and Lewin (2006). The authors assert that the most important indicator of success for a customer is the scope and quality of results. Cost and time schedule are often of secondary importance. In turn, the design team focuses on activities and processes that guarantee the delivery of the desired product in the most efficient and cost-effective way possible. In contrast, the definition of success indicators refers to the category of project management activities, and these are all activities related to team factors that must be managed a proper manner, regardless of the phase and changes in the scope of work, costs, and time schedule.

In 2006, Fortune & White developed a list of CSFs for the project based on 63 publications. The list includes support from senior management, clear realistic objectives, strong/detailed plan kept up to date, good communication/feedback, user/client involvement, skilled/suitably qualified sufficient staff/team, effective change management, competent project manager, strong business case/sound basis for project, sufficient/well allocated resources, good leadership, proven/familiar technology, realistic schedule, risks addressed/assessed/managed, project sponsor/champion, effective monitoring/control, adequate budget, organizational adaptation/culture/structure, and others.

In turn, the report of the Standish Group highlights the following factors affecting the success of the project: management support; user involvement; experience of the project manager; clearly defined business goals; minimized scope of the project; standardization of application infrastructure; stable, base solutions; formal methodology; reliable estimates; and other factors.

As it has already been emphasized, the CSF issue is particularly important in IT project management. Many consulting companies have developed their own lists of CSFs and measures of the success of IT projects (including BI). For example, Deloitte has identified the following CSFs: close links between the project and organization's strategy and needs, project sponsor (management board), project organization, allocation of qualified resources to the project, project preparation, appropriate project management methodology, and quality control.

The concept of CSFs has also been described in CobIT management guidelines (COBIT, 2012) They are defined as the most important management issues or actions to achieve control over and within IT processes. They relate to strategic, organizational, technical, process, procedural tasks as well as relevant skills and capabilities. The CobIT management guidelines include the following list of CSFs: defined and documented processes, defined and documented policies, clearly defined responsibility, strong management support, proper communication with internal and external stakeholders, and continuous measurement practices.

CSFs for Business Intelligence and Big Data Use

It is hard to disagree that the theory of CSFs gives good basis for stating what criteria should be followed during implementation of BI applications (Olszak, 2016). CSFs in BI context can be perceived as a set of tasks and procedures that should be addressed in order to ensure BI systems accomplishment (Scholtz et al., 2010). Some authors identify CSFs for BI in the dimensions of organization, environment, and project planning. They find especially strong support for organizational factors (Hwang et al., 2004). Furthermore, earlier works reviled the importance of various issues: technical (Wixom & Watson, 2010) as well as personal, educational, and business. Ariyachandra and Watson (2006), analyzing CSFs for BI implementation, consider two key dimensions: process performance (e.g., how well the process of a BI system implementation was conducted) and infrastructure performance (e.g., the quality of the system and the standard of output). According to Yeoh and Koronios (2010), CSFs can be generally classified into three dimensions: organization, process, and technology. The organizational dimension includes such elements as committed management support and sponsorship, clear vision, well-established business case. In turn, the process dimension includes business-centric support and balanced team composition, business-driven and interactive development approach, and user-oriented change management. Technological dimension regards such elements as business-driven, scalable and flexible technical framework as well as sustainable data quality, and integrity.

Davenport and Harris (2007) report that the most important elements contributing to the success of BI projects in organizations include quality of data and used technologies, skills, sponsorship, alignment between BI and business, and BI utilization. Other elements concern organizational culture, information requirements, and politics.

According to Olszak and Ziemba (2012), the biggest barriers that organizations encounter during the implementation of BI systems have a business and organizational nature. Among the business barriers, the most frequently mentioned are the lack of well-defined business problem, not determining the expectations toward BI, and the lack of connection between the business and the vision of BI system, whereas as the key organizational barriers, the enterprises enumerate lack of management support, lack of knowledge about the BI system and its capabilities, exceeded BI implementation budget, ineffective BI project management and complexity of BI project, and lack of user training and support.

The analysis of various BI&BD cases presented in the research literature indicates that the reasons for their implementation failures are extremely complex. They are often underpinned by organizational and mental factors, and not always, as it might seem, by typically IT factors. The most frequently cited are as follows:

1. BI&BD is a kind of a specific methodology of work, thinking and acting, requiring the introduction of a comprehensive pro-information policy to an organization. While, today, many organizations deal well with various IT-related problems, they are not yet prepared enough to share knowledge and utilize it to create a competitive advantage. Without promotion, increasing awareness, and level of knowledge about BI&BD ideas, it is hard to expect satisfaction from their use.

2. Internal staff resistance, weak support from the top management. BI&BD are not only a powerful analytical tool but also a control and monitoring tool. Hence, there may be resistance and reluctance of many people to use them. All the time, organizations have a strong drive to preserve existing organizational and power structures, and decision-making methods.

3. The issue of data privacy. Advanced BI&BD analytics helps detect various links between data and facts. This can cause a lot of controversy and resistance from different users.

4. BI&BD technologies are new solutions that are constantly developing and burdened with relatively high costs. In this situation, organizations, being aware of the lack of experience in this area, remain very cautious about their application.

5. Information and knowledge management in many organizations operates following the old order all the time. There are no interdisciplinary teams that would act as the BI competence center. It is necessary to reorganize many existing IT departments that would be responsible not only for processing information resources but also for developing and promoting new ways of working with information.

6. Users of BI&BD systems should take an active part in both the process of their development and utilization. They are required to be more proactive, to have skills in data transformation, extracting new knowledge from current information resources, and willingness to share knowledge and work in a team. This situation means the need to reorganize existing systems of motivation, rewarding, and promotion of employees in many organizations.

7. In the decision support environment, full specification of users' information needs is not possible. Therefore, BI&BD applications should be developed with caution and sensitivity so that new requirements can be taken into account in the future.

Big Data-Based Business Value Creation

The sense of business intelligence development and the benefits that organizations derive from BD resource analysis can be explained on the basis of value creation theory. According to some authors (Davenport & Harris, 2007; Gunther et al., 2017), the economic value of BD utilization can be measured by organizations in terms of profit, business expansion, or increased competitive advantage. BD analysis can mainly contribute to the creation of innovative products and services (Davenport et al., 2012; McAfee & Brynjolfsson, 2012). It is also argued that it can aid firms in optimizing the supply chain, pricing of products, selecting people to perform specific tasks and professions, minimizing various mistakes, as well as in improving the quality, and strengthening customer relations (Chen et al., 2012; McAfee & Brynjolfsson, 2012). Other economic and social values resulting from BD analysis may be manifested in enhanced decision-making and more informed strategizing, improved business processes, and creation of innovative business models (e-commerce, security) (Das & Kumar, 2013; Manyika et al., 2011; O'Driscoll, 2014) as well as tracking and monitoring various socioeconomic phenomena and dealing with unexpected situations (Erickson & Rothberg, 2013; Schmarzo, 2013; Wamba et al., 2014). Many researchers point to the role of BD in the context of solving contemporary environmental problems (An et al., 2017), sustainable development (Bibri & Krogstie, 2017), development of smart healthcare and smart cities (Sampri, Mavragani, & Tsagarakis, 2016; Wang et al., 2018), as well as other issues related to the world's development.

Some authors (Davenport & Harris, 2007; Parise et al., 2012; Schmarzo, 2013) argue that proper analysis of BD resources can contribute to the transformation of an organization, consisting in moving from a retrospective perspective toward a predictive and real-time perspective. At the same time, they point up that without an appropriate strategy focused on BD exploration, achieving original values from these resources may be difficult or even impossible.

Himmi et al. (2017) proposed four approaches (strategies) focused on developing and obtaining value from BD in organizations: routine, integration, strategic, and excellence. These approaches illustrate the relationship between operational activities, decision-making dynamics, and BD ability to analyze. The first approach means that operational activity in organizations is dominant, and organizations have limited capabilities in accessing and analyzing large volumes of data. Data analysis is at a low level and limited to simple mathematical and logical procedures. The second approach is when organizations face the need to make prompt decisions and respond dynamically to changing business conditions. However, they have limited analytical skills. In turn, the combination of a high level of analytical capabilities and dynamic decision-making is identified with a strategic approach and utilization BD to analyze the market, customers, competitors, etc. The latest approach (excellence) means that organizations owe their competitive advantage and market position to the comprehensive utilization of BD.

In turn, Parise, Iyer, and Vesset (2012) proposed four strategies for BD-based value creation that concern business goals as well as data type and conducted analyses. They are referred to as performance management, data mining, analytics, and decision science. Performance management mainly pertains to the analysis of corporate databases with the aid of defined queries and multidimensional analyses. The data used in this type of analysis are usually transactional. The second strategy, "data mining," is aimed at using a variety of statistical tools to analyze transactional data. In turn, the "analyst" strategy enables advanced experimentation on data and obtaining answers to questions regarding, inter alia, user behaviors based on their previous transactions and preferences. The last strategy refers to experiments and analyses of non-transactional data, such as surveying users' opinions on social media about products. Unlike the previous strategy – "analytics," focusing on measuring known goals, the "decision science" strategy addresses examination of these technologies and testing hypotheses.

Organizations that intend to derive value from BD should primarily develop their analytical skills. LaValle et al. (2011) distinguish three levels of analytical adaptation: aspirational, experimental, and transformational. The first level means that organizations focus on improving organizational efficiency and automating existing processes and are looking for the ways to reduce their operating expenses. The second level refers to organizations that have already acquired some analytical skills. They seek to create better ways to collect and combine data and to utilize analytics and optimize their decisions in a more efficient manner. The third level concerns those organizations that utilize their analytical experience to improve their competitiveness.

McAfee and Brynjolfsson (2012) identified five management components related to BD-driven value creation that included leadership, talent management, technology, decision-making, and structure of an organization. Research conducted by the authors shows that organizations that were successful in BD utilization had clearly defined goals and identified measures of success. The leaders of such organizations perfectly understood the mechanisms of market functioning; they thought creatively and were focused on creating an innovative market offer. Talent management plays up the growing role of "data scientists" and other highly qualified employees who are able to work with huge volumes of data. Another element that is crucial in creating BD-driven value is technology. Although the technology itself, in the opinion of the authors, is insufficient, it is an important component. They assert a major role of integrated platforms, such as Hadoop. The last component of this value creation strategy refers to decision-making and organizational culture. Knowledge of business problems, working with the right data, and knowledge of problem-solving techniques go together to make up a set of instruments that contribute to business value creation.

In turn, Bharadwaj et al. (2013) are of the opinion that BD-driven value creation relies on (1) the utilization of diverse information and far-reaching digitalization, (2) the utilization of multilateral business models, (3) coordination of models in networks, and (4) control of network architecture. Referring to the first element, it should be noted that the increase in value can occur through the mere fact of unlimited access to various information resources. This is becoming crucial, especially today, in the context of the need to address customer requirements. BD technology provides the opportunity to increase the availability of data posted on blogs, social networks as well as their effective processing and analysis. An increasing number of firms are personalizing their offer based on information collected, e.g., on Facebook. Sharing and redistribution of information is becoming easier. An increasing number of firms are also building their competitive advantage on advanced equipment, specialized software and applications as well as Internet communication. Value creation through BD utilization can be carried out adopting multilateral business models. The delivery of specific products and services is more and more often closely related to other firms, e.g., telecommunications operators. Firms can operate more efficiently and optimize supply chain orchestration and manage their innovation. The logical extension of multilateral business models is complex, dynamic coordination within many firms. Advanced BD platforms and computer hardware enable traditional sector barriers to break down and opportunities to operate in new business space and market niches arise (D'Adderio, 2001). Firms cooperate closely together, contribute to shared value in networks, and share that value. Addressing to the last element affecting the increase in value (control of digital architecture), it should be stressed that firms benefit not only from their innovative products but also from the original partnership and ICT impact both on a single firm and on the entire industry.

Unfortunately, the survey conducted by Olszak and Zurada (2019) among 20 organizations clearly indicated that most organizations do not have consistent, comprehensive strategies and business practices focused on BD exploration and exploitation. Organizations do not perform professional analyses on the needs of BD analysis; they also do not know who should be responsible for exploring BD, developing strategies for using BD resources as well as taking care of security issues, and BD resource protection. Only some departments in the surveyed organizations developed BD exploration strategies on their own (e.g., sales and marketing departments). The research demonstrated that the majority of the surveyed organizations are not aware of the importance and need to develop such a BD exploration strategy. Only two organizations (from the service sector) had a coherent overall strategy of BD, related to the business strategy. In seven organizations, such strategies were developed for specific departments. Other organizations did not have such strategies. The study showed a strong correlation between having a BD exploration strategy and organizational culture. The organizations with good leadership and open to new products; change and innovation had real interest in competing on the basis of information and intellectual resources.

Conclusions

The theory and practice demonstrate that modern organizations are clearly divided when it comes to BI&BD utilization. Advanced implementations can be found particularly in banks, financial institutions as well as large production and commercial firms. There, BI&BD are used for customer segmentation and profiling, predicting customer loyalty and migration, assessing credit risk, detecting fraud, forecasting the development of strategic business processes, optimizing logistics processes, as well as designing and analyzing advertising campaigns. Interestingly, organizations that utilize BI&BD are also usually the users of MRP II and ERP class systems. Good business cooperation with the IT department and knowledge management center plays a key role in the implementation of both systems. Firms that use BI&BD can be classified into organizations with both a high business culture and high analytical culture.

The SME (small- and medium-sized enterprise) sector opts for rather simple systems, focused mainly on current reporting. These systems are not comprehensive solutions and often fail to meet the ever-increasing amount of data and organization's actual needs. They show a direct impact neither on decision-making processes nor on the development of new business models nor on the creation of original logistics chains.

The most popular BI applications remain reporting systems and databases with OLAP functions and thematic data warehouses, focused primarily on the analysis of financial and commercial information. Increasingly, however, it will be necessary to deal not only with an in-depth financial analysis, planning, and budgeting but also with HR, logistics, product placement as well as planning of advertising and marketing campaigns. The role of real-time analysis, including business performance management (BPM) and the creation and analysis of customer profiles, is clearly growing. There is an escalating demand for forecasting analysis, which uses high-level algorithms based on artificial intelligence and neural networks. Online shopping applications, among which Amazon.com is the leader, is a classic example of the need for such extensive analyses. They exploit advanced analytical technologies for processing data from monitoring customer interactions in real time (Casado, 2004; Thuraisingham, 2003).

Results of many studies (Davenport & Harris, 2007), as well as research carried out by Olszak (2016) and Olszak and Zurada (2019), showed that most organizations need to raise their analytical capabilities and to think more creatively about the potential of data sources. The employees in organizations have a relatively high level of technical competences (they know hardware, software, and variety of tools). Unfortunately, staff skills do not correspond with other BI&BD capabilities, e.g., strategic alignment of IT and business strategy, establishing a fact-based and learning culture, entrepreneurship and innovation, change management, and creativity. The organizations that have been classified into the category of the highest maturity level in BI use were highly determined to collect, process, analyze, and share information. Corporate culture based on facts and learning helped them to exploit opportunities offered by BI. The most important factors determining the success of BI initiatives referred not to the technology but all users' strong belief in BI as well as soft competences and skills needed for BI, e.g., culture-based on facts and knowledge, trust, human resources management, managing analytical/creativity people.

The studies conducted by Olszak (2016) showed that organizations use BI systems, above all to optimize operational decisions, improve internal business processes and decision-making on operational level, and gain better access to data and static reporting. BI applications are mostly used in customer relationship management, identification of sales and inventory, optimization orders, and building relationships. Most of the organizations indicated the benefits from using BI, such as integrated analysis for finance, marketing, improvement of decision-making on all levels of management, and the possibility of demand forecasting.

Research by Olszak and Zurada (2019) revealed that most organizations do not consider information resources, including BD resources, in terms of strategic resources. Unfortunately, only a small group of organizations conducted strictly exploratory information analysis. The vast majority of analyses were operational and static. Organizations still attach more importance to the management of internal resources and internal business processes. Few organizations systematically analyze BD resources to improve their competitive position. Analyzing BD resources in many surveyed organizations is actually limited to simple search functions (using search engines), tracking customer interests in the products of a given firm and tracking the impact of advertising on the increase in purchases of selected products and services.

In general, most of the organizations surveyed used rather simple tools to analyze and manage their information resources. The most commonly used tools included tools for searching information on the Internet, spreadsheets and databases, tools for internal integration of business processes and document management, and tools for data visualization. The organizations much less frequently used typical analytical tools, such as BI, supply chain integration tools, CRM, group work systems, expert systems, discussion forums, complex computer simulations, specialized BD processing tools, SWD. The use of simple analytical tools in organizations, in the opinion of the surveyed organizations, results primarily from the lack of (1) sufficient knowledge about the capabilities of various ICT tools, (2) sufficient skills to use them, (3) time to learn about new tools, and (4) personalized ICT tools and sufficient motivation to use more complex data analysis tools.

References

An, Q., Wen, Y., Xiong, B., Yang, M., & Chen, X. (2017). Allocation of carbon dioxide emission permits with the minimum cost for Chinese provinces in big data environment. *Journal of Clear Production, 142*, 889–893.

Ariyachandra, T., & Watson, H. (2006). Which data warehouse architecture is most successful? *Business Intelligence Journal, 11*(1), 4–6.

Becker, J., Knackstedt, R., & Poppelbub, J. (2009). Developing maturity models for IT management – a procedure model and its application . *Business & Information Systems Engineering, 1*, 213–222.

Bharadwaj, A., El Sawy, O. A., Pavlou, P. A., & Venkatraman, N. (2013). Digital business strategy: Toward a next generation of insights. Special Issue: *Digital Business Strategy MIS Quarterly, 37*(2), 471–482. doi: 10.25300/MISQ.

Bibri, S., & Krogstie, J. (2017). ICT of the new wave of computing for sustainable urban forms: Their big data and context-aware augmented typologies and design concepts. Sustainable Cities and Society, 32, 449–474. doi: 10.1016/j.scs.2017.04.012.

Braun, H. (2015). Evaluation of Big Data Maturity Models: A benchmarking study to support big data assessment in organizations. Masters Thesis – Tampere University of Technology.

de Bruin, T., Rosemann, M., Freeze, R., & Kulkarni, U. (2013). *Understanding the main phases of developing a maturity assessment model.* Sydney: EFQM Publication.

Bullen, C., & Rockart J. F. (1981). *A primer on critical success factors. Center for Information System Research.* Sloan School Management. Massachusetts Institute of Technology. Retrieved from https://www.researchgate.net/publication/5175561_A_primer_on_critical_success_factors.

Burton, B. (2009). *Toolkit: Maturity checklist for business intelligence and performance management.* Stamford, CT: Gartner Research, Inc.

Cates, J. E., Gill, S. S., & Zeituny, N. (2005). The Ladder of Business Intelligence (LOBI): A framework for enterprise IT planning and architecture. *International Journal of Business Information Systems, 1*(1), 220–238. doi: 10.1504/IJBIS.2005.007408.

Chae, B. K., & Olson, D.L. (2013). Business analytics for supply chain: A dynamic-capabilities framework. *International Journal of Information Technology & Decision Making, 12*(1), 9–26.

Chen, H., Chiang, R. H. L., & Storey, V. C. (2012). Business intelligence and analytics: From Big data to big impact. *MIS Quarterly, 36*(4), 1–24. doi: 10.2307/41703503.

Chen, M., Mao, S., & Liu, Y. (2014). Big data: A survey. *Mobile Networks and Applications, 19*(2), 171–209. doi: 10.1007/s11036-013-0489-0.

COBIT (2012). A Business Framework for the Governance and Management of Enterprise IT. ISACA. Retrieved from https://static1.squarespace.com/static/56b3cadb59827ecd82b02b43/t/56d8c0d84d088e673055c308/1457045725120/COBIT-5_res_eng_1012.pdf.

Davenport, T. H., & Harris, J. G. (2007). *Competing on analytics. The new science on winning.* Boston, MA: Harvard Business School Press.

Deng, R. (2011). *Business intelligence maturity hierarchy. A new perspective from knowledge management.* Retrieved from http://www.informationmanagement.com/infodirect/20070323/1079089-1.html.

Eckerson, W. W. (2004). Gauge your data warehousing maturity. *DM Review, 14*(11), 34.

Erickson, G., & Rothberg, H. (2013). Competitors, intelligence, and big data. In: J. Liebowitz (Eds.), Big data and business analytics (pp. 103–115). Boca Raton, FL: CRC Press, Taylor & Francis Group, LLC.

Fraser, P., Moultrie, J., & Gregory, M. (2002). The use of maturity models/grids as a tool in assessing product development capability. In: *Proceedings of IEM*, Cambridge, 244–249.

Daniel, D. R. (1961). Management information crises. *Harvard Business Review, 39*(5), 111–116.

Davenport, T., Barth, P., & Bean, R. (2012). How big data is different. *MIT Sloan Management Review, 54*, 1.

Davenport, T. H., & Harris, J. G. (2007). *Competing on analytics. The new science on winning.* Boston, MA: Harvard Business School Press.

D'Adderio, L. (2001). Crafting the virtual prototype how firms integrate knowledge and capabilities cross organizational boundaries. *Research Policy, 30*(9), 1409–1424. doi: 10.1016/S0048-7333(01)00159-7.

Dell (2016). The Four Stages of the Data Maturity Model Retrieved from https://www.cio.com/article/3077871/the-four-stages-of-the-data-maturity-model.html.

Gibson, C. F., & Nolan, R. L. (1974). Managing the four stages of EPD growth. *Harvard Business Review, 52*(1), 76–88.

Günther, W. A., RezazadeMehrizi, M. H., Huysman, M., & Feldberg, F. (2017). Debating big data: A literature review on realizing value from big data. *Journal of Strategic Information Systems, 26*, 191–209. doi: 10.1016/j.jsis.2017.07.003.

Hagerty, J. (2011). AMR Research's Business Intelligence/Performance Management Maturity Model. Retrieved from http://www.eurim.org.uk/activities/ig/voi/AMR_Researchs_Business_Intelligence.pdf.

Halper, F., & Krishnan, K. (2014). *TDWI Big Data Maturity Model Guide.* TDWI Research.

Himmi, K., Arcondara, J., Guan, P., & Zhou, W. (2017). Value oriented Big Data strategy: Analysis & case study. *Proceedings of 50th Hawaii International Conference on System Sciences*, Hawaii, Big Island.

Hwang, H. G., Ku, C. Y., Yen, D. V., & Cheng, C. C. (2004). Critical factors influencing the adoption of data warehouse technology: A study of the banking industry in Taiwan. *Decision Support Systems, 37*(1), 1–21. doi: 10.1016/S0167- 9236(02)00191-4.

H.P. (2011). The HP Business Intelligence Maturity Model, Describing the BI Journal, Hewlett-Packard. Retrieved from http://www.techrepublic.com/whitepapers/the-hpbusiness-intelligence-maturity-model-describing-the-bijourney/1129995.

Hortonworks Big Data Maturity Model (2016). Retrieved from https://infotech.report/whitepapers/hortonworks-big-data-maturity-model/8409.

Isik, O., Jones, M. C., & Sidorova, A. (2011). Business Intelligence (BI) success and the role of BI capabilities. *Intelligent Systems in Accounting, Finance and Management, 18*, 161–176. doi: 10.1002/isaf.v18.4.

Lloyd V. (2002). *Planning to implement service management (ITIL)*, OGC.

Kasse T. (2008). Practical Insight into CMMI®, ARTECH HOUSE.

Kerzner, H., (2009). *Project management: A systems approach to planning, scheduling, and controlling.* New Jersey: John Wiley and Sons.

Lahramnn, G., Marx, F., Winter, R., & Wortmann, F. (2011). Business intelligence maturity: Development and evaluation of a theoretical model. In: *Proceedings of the 44 Hawaii International Conference on System Science.* Kauai, HI.

Lavie, D., Stettner, U., & Tushman M. L. (2010). Exploration and exploitation within and across organizations. *The Academy of Management Annals, 4*(1), 109–155.

LaValle, S., Lesser, E., Shockley, R., Hopkins, M., & Kruschwitz, N. (2011). Big data, analytics and the path from insights to value. *MIT Sloan Management Review, 52*(2), 21–31.

Looly, A. V. (2014). Business Process Maturity: A Comparative Study on a Sample of Business Process Maturity Models. Heidelberg: Springer.

Maier, A. M., Moultrie, J., & Clarkson, P. J. (2009). *Developing maturity grids for assessing organisational capabilities: Practitioner guidance.* Vienna: Academy of Management (MCD).

Manyika, J., Chui, M., Brown, B., Bughin, J., Dobbs, R., Roxburgh, C., & Byers, A. H. (2011). *Big data: The next frontier for innovation, competition, and productivity.* KY: McKinsey Global Institute.

Mettler, T., & Rosner P. (2009). Situational maturity models as instruments artifacts for organizational design. In: *Proceedings of DESRIST*, New York.

McAfee, A., & Brynjolfsson, E. (2012). Big data: The management revolution. *Harvard Business Review*, October, 59–69.

Miller, L., Schiller, D., & Rhone, M. (2011). Data warehouse maturity assessment service. TERADATA. Retrieved from http://www.teradata.com/assets/0/206/276/3457d 45f-7327-4.

Nott, C. (2015). A maturity model for big data and analytics. Retrieved from https://www. ibmbigdatahub.com/blog/maturity-model-big-data-and-analytics.

Olszak, C. M. (2016). Toward better understanding and use of business intelligence in organizations. *Information Systems Management, 33*(2), 105–123.

Olszak, C. M. (2014). Towards an understanding business intelligence. A dynamic capability-based framework for business intelligence. In: M. Ganzha, L. Maciaszek, M. Paprzycki (Eds.), *Annals of Computer Science and Information Systems, Federated Conferences on Computer Science and Information Systems*, Vol 2, IEEE, Warsaw, Poland, 1103–1110.

Olszak, C. M., & Ziemba, E. (2012). Critical success factors for implementing business intelligence systems in small and medium enterprises on the example of Upper Silesia, Poland. *Interdisciplinary Journal of Information, Knowledge, and Management, 7*, 129–150.

Olszak, C. M., & Zurada, J. (2019): Big Data in capturing business value. *Information Systems Management*, doi: 10.1080/10580530.2020.1696551.

Ortbach, K., Plattfaut, R., Poppelbuss, J., & Niehaves, B. (2012). A dynamic capability-based framework for business process management: Theorizing and empirical application. Paper presented at the IEEE 45th Hawaii International Conference on System Sciences, Maui, HI, 4287–4296.

Parise, S., Iyer, B., & Vesset, D. (2012, July). Four strategies to capture and crate value from big data. *Ivey Business Journal, 76*(4), 1–5. Retrieved from http://iveybusiness-journal.com/publication/four-strategies-to-capture-andcreatehttp://iveybusiness-journal.com/publication/four-strategies-to-captureand-create-value-from-big-data/ value-from-big-data/.

Poppelbub, J., & Roglinger, M. (2011). What makes a useful maturity model? A framework of general design principles for maturity models and its demonstration in BPM, ECIS.

Rad, P. F., & Lewin, G. (2006). *Project Management Office – podejściekompleksowe*. Warszawa: Wydawnictwo PROED.

Rajteric, I. H. (2010). Overview of business intelligence maturity models. *Management, 15*, 47–67.

Rayner, N., & Schlegel, K. (2008). *Maturity model of overview for business intelligence and performance management*. Stamford: Gartner Inc. Research. Retrieved from http://www.gartner.com.

Rockart, J. (1979). Chief executives define their own information needs. *Harvard Business Review, 52*(2), 81–92.

Shenhar A.J., & Dvir D. (2007). *Reinventing project management: the diamond approach to successful growth and innovation*. Boston: Harvard Business.

Sacu, C., & Spruit, M. (2010). BIDM: The Business Intelligence Development Model. *Proceedings of the 12th International Conference on Enterprise Information Systems*, Funchal, Madeira-Portugal 2010, 3.

Sampri, A., Mavragani, A., & Tsagarakis, K. (2016). Evaluating Google trends as a tool for integrating the smart health concept in the smart cities governance in USA. Procedia Engineering, *162*, 585–592. doi: 10.1016/j. proeng.2016.11.104.

SAS. (2011). Information evaluation model. Retrieved from http://www.sas.com/software/iem/.

Schmarzo, B. (2013). *Big data. Understanding how data powers big business*. Indianapolis, IN: Wiley.

Scholz, P., Schieder, C., Kurze, C., Gluchowski, P., & Boehringer, M. (2010). Benefits and challenges of business intelligence adoption in small and medium-sized enterprises. Paper presented at the 18th European Conference on Information Systems (ECIS2010), Pretoria, June, South Africa.

Teece, D.J., Pisano, G., & Shuen, A. (1997). Dynamic capabilities and strategic management. *Strategic Management Journal, 18*(7), 509–533.

Wamba, S., Akter, S., Edwards, A., Chopin, G., & Gnanzou, D. (2015). How big data can make big impact: Findings from a systematic review and a longitudinal case study. *International Journal of Production Economics, 165,* 234–246. doi: 10.1016/j. ijpe.2014.12.031.

Wang, Y., Kung, L., Wang, W. Y. C., & Cegielski, C. C. (2018). An integrated big data analytics-enabled transformation model: Application to health care. *Information & Management, 55,* 64–79. doi: 10.1016/j.im.2017.04.001.

Watson, H. J., Ariyachandra, T., & Matyska, R. J. (2011). Data warehousing stages of growth. *Information Systems Management, 18*(3), 42–50. doi: 10.1201/1078/43196. 18.3.20010601/31289.6.

Williams, S., & Williams, N. (2007). *The profit impact of Business Intelligence.* San Francisco, CA: Morgan Kaufmann.

Wixom, B. H., & Watson, H. J. (2010). The BI-based organization. *International Journal of Business Intelligence Research, 1*(1), 13–28. doi: 10.4018/IJBIR.

Wixom, B. H., Watson, H. J., & Werner, T. (2011). Developing an enterprise business intelligence capability: The Norfolk Southern journey. *MIS Quarterly Executive, 10*(2), 61–71.

Yeoh, W., & Koronios, A. (2010). Critical success factors for Business Intelligence systems. *Journal of Computer Information Systems, 50*(3), 23–32.

Index

Note: Page numbers in **bold** refer to tables.